Selections from

MEDIEVAL EUROPE

A Short History

Eighth Edition

C. Warren Hollister

University of California
Santa Barbara

Mc Graw Hill **Custom Publishing**

Boston   Burr Ridge, IL   Dubuque, IA   Madison, WI   New York
San Francisco   St. Louis   Bangkok   Bogotá   Caracas   Kuala Lumpur
Lisbon   London   Madrid   Mexico City   Milan   Montreal   New Delhi
Santiago   Seoul   Singapore   Sydney   Taipei   Toronto

Selections from
MEDIEVAL EUROPE
A Short History
Eighth Edition

This book is a McGraw-Hill Custom Publishing textbook and contains select material from *Medieval Europe: A Short Story*, Eighth Edition by C. Warren Hollister. Copyright © 19998, 1994, 1990, 1982, 1978, 1974, 1968, 1964 by The McGraw-Hill Companies, Inc. Reprinted with permission of the publisher. Many custom published texts are modified versions or adaptations of our best-selling textbooks. Some adaptations are printed in black and white to keep prices at a minimum, while others are in color.

5 6 7 8 9 0 OFC OFC 0 9 8 7

ISBN 0-07-312359-5

Editor: Robin E. Havens
Production Editor: Kathy Phelan
Printer/Binder: Ohio Full Court Press

CONTENTS

PART ONE

The Early Middle Ages

The Birth of Europe

THE EARLY MIDDLE AGES:
AN OVERVIEW

This book is divided into three parts. The first, "The Early Middle Ages," spans the troubled, formative centuries between the collapse of the Roman Empire in the West and the emergence of Western Europe as a major civilization, growing in population, wealth, territory, and cultural creativity. By the end of the fifth century the Western Roman Empire had disintegrated; by the mid-eleventh century the revival of Western Europe was well under way. Accordingly, the term "early Middle Ages" refers here to the period between about AD 500 and 1050, though such dividing lines are of course arbitrary and would have passed unnoticed at the time.

Rather than descending suddenly from the sky onto Europe in AD 500, we will approach it on foot from out of the Roman past, beginning with the reign of Augustus, when the old Roman Republic gave way to the Roman Empire. Looking briefly at the Empire at its height, in the first and second centuries AD, we will then explore the ways in which Roman civilization was transformed during the third, fourth, and fifth centuries. The Christianization of the Roman Empire will receive particular attention because Rome's conversion to Christianity was of decisive importance to the future of Europe, both Western and Eastern. We will trace the collapse of Roman imperial authority in the West, the Germanic settlements and invasions, and the establishment of Germanic kingdoms across vast stretches of Western Europe and North Africa once ruled by Rome. With this running start we will have arrived at AD 500.

Roman civilization gave way to three successor civilizations, three heirs: Byzantine, Islamic, and Western European. Since the subject of this book is medieval Western Europe, the other two inheriting civilizations will receive only a chapter each. These chapters will stress the influence of Byzantine and Islamic civilization on the emerging culture of Western Christendom.

The early Middle Ages witnessed repeated invasions of the West, accompanied by political and economic turmoil. Illiterate, hard-bitten landholders led their retinues in battle, often in losing causes, against Muslim armies of the expanding Islamic empire. More often, the warrior-landholders of Western Christendom fought among themselves. Western cities became underpopulated and ruinous, while the countryside suffered periodic famines and plagues along with the ravages of war. Nevertheless, Christianity gradually expanded as monks carried their missionary work to pagan peoples (i.e., non-Christians) in Germany, the Netherlands, and Anglo-Saxon England. Monasteries, planted in the wilderness, became centers of prayer, agricultural production, and learning— outposts of civilization where the Latin literary heritage of ancient Rome was kept alive through the copying and study of old manuscripts.

Around AD 700 a new Christian dynasty, the Carolingian, began to extend its authority over France, western Germany, and, later, northern Italy. Working closely with the Church, the Carolingians built an empire that eventually stretched across most of Western Christendom. Charlemagne, the greatest of the Carolingians, assumed the title "Roman Emperor" in AD 800. But lacking large cities and an educated bureaucracy, Charlemagne's empire was fragile. It collapsed during the 800s amidst a new wave of invaders: Vikings, Muslims, and Hungarians. In the course of these invasions, and partly in response to them, strong kingdoms emerged in England and Germany. In France, where the monarchy long remained feeble, the burden of defense fell to dukes and counts, who fortified their lands with castles and gradually tightened their control over lesser landholders.

By about 1050 the invasions had run their course. The Muslims were in retreat. The Vikings and Hungarians had adopted Christianity and become participants in Western civilization rather than predators of it. Cities were growing once again in the Western European heartlands and commerce was increasing. The Church was entering a period of reform and spiritual renewal, and literacy was spreading.

This revitalization can be described (crudely but conveniently) as the coming of a new era. The early Middle Ages began with the decaying of an old and powerful civilization and ended with the maturing of a new one, radically different from ancient Rome yet, in a sense, its child.

Chronology of the Later Roman Empire and the Early Middle Ages to AD 800

	Rome	Byzantium	Islam	Western Christendom
200–	•205–270 Plotinus			
	•235–284 Height of third-century anarchy			
				•c. 258 Martyrdom of St. Denis, Bishop of Paris
300–	•284–305 Diocletian			
	•306–337 Constantine			
	•325 Council of Nicaea			
	•330 Founding of Constantinople	•330 Constantine founds Constantinople		
	•354–430 St. Augustine of Hippo			
				•372–397 St. Martin is Bishop of Tours
	•378 Battle of Adrianople			
	•378–395 Theodosius I			
	•395 Final division of Eastern and Western empires	•395 Final division of Eastern and Western empires		
400–	•410 Visigoths sack Rome			
	•430 Vandals capture Hippo			
	•451–452 Huns invade West			
	•476 Last Western emperor deposed			
500–				•c.480–c.550 St. Benedict of Nursia
				•481–511 Clovis rules Franks, conquers Gaul
				•493–526 Theodoric rules Ostrogothic Italy
		•527–565 Reign of Justinian		
		•533–555 Conquest of North Africa and Italy		
		•541 ff Great plague		
		•548 Death of Empress Theodora		
		•568 Lombards invade Italy		
			•c. 571–632 Muhammad	
				•590–604 Pontificate of Gregory the Great
				•594 Death of Gregory of Tours
				•597 Augustine converts Kent

4

Chronology of the Later Roman Empire and the Early Middle Ages to AD 800 (continued)

Rome	Byzantium	Islam	Western Christendom
600–	•610–641 Reign of Heraclius; Islamic conquests of Syria and Palestine	•622 The Hijrah	•622–638 Reign of Dagobert
		•632–655 Arabs conquer Syria, Persian Empire, and Egypt	•636 Death of Isidore of Seville
		•655–661 Civil war: Umayyads vs. Ali	
	•680 Council of Constantinople; triumph of Orthodoxy	•661–750 Umayyad dynasty; conquest of North Africa and Spain	•687 Pepin of Heristal establishes Carolingian hegemony by defeating Neustria at Tertry
700–			
	•717–718 Great Muslim siege of Constantinople	•717–718 Great Muslim siege of Constantinople	•714–741 Reign of Charles Martel
		•732 Arabs defeated at Tours	•732 Arabs defeated at Tours
			•735 Death of Bede
		•750–1258 Abbasid dynasty	•741–768 Reign of Pepin the Short
			•751 Pepin crowned king of the Franks
		•786–809 Reign of Harun-al Rashid	•768–814 Reign of Charlemagne
			•793 First Viking raid against England

Chronology of Early Middle Ages, AD 800–1100

Byzantium	Carolingian Empire	France	Germany and Italy	England
800–	•800 Charlemagne crowned Roman emperor			
	•814–840 Reign of Louis the Pious	•840–877 Reign of Charles the Bald	•840–876 Reign of Louis the German	
	•842 Oaths of Strasbourg			
	•843 Treaty of Verdun	•843 Treaty of Verdun	•843 Treaty of Verdun	
		•845 Vikings plunder Paris		
				•871–899 Reign of Alfred the Great
900– •867–1056 Macedonian dynasty, reconquest of Balkans, conversion of south Slavs		•911 Charles the Simple recognizes Normandy		
			•936–973 Reign of Otto I	•954 Reconquest of Danelaw completed
			•962 Otto I crowned Roman emperor	
		•987 Capetian dynasty replaces Carolingians	•973–983 Reign of Otto II	•978–1016 Reign of Ethelred the Unready
1000– •976–1025 Reign of Basil the Bulgar-Slayer			•983–1002 Reign of Otto III	
•c.980–1015 Reign of Prince Vladimir of Kiev, who converts to Byzantine Christianity			•1003 Gerbert of Aurillac dies	•1017–1035 Reign of Canute
•1071 Seljuk Turks rout Byzantines at Manzikert; loss of Asia Minor			•1039–1056 Reign of Henry III	•1042–1066 Reign of Edward the Confessor
				•1066 Norman Conquest

CHAPTER 1

Rome Becomes Christian

THE "GOLDEN AGE" OF ROME

The Extent of the Empire and Its Governance

The Roman Empire at its height was the largest the world had ever known. It encompassed the entire Mediterranean basin and bulged far northward through present-day France and England. During its first two centuries, between the reign of the emperor Augustus (c. 31 BC–AD 14) and the death of Marcus Aurelius (AD 180), the Roman Empire extended across the vast area from the Euphrates River in modern Iraq to the shores of the Atlantic, and from the Sahara Desert of North Africa to the Danube and Rhine rivers of central Europe and the Cheviot Hills of northern Britain (see map, pp. 10–11).

The emperors of this era ruled their peoples in relative peace, but not all of them ruled wisely. Several were decidedly dull-witted and a couple were (to put it charitably) mentally ill. The first-century emperor Caligula used to have his favorite horse wined and dined at imperial banquets and made plans to have the beast raised to the office of Roman consul. (The project was cut short by Caligula's assassination.) And the less said about the emperor Nero, the better. But a number of the early emperors were able and farsighted, and even under the worst of them the imperial government continued to function. An army of some 300,000 to 500,000 men guarded the far-flung imperial frontiers, a superb system of paved roads tied the provinces to Rome, and Roman ships sailed the Mediterranean and Black seas, rarely troubled by pirates or enemy fleets. Scattered across the Empire were cities built in the classical Roman style with temples, public buildings, baths, schools, theaters, amphitheaters, and triumphal arches. Their ruins are still to be seen all around the Mediterranean and beyond—in Italy, France, Spain, Portugal, England, North Africa, the Balkans, Turkey, and the eastern Mediterranean—bearing witness even now to the tremendous scope of Roman authority and the tasteful uniformity of Roman architecture.

The Empire extended about three thousand miles from east to west, the approximate length of the United States. According to the best scholarly guesses, its inhabitants numbered something like fifty million, heavily concentrated in the eastern provinces where commerce and civilization had flourished for thousands of years. Egypt, Israel, Mesopotamia, and Greece had all fallen

Roman Empire

Areas temporarily under the influence of the Roman Empire

by now under Roman rule, although Greece—with its distinctive religion, literature, art, and urban-based political institutions—exerted such a dominating influence on Roman culture that Romans could express some doubt as to who had conquered whom.

To the east Rome shared a boundary with the Parthian Empire, which gave way during the third century to a new and aggressive Persian Empire. But elsewhere Rome's expansion from the Mediterranean Basin was halted only by the

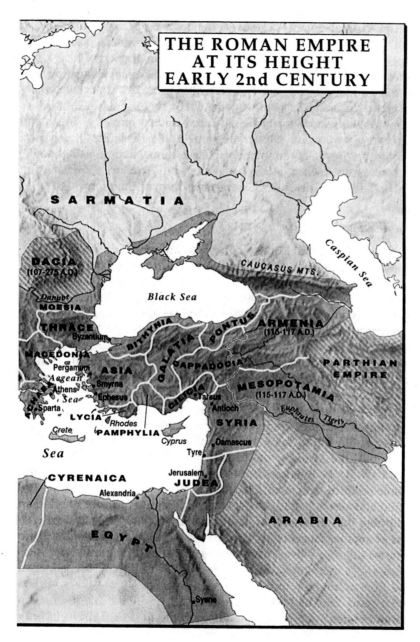

THE ROMAN EMPIRE
AT ITS HEIGHT
EARLY 2nd CENTURY

Arabian and Sahara deserts, the Caucasus Mountains, the dense forests of central Europe beyond the Rhine and Danube rivers, the barren highlands of Scotland, and the Atlantic Ocean. In short, the Roman frontiers encompassed virtually all the lands that could be reached by Roman armies and cultivated profitably by Roman landowners.

Roman institutions and classical culture spread far and wide across the empire under the canopy of the *pax Romana*, the "Roman Peace." As distant provinces became progressively Romanized, the meaning of the words "Rome" and "Roman" gradually broadened. By the time of Augustus, these terms embraced not simply a city and its inhabitants but the greater part of Italy. Later, as the decades of the *pax Romana* followed one another, Roman citizenship was extended to more and more provincials until finally, in AD 212, every free inhabitant of the Empire received citizenship. By then the Roman emperors themselves often came from the provinces: the talented second-century emperors Trajan and Hadrian, for example, were both natives of Spain. In time the terms "Rome" and "Roman" acquired a universal connotation: a Greek monarch in Constantinople, a Frankish monarch in Aachen, a Saxon monarch in Germany, a Hapsburg in Vienna could, in later centuries, all call themselves Roman emperors.

Economic and Social Conditions

The most conspicuous effect of Romanization was the spread of cities. The city-state, the characteristic political unit of the Greco-Roman world, now extended to the outermost provinces, including even remote Britain. The city still retained much local self-government and normally controlled the rural territories in its vicinity. In other words, the city was the key unit of local administration; the government of the Roman state remained fundamentally urban.

Conversely, the cities of the Empire, especially in the West, were of only modest importance as commercial and manufacturing centers. Although small-scale urban industry often flourished, particularly in the East, the economy of the Roman Empire remained fundamentally agrarian. Many of the western cities, including Rome itself, consumed far more than they produced. Like the modern Washington, DC, they were primarily administrative and military centers whose mercantile significance was secondary. During the first two centuries of the Empire, the economy was prosperous enough to support them, but this would not always be the case. In time the cities would decline, and with them the whole political structure of the Roman West.

By the first and second centuries AD, the small family farms of the Roman past were slipping into the hands of great aristocrats, who came to hold conglomerations of smaller farms or who, in many instances, consolidated them into large estates tilled by slaves or half-free peasants. Although the products of Roman farming varied considerably from region to region, the principal crops of the Roman Empire were grain, grapes, and olives—the so-called Mediterranean triad that had dominated agriculture in the Mediterranean Basin for countless generations and would continue to do so. Grain (chiefly wheat and barley) and grape vines were cultivated throughout most of the Empire. From these the Romans produced two of the basic staples of their diet: bread and wine. Olive trees were also grown in abundance, though their vulnerability to cold restricted their cultivation to the frost-free lowlands around the Mediterranean Sea. The inhabitants of the Mediterranean Basin used olive oil in place of butter, which was favored by the Germanic tribes to the north but turned rancid in the southern heat. Through much of Italy, grain production had been giving way to the more profitable enterprises of sheep and cattle raising, and the fertile wheat-growing provinces of Egypt and North Africa had by now become the primary suppliers of bread for the teeming populace of the city of Rome (perhaps half a million at its height).

In the early Roman Empire, as in the late Roman Republic, slaves played a crucial role in the economy, especially in agriculture. But as the frontiers jelled and the flow of war captives dwindled, the chief source of slaves was cut off. Landowners now began to lease major portions of their estates to sharecroppers called *coloni*, who tended to fall more and more under the control of their landlords and sank into a semi-servile status half way between slave and free, akin to the status of medieval serfs. Agricultural slavery persisted, however, far into the Middle Ages, dying out only during the decades around AD 1000.

The condition of the slaves, *coloni*, and urban poor should warn us against viewing imperial Rome through the rose-tinted microscopes of nineteenth-century historians, who considered it humanity's happiest age. Roman imperial culture at its height was impressive, but it was also narrowly limited, shared only by the Empire's upper crust. And although all inhabitants benefited from the Roman Peace, the great majority of them were impoverished and under-nourished. Such conditions persisted throughout the "golden age" and beyond, not as economic misfortunes that might be remedied by economic stimulus programs but as the means necessary for the functioning of great estates, mines, and wealthy households. The leisured lives of the Empire's elite, and the very survival of the imperial economy, depended on the muscles of slaves and poor laborers, who constituted 80 to 90 percent of the population.

Nor was the Roman Peace as peaceful as one might suppose. Germanic tribes hammered repeatedly at the imperial frontiers and often penetrated them, while, as recent research has made clear, towns and countryside deep within the Empire were afflicted by local violence and mayhem to a degree unimagined by earlier historians. The Roman provinces of the golden age were drastically underpoliced and undergoverned.

Roman women, even the wealthiest, were forbidden to hold any political office. By long tradition they were expected to stay home and obey their husbands; but during the imperial era, as in the late Republic, many Roman wives held property and most of them traveled freely within their cities. Indeed, in the Empire's later centuries women acquired considerable independence with respect to marriage, divorce, and the holding of property, and many upper-class women were well educated. The Roman father, however, was the master of his family and exercised the power of life or death over his newborn children. If he liked their looks, he kept them; if they were weak or physically handicapped, or if the father already had enough children (particularly female children), they were taken from the home and abandoned. Some had the good fortune to be rescued by adults in need of children; others simply died of exposure. Infanticide was yet another brutal consequence of Rome's marginal economy: the Empire could not afford excess mouths.

But virtually all ancient civilizations were afflicted by mass enslavement, impoverishment, malnutrition, internal violence, the suppression of women, and the abandonment of unwanted infants (although the religion of the Hebrews prohibited infanticide). In these respects, Roman imperial civilization was no worse than the others, and in the larger cities, where public baths and other amenities were available (such as free bread in the city of Rome), it was significantly better. Life in Rome's "golden age" could be pleasant enough if one were male, adult, very wealthy, and naturally immune to various epidemic diseases. But if this was humanity's happiest time, God help us all!

THE THIRD AND FOURTH CENTURIES

Anarchy and Recovery

During the third century, conditions grew still worse. Invading tribes broke through the frontiers again and again, forcing cities to construct protective walls and threatening for a time to tear the Empire to pieces. Imperial survival depended increasingly on military defense, and the Roman legions, well aware of that fact, made and unmade emperors. Roman armies repeatedly battled one another for control of the imperial office until (to exaggerate only slightly) a man might be a general one day, emperor the next, and dead the third. Twenty-odd emperors (depending on whom you count) reigned during the calamitous half-century between 235 and 285, and all but one were murdered, killed in combat, or died in captivity. With political anarchy came social and economic breakdown. The cost of living soared 1,000 percent between AD 256 and 280, and the increase in numbers of soldiers and administrators forced the government, in order to pay their salaries, to levy higher and higher taxes on its peasants and townspeople. Many fled their homes and jobs to escape the tax collector. The "golden age" had given way to what one third-century writer described as an "age of iron and rust."

The Empire was saved, though just barely, by a series of warrior-emperors of the late third and early fourth centuries. By tremendous military effort they threw back Germanic raiders and Persian armies, recovered the lost provinces, and restored the old frontiers. They also took measures to arrest the social and economic decay and to reconstruct the Roman administration, on severely authoritarian lines. These measures have often been criticized, and with some justice. But they enabled the faltering Empire to survive for nearly two more centuries in the West and for over a thousand years in the East.

The two chief architects of the new policy were the emperors Diocletian (284–305) and Constantine (306–337). It was they, more than any others, who rebuilt the loosely governed Empire of earlier days into an autocracy supported by a huge army and bureaucracy. Workers and peasants were tied by law to their jobs and frozen into a hereditary caste system. The status of the emperor himself assumed godlike proportions. Borrowing from Greek and Persian court ceremonial, the new emperors employed all the known arts of costume, cosmetic makeup, and drama to make themselves appear majestic. Everyone had to fall prostrate in the emperor's presence, and Constantine added the touch of wearing a diadem on his head. Back in the first and second centuries, emperors had striven to work harmoniously with the political institutions of the former Roman Republic—the Senate, the civic magistrates—which, during the

Chapter 1 Rome Becomes Christian

Chronology of the Later Empire

All Dated AD	
205–270:	Plotinus
235–284:	Height of the third-century anarchy
284–305:	Reign of Diocletian
306–337:	Reign of Constantine
325:	Council of Nicaea
330:	Founding of Constantinople
354–430:	St. Augustine of Hippo
376:	Goths cross Danube
378:	Battle of Adrianople
378–395:	Reign of Theodosius I
395:	Final division of Eastern and Western Empires
410:	Alaric leads Gothic sack of Rome
430:	Vandals capture Hippo
451–452:	Huns invade Western Europe
440–461:	Pontificate of Leo I
476:	Last Western emperor deposed by Odovacar
481–511:	Clovis rules Franks, conquers Gaul
493–526:	Theodoric the Ostrogoth rules Italy

"golden age", had continued to enjoy much prestige although little independent power. Under the new regimes of Diocletian and Constantine, the Senate was drained of authority and the emperor became *dominus et deus*, "lord and god." The imperial dignity, so debased during the third-century anarchy, was now exalted in every possible way.

The New Religious Mood

Amidst the invasions and economic crises of the third century and the rigid autocracy of the fourth, the upper-crust civilization of classical Rome began giving way to styles and hopes that had long been percolating among the Empire's masses. Veneration of the traditional gods of hearth and household, clan and city, slowly succumbed to the worship of more mystical deities imported from the Near East. The gods of old Rome, like the Greek gods of Mount Olympus, had safeguarded the welfare of social and political groups; the gods of the new Near Eastern cults—known as "mystery religions"— appealed instead to the individual. As these subterranean ideas floated up to the surface, the elegant, worldly culture of the "golden age" became more mystical and impressionistic. Fundamental changes occurred not only in court ceremonial but also in such areas as literature, philosophy, and art.[1] Underlying them all was a basic shift in religious outlook that shaped the intellectual world of the late Empire and the civilizations that would succeed it.

---

[1]Late Roman art is discussed on pp. 44–45 and illustrated on pp. 21–22, 45–47. Art lovers are welcome to look ahead; others can be patient and read on.

Tormented by growing economic hardship and insecurity, the urban poor of the third- and fourth-century Empire turned more and more from the boisterous and unlikely gods of the Greco-Roman Olympic cult—Jupiter, Juno, Apollo, Mars, Minerva, and the rest—to compelling new religions that offered release from individual guilt and the promise of personal salvation and eternal life. These new mystery religions originated in the older, Eastern cultures that Rome had absorbed into its Empire. From Egypt came the cult of the goddess Isis, from Persia came the cult of the savior Mithras, from Asia Minor came the worship of the Great Earth Mother, and from Palestine came Christianity. The shift from civic god to savior god, from this world to the next, gained enormous momentum as the peace of the second century gave way to the anarchy of the third, making the high hopes of classical humanism—the dream of a rational universe, an ideal republic, a good life—seem like cruel illusions.

The older pagan cults were by no means dead, but they were altered by the growth of otherworldliness. The trend is especially conspicuous in the leading philosophical movement of the third century, "Neoplatonism" (based loosely on the much earlier thought of the Greek philosopher Plato). Neoplatonism was the creation of the third-century philosopher Plotinus, one of the most influential minds of the Roman imperial era. Plotinus taught the doctrine of one god, who was infinite, unknowable, and unapproachable, except through a mystical experience. This deity was the ultimate source of everything, spiritual and physical. All existence was conceived of as a series of circles radiating outward from him, like concentric ripples in a pond, diminishing in excellence and significance as they grew more distant from their divine source. Human reason, which the Greeks had earlier exalted, now lost its fascination, for at the core of reality was a god that lay beyond reason's scope.

Plotinus and his followers regarded the pagan gods and goddesses as crude but useful symbols of the true Neoplatonic god. Though poorly suited to the deepening mood of otherworldliness, the pagan cults acquired new life under the canopy of Neoplatonic philosophy, which brought them into line with the trend toward mysticism and monotheism. The distinction between Jupiter and the new Eastern deities was steadily blurring.

By the fourth century, Greco-Roman rationalism and humanism had been superseded almost entirely by a spirit of otherworldliness and a yearning for eternal life. Neoplatonic philosophy and Near Eastern religion were accompanied by a surge of interest in astrology, magic, and similar arcane practices, which had never been absent from Greco-Roman culture but which now dominated popular thinking as never before.

CHRISTIANITY

It was in this supernatural atmosphere that the Christians converted the Roman Empire. Some of their beliefs and practices resembled those of older and competing religions: baptism, eternal salvation, the death and resurrection of a savior-god, the sacramental meal, human brotherhood under a divine father—none of these was new. Yet Christianity differed from the mystery religions in two fundamental ways: (1) its founder and savior was an actual historical personage; compared with Jesus, such mythical idealizations as Isis and Mithras would have seemed faint and unreal; and (2) its god was not merely the best of many gods but the One God, the God of the Jews, unique in all antiquity in his claims to exclusiveness and omnipotence, and now detached by Christianity from his association with the Jewish people to become the God of all peoples.

Jesus had lived and died a Jew. He announced that he had come not to abolish the Jewish laws but to fulfill them. In his earliest biographies, the four Gospels, he is pictured as a warm, magnetic leader who miraculously healed the sick, raised the dead, and stilled the winds. His miracles were seen as credentials of the divine authority with which he claimed to speak. His ministry was chiefly to the poor and outcast, and in Christianity's early decades it was they who accepted the new faith most readily. He preached a doctrine of love, compassion, and humility; like the earlier Hebrew prophets, he scorned empty formalism in religion and favored a simple life of generosity toward both friend and enemy and devotion to God. He did not object to ritual as such, but only to ritual infected with pride and divorced from love of God and neighbor. He angered leaders of the Jewish priesthood by criticizing their complacency and by claiming to speak with divine authority. In the end, they accused him before the Roman governor Pontius Pilate of claiming to be king of the Jews, which could be taken as an act of treason against the emperor. Pilate had him lashed and condemned him to crucifixion, a common means of executing non-Romans.

According to the Gospels, Jesus' greatest miracle was his resurrection—his return to life on the third day after his death on the cross. He is said to have remained on earth for a short period thereafter, giving solace and instruction to his disciples, and then to have ascended into heaven with the promise that he would return in glory to judge all souls and bring the world to an end. The early generations of Christians expected this second coming to occur quickly, which may be one of the reasons that formal organization was not stressed in the primitive Church.

From the beginning, Christians not only accepted the ethical teachings of Jesus but also worshiped him as the Christ, the incarnation of God. In the Gospels, Jesus distinguishes repeatedly between himself—"the Son of Man"—and God—"the Father"—but he also makes the statement, "I and the Father are one." And in one account he instructs his followers to baptize all persons "in the name of the Father and the Son and the Holy Spirit." Hence, Christianity became committed to the difficult and sophisticated notion of a single divinity with three aspects. Christ was the Son, or Second Person, in a Holy Trinity that was nevertheless one God. The doctrine of the Trinity produced a great deal of theological controversy over the centuries. But it also gave Christians the unique advantage of a single, infinite, philosophically respectable God who could be worshiped and adored in the person of the charismatic, lovable, tragic Jesus.

The Early Church

The first generation of Christianity witnessed the beginning of a deeply significant process whereby the Judeo-Christian heritage was modified and enriched through contact with Greco-Roman culture. Jesus' own apostles were little influenced by Greek thought, and some of them sought to keep Christianity strictly within the ritualistic framework of Judaism. But St. Paul, an early convert who was both a Jew and a Roman citizen, succeeded in steering the Church toward a more encompassing goal. Christians were not to be bound by the strict Jewish dietary laws or the requirement of circumcision (which would have severely diminished Christianity's attraction to adult, non-Jewish males). The new faith would be open to all people everywhere who would accept Jesus as God and Savior—and open also to the bracing winds of Greco-Roman thought.

St. Paul traveled far and wide across the Empire, winning converts and establishing Christian communities in many towns and cities of the Mediterranean Basin. Other Christian missionaries, among them St. Peter and Jesus' other apostles, devoted their lives as St. Paul did to traveling, preaching, and organizing, often at the cost of martyrdom. Their work was tremendously effective, for by the end of the apostolic generation Christianity had become a force to be reckoned with among the impoverished townspeople of Italy and the East. Within another century it had spread through most of the Roman Empire. The urban poor found it easy to accept a savior who had worked as a carpenter; had consorted with fishermen, ex-prostitutes, and similar riffraff; had been crucified by the imperial authorities; and had promised salvation to all who followed him—free or slave, man or woman.

From the first, Christians engaged regularly in a sacramental meal of bread and wine that came to be called the "Eucharist" (the Greek word for thanksgiving) or "holy communion." It was viewed as an indispensable channel of divine grace through which the Christian was infused with the spirit of Christ. By means of another sacrament, baptism, one was initiated into the Church, had all sins forgiven, and received the grace (moral strength) of the Holy Spirit. Because baptism erased all sins, some put it off until they were nearing death.

As Christian historical documents become more common, in the second and third centuries, the organization of the Church begins to emerge more sharply. These documents disclose a distinction between the clergy, who governed the Church and administered the sacraments, and the laity whom they served. The clergy, initiated into the Christian priesthood through the ceremony of ordination, were divided into several ranks; the most important were the bishops,[2] who served as spiritual leaders of Christian urban communities, and the ordinary priests, who conducted religious services and administered

---

[2]The Latin word for bishop is *episcopus*, from which is derived such English words as "episcopal" (having to do with a bishop or bishops) and "Episcopalian" (a member of the Anglican church in America—a church governed by bishops). One medieval writer referred slightingly to a bishop's concubine as an *episcopissa*, but since medieval bishops were supposed to be chaste, the term was very seldom used.

the Eucharist under a bishop's jurisdiction. The most powerful of the bishops were the *metropolitans* or *archbishops* of the more important cities, who supervised the bishops of their districts. Atop the hierarchy were the bishops of the three or four greatest cities of the Empire: Rome, Alexandria, Antioch, and later Constantinople. These leaders, known as *patriarchs*, governed the Church across vast areas of the Mediterranean world.

In time the bishop of Rome came to be regarded more and more as the highest of the patriarchs. His preeminence was based on the tradition that St. Peter, foremost among Jesus' twelve apostles, had spent his last years in Rome and suffered martyrdom there. St. Peter was held to have been the first bishop of Rome—the first *pope*—and later popes regarded themselves as his direct successors. Nevertheless, the establishment of effective papal authority over even the Western part of the Church required the efforts of many centuries.

Christianity and Classical Culture

Medieval and modern Christian theology is a product of both Jewish and Greek traditions. The synthesis began not among Christians but among Jews, especially those who had migrated in large numbers to the Greco-Egyptian metropolis of Alexandria. Here Jewish scholars—in particular a religious philosopher of the early first century AD named Philo Judaeus—worked toward the reconciliation of Jewish Biblical revelation and Greek philosophy. Drawing from several Greek philosophical schools, they developed a symbolic interpretation of the Hebrew Scriptures that was to influence both Jewish and Christian thought across the centuries.

Following the lead of Philo Judaeus, Christian theologians strove to demonstrate that their religion was more than merely an appealing myth—that it could hold its own in the highest intellectual circles. Plato and the Bible agreed, so they argued, on the existence of a single God and the importance of living an ethical life. As the expectation of an immediate second coming faded and Christians started to explore their faith more analytically, they began to differ among themselves on such difficult issues as the nature of Christ (how could he be both God and man?) and the Trinity (how can three be one?). Some opinions were so inconsistent with the views of most Christian leaders that they were condemned as "heresies." As questions were raised and orthodox solutions agreed on, Christian doctrine became increasingly specific and elaborate.

The early heresies sought to simplify the nature of Christ and the Trinity. One group, the Gnostics, taught that Christ was not truly human but only a divine phantom—that because the physical world was evil, God could not have degraded himself by assuming a flesh-and-blood body. Others maintained that Christ was not fully divine, not an equal member of the Trinity. This last position was taken up in the fourth century by a group of Christians known as Arians (after their leader, Arius), who spread their view throughout the Empire and beyond.

The position that came to be defined as orthodox lay midway between Gnosticism and Arianism: Christ was fully human and fully divine. He was a coequal member of the Holy Trinity who had always existed and always would, but who had assumed human form and flesh at a particular moment in time and had walked the earth, taught, suffered, and died as the man Jesus. In this way the characteristic Christian synthesis between matter and spirit was strictly preserved, and Christ remained the bridge between the two worlds.

Christianity and the Empire

From the first the Christians of the Roman Empire had been a people apart, convinced that they alone possessed the truth and that the truth would one day triumph. They were eager to win new converts and uncompromising in their rejection of all other religions. They were willing to learn from the pagan world but unwilling ever to submit to it. Consequently, Christians were often objects of suspicion and hatred. Their refusal to offer sacrifices to the state gods resulted in imperial persecution, but only intermittently. Violent purges alternated with long periods of official inaction. The persecutions could be cruel and terrifying, but they were neither sufficiently ruthless nor sufficiently sustained to exterminate the whole Christian community, and martyrdoms only strengthened the resolve of those who survived. (The pagan emperors might have learned much from Christian inquisitors of sixteenth-century Spain on the subject of liquidating troublesome religious minorities.) The most severe imperial persecution, and the last, occurred at the beginning of the fourth century under Emperor Diocletian. By then Christianity was too well entrenched to be destroyed, and the failure of Diocletian's persecution made it evident that the Empire had little choice but to accommodate itself to the Church.

A decade thereafter, Emperor Constantine undertook a momentous reversal of imperial religious policy. He himself became a Christian convert, and in 313 he granted the Church official toleration and protection. In the generations that followed, Christianity enjoyed the active support of a line of Christian emperors. Great aisled churches were built at imperial expense. The combats of gladiators, which had traditionally provided savage amusement for the urban masses, gave way under Christian influence to the less bloodthirsty sport of chariot racing. The practice of crucifixion was brought to an abrupt end. And the abandonment of infants was prohibited by imperial law. Infanticide was repugnant to Christians, as it had always been to Jews, and it was losing much of its social utility in an era of declining population. Slavery continued, for the imperial economy could not survive without it. The Church generally accepted it, recognizing that the freeing of slaves would result in economic ruin.

The gratitude of some churchmen toward the Christian emperors rose to the point of adulation. Constantine could no longer claim to be a god, but he was lauded as the thirteenth apostle, the master of all churches, the divinely chosen ruler of the Roman people. The first empire-wide council of the Church, the Council of Nicaea in 325, was dominated by his magisterial presence.

Church of Santa Sabina, Rome, nave and apse (begun AD 425). This is one of several great, late antique churches in Rome, still standing, built in the Roman basilica style that served as a model for Christian churches of later centuries.

Rich and poor alike now flocked into the Christian faith. Although paganism long survived, particularly in the countryside, Christianity had grown by the end of the fourth century to become the dominant religion of the Mediterranean world. No longer persecuted and disreputable, it was now official, conventional, respectable. Of course it lost some of its former spiritual intensity in the process. Bishops and patriarchs now tended to come from wealthy aristocratic families. And as so often occurs in human institutions, victory was accompanied by an intensification of internal disputes. Fourth-century Christianity was marked by bitter doctrinal struggles, and here too the Christian emperors played a commanding role. Arianism, the most powerful of the fourth-century heresies, was condemned by Constantine and the majority of churchmen at the Council of Nicaea in 325. But thereafter the imperial government vacillated: some emperors opposed Arianism while others supported it, and orthodox and Arian leaders trudged in and out of exile at the imperial whim. At length, the severely orthodox Emperor Theodosius I (378–395) banned the teachings of the Arians and broke their power, making orthodox Christianity the official religion of the Roman state. Theodosius outlawed paganism as well, and the tired old gods of Rome, deprived of imperial sanction, gradually shuffled off stage.

Although Arianism was now prohibited in the Empire, it survived among some of the Germanic tribes along the frontiers. These peoples had been converted by missionaries sympathetic to Arianism around the middle of the fourth century, at a time when Arianism was still strong in the Empire, and the

Colossal marble head of the emperor Constantine,
Rome, early fourth century. The huge eyes—windows
into the soul—are typical of late antique art. The
impression that the emperor is crying and drooling is
the unintended result of stains from later centuries.

persecutions of Emperor Theodosius had no effect on the faith of Germanic
tribes. Consequently, when in time groups of Germanic peoples established
successor states on the ruins of the Western Empire, they found themselves
divided from their Roman subjects not only by culture but by bitter religious
antagonisms as well.

Before the collapse of the Roman Empire in the West, despite the Arian
menace, Trinitarian Christianity had absorbed and turned to its own purposes
much of Rome's heritage in political organization and law, carrying on the
Roman administrative and legal tradition into the medieval and modern
world. The Church modeled its canon law on Roman civil law. The secular
leadership of the Roman Empire gave way to the spiritual leadership of the
Roman Church. The pope assumed the old Roman republican and imperial

title of *pontifex maximus* (supreme pontiff) and preserved much of the imperi ritual of the later Empire. In this organizational sense, the medieval Churc has been described as a ghost of the Roman Empire. Yet it was far more thaï that, for the Church reached its people as Rome never had, giving the impov- erished majority a sense of participation and involvement that the Empire had failed to provide.

The Latin Doctors

Constantine's conversion hastened the process of fusion between Christianity and Greco-Roman culture. During the generations following his death, the process was brought to completion by three Christian scholars—St. Ambrose, St. Jerome, and St. Augustine—honored in later years as "Doctors of the Latin Church." Working at a time when the Empire was swiftly becoming Christian- ized, yet before the intellectual vigor of classical antiquity had diminished, they used their mastery of Greco-Roman thought to interpret the Christian faith. Nearly seven centuries were to pass before Western Europe regained the intel- lectual level of late antiquity, and the writings of these three Latin Doctors therefore exerted a commanding influence on succeeding generations.

Although Ambrose, Jerome, and Augustine made their chief impact in the realm of thought, all three were immersed in the political and ecclesiastical affairs of their day. Ambrose (c. 340–397) was bishop of Milan, a great city of northern Italy that in the later fourth century replaced Rome as the imperial capital in the West. Ambrose was a superb administrator, a powerful orator, and a vigorous opponent of Arianism. Thoroughly grounded in the literary and philosophical traditions of Greco-Roman civilization, he enriched his Christian writings by drawing heavily from Plato, Cicero, Virgil, and other giants of the pagan past. Significantly, he was the first major churchman to assert that in the realm of morality the emperor himself is accountable to the Christian priest- hood. When Emperor Theodosius I massacred the rebellious inhabitants of Thessalonica, Ambrose barred him from the church of Milan, the imperial cap- ital, until he had formally and publicly repented. Ambrose's bold stand and the emperor's public submission set a long-remembered precedent for the princi- ple of ecclesiastical supremacy in matters of faith and morals.

Jerome (c. 340–420) was the most celebrated Biblical scholar of his time. A restless, troubled man with a touch of acid in his tongue, he once remarked to an opponent, "You have the will to lie, good sir, but not the skill to lie." Wan- dering far and wide through the Empire, Jerome lived in Rome for a time, then fled the worldly city to found a monastery in Bethlehem. Jerome's monks devoted themselves to the copying of Latin manuscripts, a task that was to be taken up by countless monks in centuries to come and which, in the long run, resulted in the preservation of important works of Greco-Roman antiquity that would otherwise have perished. The modern world owes a great debt to Jerome and his successors for preserving and transmitting the tradition of Latin letters.

Jerome himself was torn by doubts as to the propriety of a Christian immersing himself in the works of pagan literary figures such as Homer and

Virgil, Horace and Cicero. He was terrified by a dream in which Jesus banished him from heaven with the words, "You are a Ciceronian, not a Christian." For a time Jerome renounced all pagan writings, but he was much too devoted to the charms of classical literature to persevere. In the end he concluded that Greco-Roman letters might properly be used in the service of the Christian faith.

Jerome's supreme achievement lay in the field of scriptural commentary and translation. It was he who produced the definitive translation of the Bible from its original Hebrew and Greek into Latin, the language of the Western Roman Empire and medieval Western Europe. The result of Jerome's efforts was the Latin Vulgate Bible, which Catholics have used up to the twentieth century, and which has served as the basis of innumerable translations into modern languages. It was an achievement of incalculable significance to Western civilization.

Augustine of Hippo (354–430), whose conversion and career are sketched in the boxed biography at the end of this chapter, was the foremost philosopher of Roman antiquity. As bishop of Hippo (an important city in North Africa), he was deeply involved in the political-religious problems of his age. He wrote voluminously against various pagan and heretical doctrines that threatened Christian orthodoxy in his lifetime. In the course of these disputes, he examined many of the central problems that have occupied theologians ever since: the nature of the Trinity; the existence of evil in a world created by a good and all-powerful God; the special quality of the Christian priesthood; the nature of free will and predestination. Out of his diverse writings emerges a body of speculative thought that served as the intellectual foundation for medieval philosophy and theology.

Augustine was disturbed, as Jerome had been, by the danger of pagan thought to the Christian soul. But, like Jerome, he concluded that although a good Christian ought not to *enjoy* pagan writings, he might properly *employ* them for Christian ends. Accordingly, Augustine used the philosophy of Plato and the Neoplatonists as a basis for a new and thoroughly Christian philosophical scheme. As St. Thomas Aquinas later observed, looking back from the thirteenth century, "Whenever Augustine, who was expert in the philosophy of the Platonists, found in their teaching anything consistent with faith, he adopted it; those things which he found contrary to faith, he amended."

Plato had taught that abstract ideas were more important than tangible things. He believed that we acquire true knowledge not by observing things and events in the world of nature but by reflecting on the fundamental ideas that underlie the physical universe, just as a mathematician operates in the abstract world of pure numbers. Elaborating on Plato, the Neoplatonists viewed God as the center and source of reality and saw the natural world as merely a dim reflection of its divine source—a faint outer ripple in the concentric circles of existence, scarcely worth considering.

Augustine used Christianity to reshape the insights of Plato and Plotinus. Like the Neoplatonists, he believed that the material world was less important than the spiritual world, but it was nevertheless the creation of a good and loving God who remained actively at work in it. Augustine elaborated on the traditional Christian doctrine, rooted in Judaism, that God had created the first man and woman with the intention that they and all their descendants should attain salvation—should live forever in God's loving presence. But rather than creating mere human puppets, God gave human beings freedom to choose between good (accepting his love) and evil (rejecting it). As a consequence of Adam and Eve's choosing wrongly, humanity fell from its original state of innocence, became incorrigibly self-centered, and thus severed its relationship with God. But God reknit the relationship by assuming human form himself in the person of Jesus—suffering, dying, and rising again. The original sin of the first man, Adam, was redeemed by the crucifixion of the sinless God-man, Christ, and the possibility of human salvation was thereby restored.

Accordingly, the central goal of the Christian life is to attain the salvation that Christ has made possible. One can achieve this goal only by becoming a loving, unselfish person, and Augustine insisted that we are powerless to overcome our self-centeredness except through divine grace. He saw us as incapable of earning our own way into heaven. This being so, nobody deserves salvation, yet some achieve it because their moral characters are shaped and strengthened by God's grace.

The necessity of divine grace to human salvation is a central theme in the greatest of Augustine's works, the *City of God*. Here he set forth a comprehensive Christian philosophy of history that was radically new and deeply influential. Rejecting the Greco-Roman notion that history repeats itself in endless meaningless cycles, he viewed it as a purposeful process of human-divine interaction beginning with the creation and continuing through Christ's incarnation to the end of the world. Augustine interpreted history not in economic or political terms but in moral terms. To him the single determining force in history is human moral character, the single goal, human salvation. God is not interested in the fate of kingdoms or empires, except insofar as they affect the spiritual destiny of individuals. And individual salvation depends not on the victories of imperial legions but on the cleansing of human moral character by divine grace. True history, therefore, had less to do with the struggles between states than with the war between good and evil that rages within each state and each soul.

Augustine divided humanity into two opposing groups: not Romans and barbarians as the pagan writers would have it, but those who live in God's grace and those who do not. The former are members of the "City of God," the latter belong to the "Earthly City." The two cities are hopelessly intertwined in this life, but their members will be separated at death by eternal salvation or damnation. Human history, therefore, has as its purpose the growth and welfare of the City of God.

The writings of St. Augustine have shaped Western thought in fundamental ways. His theory of the two cities, although often reinterpreted in later generations, influenced political ideas over the next thousand years. His Christian Platonism dominated medieval philosophy until the mid-twelfth century and remains a significant theme in religious thought to this day. His distinction between the ordained priesthood and the laity has always been basic to Catholic theology. And his emphasis on divine grace was to be a crucial source of inspiration to the Protestant leaders of the sixteenth century.

As a consequence of Augustine's work, together with that of his contemporaries, Ambrose and Jerome, Christian culture was firmly established on classical foundations. At Augustine's death in 430 the Western Empire was tottering, but the Classical-Christian fusion was by now essentially complete. The strength of the Greco-Roman tradition that underlies medieval Christianity and Western civilization owes much to the fact that these three Latin Doctors, and others like them, found it possible to be both Christians and Ciceronians.

St. Augustine of Hippo

In his *Confessions*—the first major autobiography ever written—Augustine (354–430) described his long intellectual and moral journey along a twisting path from youthful hedonism to Christian piety. He did so in the form of a prayer—a confession to God—written in the hope that others, lost as he once was, might be led into the spiritual haven of the Church.

Augustine told of his dissolute boyhood and early manhood in the North African region of the Roman Empire. Despite the prayers and admonitions of his Christian mother Monica (St. Monica—"Santa Monica"), he rejected her faith. He took a mistress, who bore him a son; he studied philosophy and rhetoric; and he drifted from one popular creed to another: from paganism to dualism, skepticism, and Neoplatonism. It was not until the age of thirty-two that he converted to Christianity.

Augustine's conversion occurred in stages, while he was teaching rhetoric in Milan. Out of curiosity he went to hear the preaching of Milan's eloquent and renowned Christian bishop, Ambrose, and he was profoundly moved. "I came to damn," Augustine said, "and stayed to praise."

Nevertheless, Augustine was not yet prepared to abandon his life of wine and women. While in Milan he became betrothed (very formally engaged) to a wealthy heiress not yet of marriageable age. Out of respect for his betrothal (and to further his quest for wealth), he parted from the mistress who had borne his son. But as one of Augustine's mid-Victorian biographers disapprovingly and discreetly remarked, "Neither the pain of this parting nor consideration for his not yet marriageable bride prevented him from forming a fresh connection of the same kind." Augustine prayed to God to deliver him from his slavery to the pleasures of the flesh, but then he added: not quite yet! "Let me wait a little longer."

But Ambrose's sermon and Augustine's own intellectual and spiritual quest were drawing him more and more deeply into the Christian religion, and the tension between his growing faith and the worldliness of his life was becoming all but unbearable. His great emotional crisis occurred late in the summer of 386, when a friend told him about the development and spread of Christian monasticism, and how two young imperial officials, betrothed as Augustine was, had abandoned the world and the prospect of marriage to become monks. Profoundly moved, Augustine said to his friend, "What's the matter with us? What does this story mean? These two men have none of our education, yet they rise up and storm the gates of heaven while we, for all our learning, lie here wallowing in this world of flesh and blood."

Overcome by his emotions, Augustine rushed from the house: "I now found myself driven by the torment in my breast to take refuge in the garden, where nobody could interrupt that fierce struggle, in which I was my own opponent, until it reached its conclusion." Augustine tore at his hair and beat his forehead. His past sins seemed to speak to him in tempting whispers: Did he really intend to renounce the joys of sex forever? His conscience countered: "Close your ears to the dirty whispers of your body." Then, as Augustine reported, "a great storm broke within me, bringing with it a deluge of tears." He flung himself beneath a fig tree, continuing to weep, when he heard a child's voice repeating the phrase over and over again: "Take it and read, take it and read."

In the belief that those words were a divine command, Augustine sought out his copy of St. Paul's *Epistles*, opened it at random, and read a passage from the Epistle to the Romans: "No drunken orgies, no promiscuity or licentiousness, and no strife or jealousy. Let your armor be the Lord Jesus Christ, and forget about satisfying your bodies with all their lusts." As Augustine wrote, "I had neither the desire nor the need to read further. When I finished the sentence, as though the light of peace had been poured into my heart, all the shadows of doubt dispersed."

Augustine gave up his wealthy bride-to-be, his licentiousness, and his teaching career. St. Ambrose baptized him in Milan the following Easter, AD 387, to the overwhelming joy of his mother, Monica, who was at his side.

Augustine subsequently returned to his native North Africa, where he formed a small religious community and headed it for a time. His writings were by now winning him fame throughout the Western Empire. In the 390s he was dragged unwillingly into Church administration, being appointed bishop of the important North African port city of Hippo. There, he produced a great quantity of literary and philosophical works of immeasurable importance to medieval intellectual history, including the *Confessions* and, much later, the *City of God*.

As he wrote, Augustine was also occupied with the day-to-day cares of his diocese and his Christian flock. His contribution to religious thought arose not from the dispassionate working out of an abstract system of theology but rather from his responses to the urgent issues of the moment. One such issue was the survival of the Roman Empire itself. And by strange coincidence, in AD 430, within months of the death of the man who wrote the *City of God*, the Vandals had seized his episcopal city of Hippo.

CHAPTER 2

The Waning of the Western Empire

DECLINE AND FALL

The Splitting of East and West

In the year 330, a century before Augustine's death, Constantine founded a new, Eastern imperial capital on a strategic waterway known as the Bosphorus, which connects the Black Sea with the Mediterranean. The city was built on a grand scale and adorned with monuments pillaged from throughout the Roman Empire. It was a second Rome, with its own senate, its own imposing palaces and public buildings, and its own hungry lower classes fed by the bread dole and diverted by chariot races in its enormous hippodrome (the oval course of which can still be traced). Constantinople was situated on the site of a Greek town called Byzantium, which was renamed Constantinople, "Constantine's City." Now renamed Istanbul, it is the metropolis of western Turkey, and with its population in excess of eleven million it is today, as it was in the Middle Ages, one of the largest cities in the world.

When in later centuries the Western Empire had fallen to Germanic invaders and the Eastern part survived alone, Constantinople became Europe's greatest urban center. The lands that its emperors ruled continued to be known as the Roman Empire, but modern historians have distinguished it from the Roman Empire of classical antiquity by calling it the "Byzantine Empire," after old Byzantium.

Ever since the late third century, the Roman imperial office had been split from time to time between a Western emperor and an Eastern emperor, and by the end of the fourth century the split had become permanent. Thenceforth, although the Roman Empire continued to be regarded as a whole, one emperor ruled the Eastern half from Constantinople, while another ruled the Western half—no longer from Rome but from some more strategically situated capital, first Milan, then Ravenna.

This political split reflected a cultural and linguistic division of long standing. The Latin tongue of the early Romans had spread across the Western provinces, but Greek remained the major language in the East. (The educated elite throughout the Empire tended to be bilingual.) The Eastern half of the

Empire—Greece, Egypt, and the eastern Mediterranean provinces—had been civilized far longer than the western lands of North Africa and Western Europe, far longer than Rome itself. The East contained the bulk of the population; its agriculture was dominated less by owners of vast plantations who, in the West, resisted imperial taxation and, to a degree, imperial authority. The Eastern cities were larger, more numerous, and more commercially active than the newer cities of the West. Indeed, the Western cities—including Rome—were chiefly military, administrative, and cultural centers rather than centers of commerce. Supported by the taxes of the country folk, they were economic parasites living off the labor and productivity of the agrarian regions around them. Under the circumstances, the West was bound to suffer from an unfavorable balance of trade with the East. In exchange for Eastern silks, spices, jewels, and grain, the West had relatively few exports to offer, apart from slaves, warhorses, and a diminishing supply of gold coins. Thus, with the coming of large-scale Germanic migrations in the fifth century, the Eastern Empire managed to survive while the more brittle political superstructure of the Western provinces disintegrated.

Reasons for the Fall of the Western Empire

The "decline and fall" of the Western Empire has fascinated historians across the centuries, for it involves not only the collapse of one of humanity's most impressive and enduring "universal states" but also the demise of Greco-Roman civilization itself. Many reasons have been proposed—no less than 210 different causes according to a recent survey. They include such factors as climatic changes, sexual orgies, bad ecological habits, slavery, Christianity, even lead poisoning. None of them makes much sense. Classical civilization began and ended with slavery. The Eastern Empire was more thoroughly Christianized than the Western, yet it survived for another thousand years. The most spectacular Roman orgies occurred in the pagan golden age. Christian conversion made them unstylish, and the Germanic migrations occurred long after the age of orgies had passed. One otherwise respectable historian proposed the bizarre idea that the fall of Rome was a result of homosexuality, a practice that is much more easily documented in the fifth century BC than the fifth century AD and might more plausibly be associated with the rise than the demise of classical civilization.

More likely causes were the failure of the Roman economy to change or expand and the parasitical character of the Western cities. Then too, the fifth-century Western emperors tended to be less competent than their Eastern colleagues and more open to the potentially hazardous policy of filling their armies with Germanic troops under Germanic generals. The first-century Empire was sufficiently entrenched to endure the rule of Nero and Caligula; the far weaker Western Empire of the fifth century was hard put to survive the rule of such imperial nincompoops as Honorius, Valentinian III, and Romulus Augustulus.

The riddle of Rome's decline and fall will probably never be completely solved, and even the question itself is misleading. For imperial Rome did not literally fall. Instead, it underwent an immense strategic withdrawal from the less productive West to the wealthy and long-civilized provinces of the eastern Mediterranean. Some historians have found it puzzling that the Western Empire endured as long as it did.

Back when the Empire was expanding, its economy had been nourished by a constant influx of booty and slaves. But once expansion ceased, the West was unable to compensate by more intensive internal development. There was no large-scale industry, no mass production. Instead of importing manufactured goods from major urban centers, the various regions of the Empire tended more and more to produce them locally, and therefore less efficiently. Industrial production was held in low esteem by the Roman aristocracy, who had always considered it unrefined to engage in commerce or industry. They preferred to draw their wealth from their great plantations, their status from high public office, and their pleasure from the good company of fellow landed aristocrats. The Bill Gateses and Ross Perots would never have been invited to their parties.

The Roman economy remained agrarian to the end, and basic farming techniques advanced very little during the imperial centuries. The Roman plow was adequate but rudimentary, and windmills were unknown. There were some water mills, but nowhere near as many as in, say, eleventh-century England. Roman landowners continued to rely on their slaves and seemed little interested in labor-saving devices.

The economic exhaustion of the Western Empire was accompanied by population decline, runaway inflation, and deepening poverty. And at the very time that the labor shortage was becoming acute, the army and bureaucracy were growing ever larger. Higher and higher taxes on fewer and fewer taxpayers resulted in the impoverishment of the urban middle classes, and by the fifth century the Western cities were declining in wealth and population. Only the small, exclusive class of great landowners managed to dodge taxes and prosper. As early as the third century they were withdrawing from civic affairs, abandoning their town houses, and retiring to their country estates. They warded off marauders and imperial tax collectors alike by assembling armies of their own and fortifying their villas. Having deserted the cities, the West European aristocracy would remain an agrarian class for the next thousand years.

The decline of the city was damaging to the urbanized administrative structure of the Western Empire. More than that, it crippled the civic culture of Greco-Roman antiquity. The civilization of Athens, Alexandria, and Rome could not survive in the fields. It is in the decay of urban society that we find the crucial connecting link between political collapse and cultural transformation. In a very real sense Greco-Roman culture had been changing its shape long before the final demise of the Western Empire. By 476 the cities were shrinking. The rational outlook of Greco-Roman classicism was transformed. All through the fifth century the Roman army and civil government were becoming Germanized just as the Germanic peoples were becoming Romanized. Indeed, the two cultures had long been merging, and during the Western Empire's final century its desperate emperors, faced with a growing shortage of resources and indigenous manpower, were turning more and more to non-Romans to defend their frontiers and keep order in their realm. Germans abounded in the army, entire tribes were hired to defend the frontiers, and Germanic military leaders came to hold positions of high authority in the Western Empire. Survival had come to depend on the success of Germanic defenders against Germanic invaders.

The Roman Legacy

In another sense, however, Greco-Roman culture never died in the West. It exerted a profound influence, as we have seen, on the Doctors of the Latin Church and, through them, on the thought of the Middle Ages. It was the basis of repeated cultural revivals, great and small, down through the centuries—in the era of Charlemagne, in the High Middle Ages, in the Italian Renaissance, and in the neoclassical movements of the eighteenth and nineteenth centuries. Roman law endured to influence Western jurisprudence. The Latin tongue remained the language of educated Europeans for well over a thousand years, while evolving in the lower levels of society into the Romance languages: Italian, French, Spanish, Portuguese, and Rumanian. And the dream of Rome inspired empire builders from Charlemagne to Napoleon.

Even though fragmented in the fifth-century West, the Roman political administration survived after a fashion in the administrative systems of the Germanic successor states, whose kings were often advised by Roman counselors and fiscal experts. Similarly, the organizational units of the Church—"dioceses" and "provinces," presided over by bishops and archbishops—were patterned on Roman administrative units that had borne identical names. The bishops of the late Empire had become increasingly involved in imperial governance, participating in numerous civic functions and checking on the activities of Roman officials. With the demise of imperial authority in the West, bishops sometimes assumed direct political control of their dioceses, seeing to the maintenance of the food supply and supervising the repair of walls and fortifications. Since most bishops were now drawn from office-holding families of the old Roman senatorial aristocracy, such duties came easily to them.

In these ways and many more, the legacy of classical antiquity was passed on to the medieval West. Europeans for centuries to come would be nourished by Greco-Roman culture and haunted by the memory of Rome.

THE GERMANIC IMPACT ON ROMAN EUROPE

The civilization of medieval Europe emerged as a synthesis of three cultures: Classical, Christian, and Germanic. The age of the Latin Doctors witnessed the virtual completion of the Classical-Christian synthesis, but the blending of Roman and Germanic cultures was as yet far from complete. Not until the eighth century or thereabouts was a fusion of Classical-Christian culture with Germanic culture fully achieved. The intervening era—the sixth and seventh centuries—provides a fascinating view of a new civilization in the making.

Germanic Customs and Institutions

In the later fourth century, Germanic peoples from central and southeastern Europe began to press harder against the imperial frontiers. They were not entirely Germanic but included considerable numbers of Celts, Slavs, and even peoples of the Middle East. It is therefore hazardous to make broad generalizations regarding their culture and institutions, for customs varied from tribe to tribe and from group to group. The Germanic tribes were themselves extremely unstable, taking form around successful war leaders, then disintegrating when their military fortunes declined and forming again around new leaders. In time the Germanic peoples tended to coalesce, under growing Roman influence, into the tribal kingdoms that emerged from the fractured remnants of Roman imperial governance in the West: those of the Franks, the Vandals, the Angles, the Saxons, the East and West Goths (Ostrogoths and Visigoths), and others. Once established as kingdoms in the Roman West, these newly formed tribes fabricated myths about their allegedly age-old origins in Eastern Europe or Scandinavia.

Before their first contacts with the Empire, all these peoples were illiterate and therefore "prehistoric." Even archaeological investigations are hindered by the fact that the barbarians did not build in stone. Our first reliable evidence of these cultures dates from a time when they had already been transformed by their contacts with Roman civilization. By the time they filtered into the Empire, or crossed the imperial frontiers en masse, they had all absorbed Roman culture to a considerable degree, and many had been converted in the fourth century to Arian Christianity.

A contemporary account of early Germanic institutions in the late first century AD is to be found in a short book entitled *Germania*, written by the Roman historian Tacitus in AD 98. This work is not altogether trustworthy; it is a morality piece written with the intention of criticizing the "degeneracy" of the Romans by comparing them unfavorably with the simple, upright Germans. And one should always bear in mind that the fourth-century Germanic settlers had fallen much more deeply under Roman influence than the Germans whom Tacitus described. Nevertheless, if used cautiously, Tacitus's *Germania* is a valuable source of information on the early Germanic peoples. We can accept his description of tall, blue-eyed people with reddish-blond hair, living in rustic villages and occasionally going on rampages. And Tacitus correctly pointed out that Germanic women enjoyed considerable independence and respect. They were valued members of Germanic communities because they performed much of the agricultural labor. German men specialized in hunting and warfare, though women occasionally joined in even these pursuits. But Tacitus's picture of Germanic sexual equality is contradicted by the evidence from early Germanic law codes, which regard women as lifelong minors under the legal guardianship of their fathers, their husbands, or, if the husband died, his nearest kinsman. Tacitus likewise exaggerated when he praised the Germans for their chastity and virtuous behavior. On the whole their vices seem to have been no less numerous than those of the Romans, but simply cruder. Their standards of personal hygiene are suggested by the observation of the fifth-century Roman gentleman, Sidonius Apollinaris: "Happy the nose that cannot smell a barbarian."

Like the Romans, the Germans used iron tools and weapons. Their chief activities were tending crops or herds and fighting wars. Violence was common, not only between tribes but within them as well. When someone was killed, all close relatives were bound to avenge the death by conducting a feud—declaring war, as it were—against the killer's family. In the boisterous and unstable milieu of the tribe, killings were all too common, and in order to keep the social fabric from being torn apart by blood feuds, it became customary for the tribe to establish a *wergeld,* a sum of money that the killer might pay to the relatives of the victim to appease their vengeance. Wergelds varied in size depending on the victim's sex, age, and social status (they were highest for aristocratic adult males and women of childbearing age). Smaller payments were established for lesser injuries such as the cutting off of a victim's arm, leg, thumb, or finger, until in time every imaginable injury was covered, down to the little toe. There was no guarantee, however, that the assaulter would agree to make the payment or that the offended kin-group would agree to accept it. Despite all efforts to control them, blood feuds continued far into the Middle Ages.

Ties of kinship were strong among the early Germans, but they were rivaled by those of the war band, or *comitatus,* a group of warriors bound together by their loyalty to a chief or king. Indeed, the leader of a comitatus that won its battles might attract sufficient followers to become chief or king of a tribe of his own. The comitatus was a kind of military brotherhood based on honor, fidelity, courage, and mutual respect between the leader and his men. In warfare the leader was expected to excel his men in courage and prowess, and should the leader be killed, his men were honor-bound to fight to the death even if their cause was hopeless. The heroic virtues of the comitatus persisted throughout the early Middle Ages as the characteristic ideology of the European warrior aristocracy.

The comitatus was usually a subdivision of a tribe, whose members were bound together by their allegiance to a chieftain or king and, after being modified by Roman civilization, by their recognition of a common body of customary law. The laws of the Germanic tribes differed significantly from those of the Roman Empire; they dealt not with broad, systematic concepts but with wergeld schedules and similar devices for controlling violence and private feuding. Legal decisions often depended on whether the parties were able to adhere precisely to complex procedural formalities. Among the Franks, for example, innocence or guilt was determined by requiring the accused to submit to a process known as the "ordeal." One might be required to grasp a bar of red-hot iron and carry it some specified distance or take a stone from a boiling cauldron. If after several days the hand was healing properly, the accused was judged innocent. If not, the verdict was guilty. Similarly, the accused might be lowered into a pond by rope to sink or float. Sinking was a proof of innocence and floating a proof of guilt: the pure water would not "accept" the guilty.

Through such appeals to divine judgment, the Germanic peoples sought to achieve community consensus—to heal the breaches in interfamily relationships created by acts of violence. Throughout the early Middle Ages it was chiefly these Germanic customs, rather than the sophisticated, impersonal concepts of Roman law, that governed jurisprudence in Western Europe. For Roman law depended not on local consensus but on the enforcement authority of a powerful state, and no such authority emerged in Western Europe until the twelfth century. Roman law survived the fall of the Western Empire in fragmentary or bastardized form, but only in the twelfth century did it undergo a fundamental revival in the West. And even then its victory over Germanic law was gradual and incomplete.

The decades just preceding the invasions witnessed the development, under Roman influence, of relatively stable royal dynasties among some Germanic tribes. Perhaps an unusually gifted warrior and his kindred would gather military followers around him to form a new tribe, rather like the formation of a new criminal gang in urban America. But if the new tribe was successful in war, its leader or leaders might claim royal status and even, in time, descent from some divine ancestor. When a king died, the assembly of the tribe chose as his successor the ablest member of his family. This might or might not be his eldest son, for the tribal assembly was given considerable latitude in its power to elect. The custom of election persisted in most Germanic kingdoms far into the Middle Ages. Its chief consequence during the fifth-century invasions was to ensure that the tribes were normally led by clever, battle-worthy kings or chieftains at a time when the Western Empire was ruled by dolts.

The Germanic Migrations

Germanic peoples from central and southeastern Europe had long been a threat to the Empire. They had defeated a Roman army in the first century; they had probed deeply into the Empire in the second century and again in the mid-third. But until the late fourth century the Romans had always managed eventually to drive the invaders out or absorb them into the Roman political structure. Beginning in the 370s, however, an overtaxed, exhausted Empire was confronted by renewed Germanic pressures of great magnitude. Lured by the relative wealth, the productive agriculture, and the sunny climate of the Mediterranean world, the Germanic peoples tended to regard the Empire as something to enjoy, not destroy. Their age-long yearning for the fair lands across the Roman frontier was suddenly made urgent by the westward thrust of a tribe of Asiatic nomads known as Huns. These mounted warriors conquered one Germanic tribe after another and turned them into satellites. They subdued the majority of the Goths and made them a subject people. A group of Gothic survivors, known subsequently as the Visigoths, sought to preserve their independence by appealing for sanctuary behind the Roman Empire's Danube frontier. The Eastern emperor Valens, an Arian, sympathized with the Arian Goths, and in 376 he took the unprecedented step of permitting a multitude of Visigoths and associated peoples to cross peacefully into the Empire.

Chapter 2 The Waning of the Western Empire

There was trouble almost immediately. Corrupt imperial officials cheated and abused the Goths, who retaliated by going on a rampage. At length, Valens himself took the field against them, but the emperor's military incapacity cost him his army and his life at the battle of Adrianople in 378. Adrianople was a military debacle of the first order. Valens's successor, Theodosius I, pacified the Goths, permitting them to settle peacefully in the Balkans and providing them with food and revenues in return for their loyalty and military backing.

When Theodosius died in 395, imperial authority was split between his two youthful sons. Arcadius, barely eighteen, became emperor in the East, and Honorius, a child of eleven, assumed authority in the West. As it happened, the two halves were never again rejoined under a single ruler. Not long after Theodosius's death, a skillful new Gothic leader named Alaric led his people on a second pillaging campaign that threatened Italy itself. In 406 the desperate Western Empire recalled most of its troops from the Rhine frontier to block Alaric's advance, with the disastrous result that in late December the Vandals and other Germanic peoples crossed the frozen, ill-guarded Rhine into Gaul. Shortly thereafter, the Roman legions abandoned distant Britain, and the island was gradually overrun by Angles, Saxons, and other Germanic war bands.

In 408 Emperor Honorius engineered the murder of his ablest general, a man of Germanic ancestry named Stilicho. Honorius was by then an adult in his mid-twenties, but the evidence suggests that he may have been mentally retarded.[1] He apparently suspected, perhaps with reason, that Stilicho's devotion to the imperial cause was less than fervent. But without Stilicho, Italy was virtually defenseless. Honorius and his court barricaded themselves behind the impregnable marshes of Ravenna, leaving Rome to the mercies of Alaric and his Visigoths. In 410 the Visigoths entered the imperial capital unopposed, and Alaric permitted them to plunder it for three days.

The sack of Rome had a devastating impact on imperial morale. "My tongue sticks to the roof of my mouth," wrote St. Jerome on hearing of the catastrophe, "and sobs choke my speech." But in historical perspective, the event was merely a single milestone in the disintegration of the Western Empire. Alaric died in 410, shortly after the sack, and the Visigoths, leaving Rome to its witless emperor, moved northward into southern Gaul and Spain. There they established a Visigothic kingdom that endured until the Muslim conquest of the eighth century.

Meanwhile other Germanic tribes, most of them newly formed, were carving out kingdoms of their own. The Vandals swept through Gaul and Spain and across the Straits of Gibraltar into Africa in the 420s and 430s. In 430, the year of St. Augustine's death, they captured his episcopal city of Hippo. They established a North African kingdom centering on ancient Carthage and took to the sea as buccaneers, devastating Mediterranean shipping and sacking coastal

---

[1]For a most ingenious, if not altogether convincing, rehabilitation of Honorius as a highly effective strategist, see Roger Collins, *Early Medieval Europe, 300–1000* (New York, 1991), pp. 51–57.

cities, including Rome itself in 455.[2] The Vandal conquest of North Africa cost Rome much of its grain supply, while Vandal piracy shattered the peace of the Mediterranean and dealt a crippling blow to the waning commerce of the Western Empire.

Midway through the fifth century the Huns themselves moved against the West, led by Attila, the "Scourge of God" (see accompanying box). Defeated by a Roman-Visigothic army in Gaul in 451, the Huns returned the following year, hurling themselves toward Rome and leaving a path of devastation behind them. The Western emperor, Valentinian III, left Rome undefended, but the bishop of Rome, Pope Leo I, somehow persuaded Attila to withdraw from Italy. Attila died shortly afterward; his empire collapsed, and the Huns themselves vanished from history. They were not mourned.

In its final years the Western Empire, whose jurisdiction now scarcely extended beyond Italy, fell under the control of hard-bitten military adventurers of Germanic birth. Emperors continued to reign for a time, but their Germanic generals were the powers behind the throne. In 476 the barbarian general Odovacar, who saw no point in perpetuating the charade, deposed the last emperor, a boy named Romulus Augustulus, "little Augustus." Odovacar sent the imperial trappings to Constantinople and asserted his sovereignty over Italy by diverting a third of the agrarian tax revenues to his Germanic troops. Odovacar claimed to rule as an agent of the Eastern Empire, but in fact he was on his own. A few years later, a group of Germanic peoples calling themselves Ostrogoths, now free of Hunnish control and led by an astute king named Theodoric, advanced into Italy. Theodoric invited Odovacar to a peace conference, murdered him, and established his own rule over Italy.

Attila the Hun, the "Scourge of God"

Attila, leader of the Huns during their invasions of the Roman Empire, is well known but not well loved. His atrocities, although reported in hair-raising detail by contemporary Roman observers, were probably no worse than those of the Roman armies. One of the most terrifying things about the Huns was that, being Asiatic nomads from Mongolia, they did not resemble Romans or Germans in appearance; they were therefore regarded by people of the West as hideously ugly: short, foul, skinny, low-browed, high-cheeked, and scar-faced. As one contemporary observer uncharitably remarked, "Their swarthy aspect was fearful and they had a kind of shapeless lump for a head, with pinholes rather than eyes."

---

[2]Historians have had few good things to say about the Vandals, but of course they are no longer here to defend their reputation. We are indebted to them for providing our language with such colorful words as "vandal," "vandalize," and "vandalism."

Less biased contemporaries described Attila as brown-skinned and broad-chested, with deep eyes, an upturned nose, and hair prematurely gray. He ruled the Huns from 433 to 453, at first jointly with his brother (who vanished under mysterious circumstances). By about 440, he and his horsemen had made themselves virtually supreme over the Germanic tribes of central Europe and had frightened the Eastern Roman Empire into paying an annual tribute. Attila established his capital in Pannonia, present-day Hungary, not far from modern Budapest.

A report by an ambassadorial mission from Constantinople in 448 provides a vivid description of Attila and his court. He walked around the wooden buildings of his headquarters with a "dignified strut" and entertained the envoys from Constantinople in his large wooden banquet hall, where attendants served food and drink in silver plates and cups. Attila himself drank from a wooden cup typical of older, less elegant days. At nightfall "torches were lit and two barbarians approached Attila and sang songs they had composed celebrating his victories and brave deeds in war." Afterward Attila retired to his bed, on a raised platform in the same hall, to sleep under "linen sheets and jewelled coverlets." The ambassadors' sense of cultural superiority over the newly rich Hun was dimmed by the fact that the mission from Constantinople had hired an assassin to murder Attila. Discovering the plot, the Hunnish chieftain contemptuously sent the envoys home.

In 450 the Eastern Empire discontinued its tribute payments to the Huns, and rather than seeking revenge on Constantinople, Attila turned to the more vulnerable West. Accompanied by his Huns and tributary Germans, he crossed the Rhine in 451. He claimed that he was coming as a kind of Prince Charming to rescue the Roman princess Honoria, who had been put under house arrest for having an affair with a palace chamberlain. In a fit of anger, Honoria had sent her ring to Attila with the plea that he marry her and carry her off to freedom. Although Honoria is said to have been beautiful, Attila's chief motive for coming west was doubtless plunder rather than marriage. His army was met by an allied Roman-Visigothic force near Troyes in central Gaul, where, after a day of mutual carnage, Attila withdrew his warriors from the battlefield and led them back home to Pannonia.

In the following year Attila descended on Italy, sacking and pillaging cities as he moved toward Rome. It was at this point that he was confronted by Pope Leo I at the head of a delegation of Roman senators. According to the best account, Pope Leo, "an old man of harmless simplicity, venerable in his gray hair and majestic clothing," was suddenly and miraculously joined by Saints Peter and Paul, swords in their hands and clad in bishops' robes. Their appearance at this critical moment was especially noteworthy because both saints had been dead for nearly four hundred years.

Whether because of this marvel or because his army was dying from heat and plague, Attila withdrew once again from the Western Empire. He died in 453 during the night following a great banquet celebrating his marriage to a young Germanic woman named Ildico. Perhaps he had too much to drink at the banquet; perhaps Ildico was more than the middle-aged Hun could cope with. There were rumors of violence, but Attila's death was more probably natural and, as one Victorian writer put it, "due to his own intemperate habits."

Theodoric and Clovis

Theodoric ruled Italy from 493 to 526 and became the dominant power in Western Europe. Although apparently illiterate, he respected Roman culture: in Italy, Arian Ostrogoths and orthodox Romans worked together harmoniously under his governance, repairing aqueducts, erecting new buildings, and bringing a degree of prosperity to the long-troubled peninsula. The improving political and economic climate gave rise to an intellectual revival that contributed to the transmission of Greco-Roman culture into the Middle Ages. At a time when the knowledge of Greek was dying out in the West, the philosopher Boethius, a high official in Theodoric's regime, produced a series of Latin translations of Greek philosophical works that served as fundamental texts in Western schools for the next 500 years. Boethius wrote his masterpiece, *The Consolation of Philosophy*, at the end of his life when he had fallen from official favor and was imprisoned. The book's central theme is that earthly misfortunes cannot affect the inner life of a virtuous individual. Although such a notion is perfectly consistent with Christianity, Boethius drew his ideas primarily from the thought of Plato and the Stoics. Boethius was himself a Christian, yet he never mentioned Christianity explicitly in his *Consolation of Philosophy*. Nevertheless, the work remained immensely popular throughout the Middle Ages.

Theodoric's secretary, Cassiodorus, was another scholar of considerable distinction (though incorrigibly long-winded). A wealthy Roman aristocrat, Cassiodorus spent his later years as abbot of a monastery that he had erected on his own lands in southern Italy. Like Jerome, he set his monks to the task of copying and preserving the literary works of antiquity, both Christian and pagan.

During the years of Theodoric's rule in Ostrogothic Italy, another Germanic king, Clovis (481/2–511), was creating a Frankish kingdom in the former Roman province of Gaul. Although much less Romanized then Theodoric, Clovis possessed a keen instinct for political survival. He adopted the straightforward policy of murdering all possible rivals (a tactic not unknown to third-century Roman emperors or to Theodoric). Bishop Gregory of Tours, writing in the late 500s, quoted Clovis as saying, "Oh woe, for I travel among strangers and have none of my kinfolk to help me!" But Bishop Gregory added, "He did not refer to their deaths out of grief, but craftily, to see if he could bring to light some new relative to kill."

It will perhaps seem odd that Gregory of Tours approved wholeheartedly of Clovis's rule. That savage monarch—who lacked even the family loyalty of a mobster—is pictured in Gregory's *History of the Franks* as one who "walked before God with an upright heart and did what was pleasing in his sight." The explanation is that, sometime in the late 490s, Clovis converted to Christianity not in its Arian but in its orthodox form. As a Trinitarian Christian he respected and favored the churches of his kingdom, whereas other Germanic rulers were handing orthodox churches over to the Arians. Clovis himself regarded Christianity as a kind of magic to help him win battles (much as Constantine had done), but the Church supported him as a hero of Christian orthodoxy.

Sidonius Apollinaris

A member of the Roman landholding elite of southern Gaul, Sidonius Apollinaris (c. 431–489) lived through the period when his homeland was overrun by the Arian Visigoths. His response to this experience provides a valuable clue as to how wealthy Romans in parts of the Western Empire managed to survive the Germanic conquests.

Sidonius was a Roman patriot, a Latin poet, the son-in-law of a Roman emperor, and, like most fifth-century aristocrats, a Catholic Christian. He served for a time as prefect of the city of Rome, and he spent the final seventeen years of his life as bishop of Clermont (in the south-central part of modern France). When Clermont was besieged by the Visigoths in the 470s, Bishop Sidonius took an active part in the successful defense of the city. He observed that he would "have endured poverty, fire, sword, and plague" rather than submit to Visigothic rule. But Sidonius was left with no choice in the matter when the Western emperor ceded Clermont and its surrounding district to the Visigoths in 475, in return for Visigothic support against other Germanic invaders.

The Visigoths banished Sidonius from Clermont for a time but afterward permitted him to return to his bishopric, where he lived out his last years. He complained to friends and readers that he could scarcely write good Latin verse while surrounded by people who spoke outlandish German and reeked of onions and rancid butter. Nevertheless, he continued to compose poetry—lines that were tinged with classical learning and rich in allusions to Roman mythology. He also followed the sensible course of striking up an acquaintance with the Visigothic king, Alaric II. He won Alaric's friendship by playing backgammon with him and making it a point always to lose. Catholic-Arian differences could be forgotten over the backgammon board, and Sidonius was permitted to rule his bishopric and enjoy his estates in peace.

Sidonius Apollinaris loved the provincial villa life and the lands surrounding him, "where pastures crown hilltops and vineyards clothe the slopes, where villas rise in the lowlands and fortresses on the mountainous rocks—forests here, clearings there, and headlands washed by rivers." Descriptions such as these, together with Sidonius's vivid accounts of feasts and garden parties, suggest that villa life in late fifth-century Gaul could still be beautiful—for a Roman aristocrat who could hold his nose, mind his business, and lose at backgammon.

Another reason for Clovis's good press was that he maintained relatively warm relations with the old landholding aristocracy (to which Bishop Gregory of Tours belonged). Because of the depopulated condition of the countryside, there were adequate lands for all—Frank and Gallo-Roman alike. The great landowning families of Roman times were for the most part left in place—to enjoy their fields, their bishoprics, and their garden parties, and to serve as high officials in the Frankish regime. From their point of view, Clovis's victory was not so much a conquest as a coup d'état.

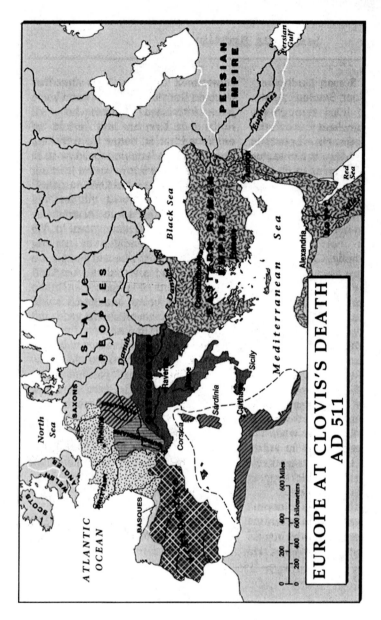

In succeeding generations, Frankish and Gallo-Roman landowners, sharing a common religion, fused through intermarriage into a single aristocratic
order. As centuries passed, the royal name "Clovis" was softened to "Louis,"
and the "Franks" became the "French." And the friendship between the Frankish monarchy and the Church developed into one of the determining elements
in European politics.

Chapter 2   The Waning of the Western Empire

Europe in AD 500

As the sixth century dawned, the Western Empire was only a memory. In its place was a group of Germanic successor states that vaguely prefigured the nations of modern Western Europe. Theodoric headed a relatively tolerant Ostrogothic-Arian regime in Italy. The orthodox Clovis was completing the Frankish conquest of Gaul. The Arian Vandals lorded it over a restive orthodox population in North Africa, seizing the wheat plantations and introducing former Roman aristocrats to the joys of field work. The Arian Visigoths were being driven out of southern Gaul by the Franks, but their regime continued to dominate Spain for the next two centuries. And the Angles and Saxons were in the process of establishing a group of small, non-Christian kingdoms in Britain that would one day coalesce into "Angle-land," or England.

While Germanic kingdoms were establishing themselves in the West, the Roman papacy was beginning to play an important independent role in European society. We have seen how Pope Leo I (440–461) assumed the task of protecting the city of Rome from the Huns, thereby winning for himself the moral leadership of Italy. Leo and his successors declared that the bishops of Rome—the popes—constituted the highest authority in the Church, and following the example of St. Ambrose, they insisted on the supremacy of Church over state in spiritual and ethical matters. In proclaiming its doctrines of papal supremacy in the Church and ecclesiastical independence from state control, the papacy was wisely disengaging itself from the faltering Western emperors. The mighty papacy of the High Middle Ages was yet far off, but it was already foreshadowed in the boldly independent stance of Leo I. The Western Empire was crumbling, but eternal Rome still claimed the allegiance of the world.

CHAPTER 4

Early Western Christendom

CONTINUITY AND CHANGE

Western Europe: The Land and Its People

Until recently, historians had visualized transalpine Western Europe in late
Roman and early medieval times as a sparsely populated and largely untamed
wilderness. This misconception turns up, among other places, in an earlier edition of the present text: "North of the Mediterranean Basin, Western Europe
was lightly settled and little developed" in AD 500.[1] But the traditional
"untamed wilderness" picture of post-Roman Europe—and pre-Roman Europe
as well—has now been discarded. Archaeological investigations throughout
much of Western Europe have demonstrated that human settlement was far
more widespread, and more complex, than had previously been suspected. As
the Romans expanded into the Balkans, Gaul, and Britain, they found populous
and flourishing agricultural villages in large numbers. They encountered hill
forts sheltering well-organized communities, farms tilled with large and highly
effective plows, and networks of fields, stock corrals, and homesteads linked
together by boundaries and trackways into what archaeologists describe as
"managed landscapes." The lands north of the Alps, which the Romans conquered in the first century BC and thereafter, had undergone many millennia of
economic and cultural development from the Stone Age to the Bronze Age
(c. 3000 BC) and finally, after 100 BC, the Iron Age. The half-millennium of
Roman occupation witnessed the building of cities on the Greco-Roman model:
Lyons, Cologne, Vienna, London, and many others.

With this new knowledge, together with the benefit of hindsight (a form of
cheating known as "history"), Europe's potential becomes obvious. Its weather
is bracing but not intimidating—a happy compromise between the languid, nar-
cotic mildness of Southern California and the torrid summers and arctic winters
that can sometimes afflict mid-America. (A guidebook for British tourists visiting the United States warns them of the violent temperature extremes of the
Middle West.) Northwestern Europe's dependable, year-round rainfall and the

---

[1]C. Warren Hollister, *Medieval Europe: A Short History*, 5th ed. (McGraw Hill-New York, 1982), p. 51.

fertile soils of its numerous river valleys encourage agricultural productivity—so much so that a first-century Greek geographer could describe the region as "producing in perfection all the fruits of the earth necessary for life."

By the fifth century, Europe's climate was better still. Between roughly AD 400 and 1200, Europe was less rainy and warmer by several degrees than it had previously been or than it is now. The summer growing season was longer, and vineyards flourished some three hundred miles farther north than they do today. Marshes and bogs receded, and the North Atlantic welcomed seafarers with less ice and milder storms.

The Western European heartlands form a vast plain that fans out from the Pyrenees and the Alps northeastward across France and Germany and on through Eastern Europe to the Ural Mountains of Russia. In Roman and early medieval times, as in preceding millennia, this fan-shaped plain was the route of countless tribes migrating westward out of Russia and beyond. Crossing the plain are several low, mineral-rich mountain ranges and a remarkable network of broad rivers fed by the year-round rains.

Europe has been shaped and nourished by its rivers. They connect interior settlements with the sea and with each other, facilitating communication and commerce. Most of Europe's major cities were built on riverbanks—Paris, London, Milan, Cologne, and many others—so that even though they lay far from the sea, they could function as ports. A further stimulus to commerce is Europe's long, irregular coastline, with its huge bays and peninsulas, and accessible offshore islands such as Sicily, Sardinia, and the British Isles. Taken altogether, Europe's climate, rich soils, rivers, and coastline create an ideal environment for human habitation and commercial enterprise.

Before the Roman conquests and long thereafter, most of Western Europe north of the Alps was inhabited by Celts—and by still-earlier settlers whom they had subdued. The Celts were a creative people, skilled at music and poetry, metalwork, and textile making. The Romans were amused at their barbaric custom of wearing pants instead of tunics ("breeches" is a Celtic word). Most Celts were farmers, living in villages set amidst cultivated fields. Others engaged in commerce across vast reaches of western, central, and even eastern Europe. The Celts built fortified towns along their trade routes, some of which became important provincial cities in Roman times. But it would be misleading to describe their far-flung settlements as a "Celtic Empire" (as some careless scholars have done), for the Celts were split into hundreds of independent tribes that united only occasionally, briefly, and grudgingly into larger confederations. They fought hard against the Romans, but in the long run they could not match the military resources of a Mediterranean empire.

Under the Roman conquerors, Celtic agricultural villages continued to function much as before. In time, the majority of these communities were incorporated into the great estates of the provincial Roman aristocracy (itself part Celtic through intermarriage). The farmer-villagers became unfree peasants and were forced to pay rents and dues to their lords. Some became slaves. But they continued to inhabit their villages and till their fields; it was in their landlords' interest that they should do so.

Physical map of Europe. Note the Alps (north of the Italian Peninsula), the Appenines (down the spine of Italy), and the Pyrenees (northeastern Spain).

The Germanic conquerors, as we have seen, took only portions of the old Roman estates (or their tax revenues) while establishing new estates on much the same pattern. And in the meantime, important churchmen—bishops and abbots—were themselves acquiring extensive lands through the accumulation of pious gifts. But whether under new lords or old, lay or ecclesiastical, the villagers worked on.

Post-Roman Europe

During the generations following the Germanic settlements, Western Europe lost much of the administrative structure of the Roman Empire. But the Church preserved a great deal of the old classical legacy, and bishops exercised both spiritual and political authority across considerable areas. During the 600s and early 700s, the municipal governments of Roman antiquity were disappearing north of the Alps; and archaeological investigations have disclosed a process of urban economic collapse in that period. But many towns endured as centers of church administration, the sites of the bishops' cathedrals and the headquarters of episcopal government over surrounding districts.

Many towns became important centers of pilgrimage. Christians from far and wide would travel to urban cathedral churches to venerate their holy relics—the bodies or clothing of deceased saints—which were regarded as agents of spiritual power and physical healing. The cathedral at Tours, for example, possessed the body of the noted miracle worker, St. Martin (bishop of Tours, 372–397), who was said to have healed many who touched his tomb. Holy men such as St. Martin were revered in their lifetimes as transmitters of God's power, wisdom, and love to the communities in which they lived, and their sacred bodies were thought to retain this function after death.

The urban bishoprics, with their relics and vast estates, played a major role in the economy of the Germanic successor states. So, too, did the large monasteries (abbeys) with their surrounding fields, and often with wonder-working relics of their own. The abbey of St. Denis near Paris, for example, housed the body of its renowned namesake, Dionysius or Denis, the martyred first bishop of Paris (d. c. 258), who, after having his head chopped off, picked it up and held it in front of him so that he could see where he was going. St. Denis later became the patron saint of France.

Bishops and abbots were the social and economic equals of the lay aristocracy, to whom they were often closely related; together they formed the landholding elite of the post-Roman West. The great estates—whether lay, ecclesiastical, or royal—were tilled by slaves or by semi-servile, rent-paying villagers in an economic environment that was becoming increasingly localized and self-contained. A small-scale luxury trade persisted, but the agrarian communities of the sixth and seventh centuries produced most of what they needed, and since lives were meager, needs were few.

There is reason to believe that some Western European farmlands were abandoned altogether and resettled only much later. Aerial photographs of the southern French countryside disclose fields of a typically medieval pattern—radiating outward from a central village. But often these radiating fields appear superimposed on earlier Roman patterns—square or rectangular fields, systematically laid out. Since no governmental authority of the early Middle Ages had either the power or the will to effect such a fundamental change in field patterns, one can only conclude that the Roman fields had reverted to wilderness, and generations thereafter had been resettled and reshaped. Aerial photographs do not permit precise dating, but the silent catastrophe they record may well have resulted from the violence and depopulation following the collapse of imperial authority in the West, aggravated by the great plague cycle that commenced in the 540s.

Germanic invasions and Germanic settlements transformed the ethnic character of Western Europe. First in Gaul, then elsewhere, the Germanic settlers gradually fused with the indigenous population. In the process, free Germanic farmers often descended into the ranks of semi-servile villagers, or even slaves. At the aristocratic level, the pattern of life was influenced by the Germanic warrior ideology—the heroic virtues of the comitatus and its warlord—while the civility of Roman villa life diminished accordingly.

On the other hand, the ideas of the late Empire and Christianity gradually liberalized Germanic legal attitudes toward women, who rose steadily from their earlier legal status as perpetual minors. Wealthy and powerful men found it increasingly difficult (though not yet impossible) to maintain flocks of wives and concubines or to divorce their wives at will and cast them aside. Nevertheless, polygamy was the standard practice among the monarchies and aristocracies of post-Roman Europe, creating intricately complex family entanglements and struggles over inheritances between contending half-brothers abetted by their various mothers.

Some women, rather than submit to unwanted marriages arranged by their families, found welcome refuge by entering monastic life. Daughters could inherit lands, and widows could now be guardians of their children and could exercise considerable power over their property. The blending of Roman and Germanic landholders into a single social order—combining elements from both cultures—gave rise to the aristocracy of medieval Europe.

Government and Intellectual Life

The Roman system of administration survived after a fashion in the West, particularly in Ostrogothic Italy and Visigothic Spain, less so in the kingdom of the Franks (Gaul, the future *Francia*, or France). But long before the imperial collapse of the fifth century, Roman government in the West had been gradually disintegrating. All through the late imperial era, government and economic life were becoming steadily more localized. Resistance to imperial taxes was growing, and great landowners were supporting private armies on their own fortified estates. The Germanic kings were by no means incompetent to manage a Roman provincial government; they were themselves the products of many generations of Roman influence, and they could always rely on the help of administrators from the indigenous population, left over from imperial days and eager to survive and prosper in the new regime. But when the Germanic kingdoms established themselves in the former Western provinces, the administrative machinery that they inherited was apt to be in bad repair. The unfavorable trade balance with the East persisted; gold coins remained scarce; violence in the countryside continued and worsened; and powerful aristocrats were no more willing to pay taxes to Germanic kings than to Roman emperors.

But although strong elements of continuity linked the late Empire to the early Germanic kingdoms, the shift was nevertheless accompanied by widespread dispossession, suffering, and violence. The Church was largely helpless to ameliorate these conditions, particularly in the troubled countryside, because its organization was confined largely to the shrinking towns and walled monasteries. Only gradually, and much later on, were rural parishes organized to meet the needs of the peasantry. In the meantime peasants were fortunate if they saw a priest once a year. Churchmen, like kings and nobles, were better known among the peasantry as grasping landlords than as fountains of justice and divine grace.

The intellectual life of the West suffered accordingly. The culture of old Rome was fading, and the new civilization of Western Europe had scarcely begun to develop. The leading scholars of the era were bishops, most of whom were from families of the old Roman aristocracy. One such bishop whom we have already encountered, Gregory of Tours (d. 594), remarked that "all but five of the bishops of the see of Tours have been connected with my family." Gregory of Tours's *History of the Franks*, our best source for the reigns of Clovis and his successors, is in some respects an impressive work of history. But it is written in ungrammatical Latin (for which he apologizes to his readers), it displays blatant political bias, and it tends to dwell on improbable miracles and all-too-probable murders and atrocities. The world that Gregory portrays was dominated by savage cruelty and beclouded by fantasy. Both the story that he presents and the way in which he presents it attest to the decline of literary culture in sixth-century Gaul.

Pope Gregory the Great (d. 604), another bishop of aristocratic Roman background, was awarded a place alongside Ambrose, Jerome, and Augustine as one of the Doctors of the Latin Church. Pope Gregory's writings are marked by profound practical wisdom and psychological insight, but they do not approach the level of the fourth-century Doctors in philosophical depth and scholarly sophistication. Pope Gregory watered down Augustinian theology for the benefit of his own naive contemporaries. The profound theological issues with which Augustine grappled are overshadowed in Gregory's thought by a concentration on such secondary matters as demons and relics.

Bishop Isidore of Seville (d. 636) was known as the foremost scholar of his generation. His most impressive work, the *Etymologies,* was intended to be an encyclopedia of all knowledge. It was a valuable work for its time and was studied for many centuries thereafter. But its value was diminished by Isidore's lack of critical powers. He included every scrap of information he could find, whether likely or unlikely, profound or superficial. In fairness to Isidore, it should be said that he was victimized by the credulity of the ancient Roman writers on whom he depended and was left adrift by the weakness of the Latin scientific tradition. Nevertheless, as the greatest mind of his age he betrayed a certain lack of sophistication. On the subject of monsters, he wrote:

> The Cynocephali are so called because they have dogs' heads and their very barking betrays them as beasts rather than men. These are born in India. The Cyclopses, too, hail from India, and they are so named because they have a single eye in the middle of their forehead. . . . The Blemmyes, born in Libya, are believed to be headless trunks, having mouth and eyes in the breast; others are born without necks, with eyes in the shoulders. . . . They say the Panotii in Scythia have ears so huge that they cover the whole body with them. . . . The race of Sciopodes is said to live in Ethiopia. They have one leg apiece, and are of a marvelous swiftness, and . . . in summertime they lie on the ground on their backs and are shaded by the greatness of their feet.

Finally, with a touch of skepticism, Isidore concluded:

> Other fabulous monstrosities of the human race are said to exist, but they do not; they are imaginary.

The Germanic Kingdoms

The century between AD 500 and 600 witnessed important changes in the political superstructure of Western Christendom. In AD 500 Theodoric's Ostrogothic regime dominated Italy, the Vandals ruled North Africa, the Visigoths governed Spain, Clovis and his Franks were conquering Gaul, and the Anglo-Saxons were expanding their settlements in Britain. A century later, two of these states had been destroyed by Justinian's armies: North Africa was now Byzantine rather than Vandal, and the Ostrogothic kingdom of Italy had collapsed.

By 600 pagan Anglo-Saxon tribes had occupied much of Britain, dispossessing and enslaving many of the indigenous Celtic inhabitants and driving others into the western hills of Cornwall, Wales, and southern Scotland. Anglo-Saxon Britain was now a confused patchwork of small, independent kingdoms in which the process of Christian conversion was just beginning.

Gaul in 600 was thoroughly dominated by the Franks under the successors of Clovis, founder of the Merovingian dynasty (named after Clovis's legendary ancestor, Merovech). The Merovingian kings developed the practice of dividing the kingdom among the sons of a deceased ruler. Often the sons would engage in civil war until, as it sometimes happened, one of them emerged as sole monarch of the Franks. At his death, the kingdom would often be divided among his own sons, and the sad story would be repeated.

There were occasions when an able Merovingian king ruled effectively over a united Frankish kingdom or a portion thereof. The most celebrated of the later Merovingians, Dagobert I, received part of the kingdom in 622 from his father Clothar II, who himself had united Francia by seizing power from his aunt, Queen Brunhilde (whom he tortured to death). Dagobert acquired the remainder of Francia on Clothar's death in 629 and thereafter ruled strongly over all the Franks until his own death in 638. He was a generous benefactor of the Church; by granting permission to his favorite abbey of St. Denis to hold an

annual fair, he managed at one blow to please God and stimulate commerce; he issued Latin charters that employed Roman legal formulas and had Latin law codes drawn up for Germanic tribes under his sway.

But Dagobert's reign was exceptional, and it was brief. His dynasty was never able to rid itself of the habit of murdering rivals, usually fellow kinsmen. With the passage of generations, the Merovingian kings became less and less effective as their power and estates slipped into the hands of aristocrats. Yet the Merovingians managed to endure in Francia for two and a half centuries—much longer than any other Germanic dynasty—before giving way in 751 to a new dynasty, the Carolingians (who will be turning up in Chapter 6).

The Arian kings of Visigothic Spain were more successful than the Merovingians in retaining vestiges of the old Roman administration, particularly the system of tax assessment and collection. During the early generations of their rule, they lacked the Merovingians' crucial advantage of a shared faith

The Visigothic church of St. John the Baptist in Baños de Cerato, Palencia, Spain, mid-seventh century. A highly original reinterpretation of the classical style.

with their Roman-provincial Catholic subjects. This problem was solved when the Visigothic king Reccared (586–601) converted from Arianism to Catholicism, bringing with him most of the Visigothic aristocracy and Arian clergy. This mass conversion—a virtual holy stampede—opened the way for the integration of the Roman and Germanic landholding classes into one. King Reccared then authorized the holding of a great church council at his capital of Toledo in 589, which provided the legislation necessary to extinguish Arianism and fuse the two churches.

The Visigothic monarchy enjoyed a further success in the 620s, when it reconquered its Mediterranean shore from the Byzantines (whose attention was focused on the Persians just then). But the Visigothic kings, like the Merovingians, allowed their power and wealth to pass little by little to the landed aristocracy. As Gregory of Tours explained, the Visigoths "had adopted the reprehensible habit of murdering on the spot any king who displeased them and replacing him with someone they preferred." The regime fell prey to the conquering Muslims in the early 700s.

The century since Theodoric's reign had been a disastrous one for Italy. The horrors of Justinian's Gothic wars were followed by the invasion of the Lombards. By 600 the decimated peninsula was divided between the Byzantines in Ravenna and the south and the Lombards in the north. The papacy, under nominal Byzantine jurisdiction, dominated the lands around Rome and sought to preserve its fragile independence by playing Lombard against Byzantine. At critical moments, however, it looked to the Byzantines as its defenders.

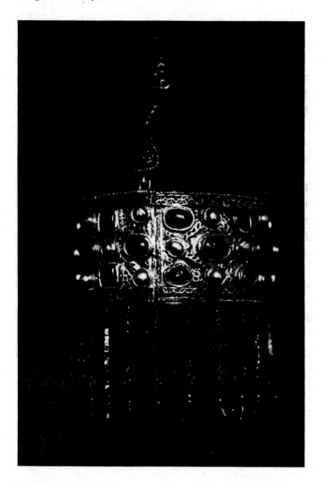

Visigothic royal crown, seventh-century Spain. Set in
gold, the jewels include sapphires, agates, pearls, and
rock crystals.

THE EARLY MEDIEVAL CHURCH

Monasticism

Encouraged by popes and supported by kings, monasticism was a potent transforming force in the early medieval West. We have already commented on the
role of monasteries, such as St. Jerome's in Bethlehem and Cassiodorus's in
southern Italy, as transmitters of classical learning. And we have seen how
wealthy monastic communities such as St. Denis served both as economic centers and as custodians of holy relics. But at heart, of course, monasteries were
places of prayer, meditation, and service to God and humanity.

Monastic life is not peculiar to Christianity but is found in many religions—Buddhism and Judaism, to name two. The Essenes, for example, whose cult may have produced the famous Dead Sea scrolls, constituted a kind of Jewish monastic order. There have always been religious people who seek to withdraw from the world and devote their lives to uninterrupted communion with God, and among late Roman and medieval Christians, this impulse was particularly strong. Monasticism came to be regarded as the most perfect form of the Christian life, the consummate embodiment of Christ's own words: "Anyone who has forsaken home, brothers, sisters, father, mother, wife, children, or lands for my name's sake will be repaid a hundred times over and inherit everlasting life" (Matthew, 19:29).

This impulse toward withdrawal and renunciation first affected Christianity in the third century when the Egyptian St. Anthony retired to the desert to live the ascetic life of a godly hermit. In time the fame of his sanctity spread, and a colony of ascetics gathered around him to draw inspiration from his holiness. Anthony thereupon organized a community of hermits who lived together but had no communication with one another—like apartment dwellers in an American city. Similar hermit communities soon arose throughout Egypt and spread into other regions of the Empire. Hermit saints abounded in the fourth and fifth centuries. One of them, a Syrian holy man named Simeon Stylites, achieved the necessary isolation by living atop a sixty-foot pillar for thirty years, evoking widespread admiration and imitation. Simeon Stylites and other pillar saints, despite their relative isolation, played a role of the most fundamental importance to their communities by serving as transmitters of divine favor and protection to those around them, sources of holy wisdom and grace, and mediators between God and humanity.

In the meantime a more down-to-earth type of monasticism was developing. Beginning in early fourth-century Egypt and then expanding quickly throughout the Eastern Empire, monastic communities of men or women, based on a cooperative rather than a hermit's life, were attracting numerous dedicated Christians who found insufficient challenge in the increasingly complacent post-Constantinian Church. By the early fifth century these East-Roman ideas of ordered communal monasticism were being carried to the West by travelers such as John Cassian, who had served as a monk in both Bethlehem and Egypt before journeying to Rome in 404 as an envoy of the patriarch of Constantinople. Remaining in the Western Empire until his death (c. 435), John Cassian wrote widely influential Latin treatises on the monastic life and founded two monasteries in Marseilles on the Mediterranean coast of Gaul, one for men and one for women.

Far to the north, in Ireland, still another strain of Christian monasticism emerged. The Celts of Ireland had been converted to Christianity in the fifth century by St. Patrick and other missionaries; by 600 the Irish had developed an astonishingly creative Celtic-Christian culture. Having never been incorporated into the Roman Empire, Ireland had no cities and therefore lacked the urban-based substructure of episcopal organization that existed on the Continent. Instead, Irish Christianity developed its own distinctive organizational

The first page of St. Matthew's Gospel, from the
Lindisfarne Gospels, British Museum, London.

structure based on great, autonomous monasteries rather than urban bishoprics. The Celtic Church did have bishops, but they did not rule dioceses; their
functions were spiritual and sacramental only. They had no administrative
power and usually lived in monasteries under the authority of an abbot.

Celtic monasticism became one of the great energizing forces of the age—
in Ireland, in Scotland, on the Continent, and, eventually, among the English.
Developing in relative isolation from the papacy, it originated a variety of customs and practices uniquely its own. During the sixth and seventh centuries,
Irish monks excelled in the rigor of their scholarship, the depth of their sanctity,
the austerity of their lives, and the scope of their missionary work. Irish monastic schools were perhaps the best in Western Europe at the time, and a rich Irish
artistic tradition culminated in the illuminated manuscripts of the eighth century, which were the wonder of their age and still excite admiration in our own.
Irish missionaries, striving to deepen and expand monastic life on the Continent, founded a number of important religious houses in Francia and as far
afield as northern Italy, and Frankish aristocratic abbey founders often adapted
Irish monastic customs, usually in modified form, for the governance of their
own monastic communities.

St. Benedict and His Rule

St. Benedict of Nursia (c. 480–c. 550) has been called the "father of Western monasticism." This is an exaggeration, for monasticism was well established in the West long before Benedict's time. His great contribution was to synthesize the ideas of John Cassian and others into a written rule of monastic life that remains deeply influential to this day.

Like other Christian leaders of his time, Benedict was a Roman of good family. Born in the province of Nursia, in the mountains of central Italy, he was sent to Rome for his education. But he fled the worldly city before completing his studies and took up the hermit's life in a cave near the ruins of Nero's country palace. In time, word of his saintliness circulated and disciples gathered around him. As it turned out, Benedict was more than a simple ascetic; he was a man of keen psychological insight—a superb organizer who learned from the varied experiences of his youth how the monastic life might best be lived. His tremendously influential monastic "Rule" discloses not only his personal genius but also a sense of order and discipline that was characteristically Roman.

Benedict founded a number of monasteries and attracted within them not only prospective saints but ordinary people as well, including the offspring of wealthy Roman families. At length he built his great monastery of Monte Cassino atop a mountain midway between Rome and Naples. His sister and disciple, St. Scholastica, established herself in a nearby hermitage and visited him once a year to talk of spiritual matters. Scholastica was to become the patron saint of all Benedictine nunneries, and Benedict's abbey at Monte Cassino remained for many centuries one of the chief centers of religious life in Western Europe.

Pope Gregory the Great described the Rule of St. Benedict as "conspicuous for its discretion." Modern scholars have discovered that it was derived from an earlier, anonymous monastic rule by a mysterious writer known only as "the Master." But St. Benedict improved on the "Rule of the Master" by giving it a novel quality of humane practicality. It provided for a busy, closely regulated life, simple but not ruthlessly austere. Although designed for communities of men, it was readily adaptable to nunneries. Benedictine monks and nuns were decently clothed, adequately fed, and seldom left to their own devices. Theirs was a life dedicated to God and the attainment of personal sanctity through prayer and service, yet it was also a life that could be led by any serious Christian. Benedictine communities were even open to children, many of whom were dedicated to religious life (without being asked) by their parents or guardians and were then educated in their monastery's school.

The monastic day was filled with carefully regulated activities: communal prayer, devotional reading, and work—field work, household work, manuscript copying, according to need and ability. Benedictine communities included priests to conduct the Eucharist and other sacraments, but it was by no means necessary that all monks be inducted into the priesthood—and most were not. Monks and nuns alike were pledged to the fundamental obligations of poverty, chastity, and obedience. Benedictines were to resist the three great worldly temptations of money, sex, and ambition by relinquishing all personal possessions, living a celibate life, and obeying the abbot or abbess. The heads of Benedictine houses were elected for life and were the unquestioned rulers of their abbeys. They were strictly responsible to God and were instructed to govern justly in accordance with the Rule. Benedict cautioned abbots not to "sadden" or "overdrive" their monks or give them cause for "just murmuring." Here especially is the quality of discretion to which Pope Gregory alludes and which was such a significant element in the Rule's success.

Contributions of the Benedictines

Within two or three centuries of Benedict's death, the Rule had spread throughout Western Christendom. The result was not a vast hierarchical monastic organization but rather a host of individual, autonomous monasteries sharing a single way of life, yet administratively unrelated. Benedict had visualized his monasteries as spiritual sanctuaries into which pious Christians might withdraw from the world. But the vast estates accumulated by many abbeys, along with the need of secular society for the discipline and learning of the monks, thrust the Benedictine order into the nexus of early medieval politics.

In reality, therefore, the Benedictines had an enormous impact on the world they renounced. Their schools produced most of the literate Europeans who kept the art of writing alive during the early Middle Ages. They served as a cultural bridge, transcribing and preserving the writings of Latin antiquity in a society that was largely nonliterate. Scribal work could be demanding and exhausting, as we learn from occasional postscripts tacked onto the ends of medieval manuscripts: "The art of writing is difficult; it tires the eyes, breaks the back and cramps the arms and legs." "The end has come; give me a pot of wine." "Give the poor scribe a pretty girl" (presumably a fleeting erotic fantasy, not to be taken literally).

This preservation of a cultural lifeline to Classical-Christian antiquity was by no means the only contribution of the Benedictines to early Western Europe. They spearheaded the penetration of Christianity into the forests of Germany and later into Scandinavia, Poland, and Hungary. They served as scribes and advisers to princes and were drafted into high ecclesiastical offices. As recipients of gifts of land from pious donors over many generations, they held and managed large estates, some of which were models of intelligent agricultural organization and technological innovation. For although each Benedictine was pledged to *personal* poverty, a Benedictine abbey might acquire immense *corporate* wealth. In time, Benedictine abbots became great landholders, responsible to their lay lords for political and legal administration and military recruitment over the large areas under their control. Above all, as islands of learning and security in an ocean of ignorance and political chaos, the Benedictine monasteries were the spiritual and intellectual centers of the developing Classical-Christian-Germanic synthesis that underlay European civilization. In short, Benedictine monasticism became the supreme civilizing influence in the early Christian West.

Pope Gregory the Great (590–604)

In its early years, however, the Benedictine movement was very nearly destroyed. A generation after Benedict's death, Monte Cassino was pillaged by the Lombards (c. 577) and its monks were scattered. Some of them took refuge in Rome, where they came into contact with the pious, well-born monk and future pope, Gregory the Great. Though not himself a Benedictine, Gregory was deeply impressed by their accounts of Benedict's holiness and his Rule. Gregory wrote a biography of the saint that achieved tremendous popularity in the years that followed and drew widespread attention and support to Benedictine monasticism. Most of the biography deals with Benedict's miracles, but Gregory also wrote admiringly of the Benedictine Rule. Some scholarly specialists doubt that Gregory had actually seen the Rule, but I suspect they are mistaken, for Gregory advised his readers that they could "find all of Benedict's administrative acts in this *Book of the Rule*," and one can reasonably suppose that the honest and unassuming pope knew whereof he spoke.

We have already encountered Pope Gregory as a scholar, a popularizer of Augustinian thought. His theology, although highly influential in subsequent centuries, failed to rise much above the intellectual level of his age. His real genius lay in his keen understanding of human nature and his ability as an administrator and organizer. His *Pastoral Care*, a treatise on the duties and obligations of a bishop, is a masterpiece of practical wisdom and common sense. It answered a great need of the times and became one of the most widely read books in the Middle Ages.

Gregory loved the monastic life and ascended the papal throne with genuine regret. On hearing of his election he went into hiding and had to be dragged into the Roman basilica of St. Peter's to be consecrated. But once resigned to his new responsibilities, Gregory bent every energy to the extension of papal authority. He believed fervently that the pope, as successor of St. Peter, was the rightful ruler of the Church. He reorganized the financial structure of the papal estates and used the increased revenues for charitable works to ameliorate the wretched poverty of his times. His integrity, wisdom, and administrative ability won him an almost regal position in Rome and central Italy, as Lombards and Byzantines struggled for control of the peninsula. The reform of the Frankish Church was beyond his immediate powers, but he set in motion a process that would one day bring both France and Germany into the papal fold when he dispatched a group of monks to convert the pagan Anglo-Saxons.

The Conversion of England

The mission to England was led by the monk St. Augustine (not to be confused with the great theologian of an earlier day, St. Augustine of Hippo). In 597, Augustine and his followers arrived in the English kingdom of Kent and began their momentous work. England was then divided into a number of independent Germanic kingdoms, of which Kent was momentarily the most powerful, and

Two Germanic Christian Queens: Bertha of Kent and Ethelberga of Northumbria

In the conversion of pagan Germanic kingdoms to Christianity, royal women often played a determining role. The conversion of Clovis and his Frankish people in the 490s, for example, owed much to the efforts of Clovis's Christian wife, Queen Clotilde, who served as the essential link between her pagan husband and the clergy of Gaul.

The pattern was repeated a century later in England when Queen Bertha, a Merovingian princess and descendant of Clovis and Clotilde, provided crucial assistance in the conversion of her husband, King Ethelbert of Kent, in 597.

Little is known of Bertha's early life; even the date of her birth (as well as of her marriage and death) is uncertain. Like all royal and aristocratic marriages of the time, Bertha's was arranged by her parents in negotiations with the bridegroom or his parents. The motive, as in all such marriages, was the advancement of family interests through a useful alliance. Bertha herself was probably not consulted. Indeed, until she crossed the English Channel to Kent for her wedding, Bertha had probably never met her future husband.

Because Bertha was a Christian princess about to marry the pagan king of a pagan people, Ethelbert had been made to agree that she could practice her religion freely and could bring a Frankish bishop with her to serve as her chaplain. King Ethelbert gave his bride an old, abandoned Romano-British church, St. Martin's, in the royal town of Canterbury ("Kent City"). St. Martin's church still stands and is of extraordinary historical interest, although, owing to modern Canterbury's diabolical one-way street system, it would have been much easier to find in the late sixth century than it is today.

Pope Gregory the Great was very likely in correspondence with Queen Bertha on the subject of St. Augustine's coming mission to Kent. Whatever the case, Bertha contributed significantly to Augustine's eventual success by instructing Ethelbert in the basic principles of her faith. According to Bede's *Ecclesiastical History,* when Augustine and his companions arrived in Kent, King Ethelbert "ordered that they should be provided with all necessities. . . . For he had already heard of the Christian religion, having a Christian wife of the Frankish royal house named Bertha." It was in Bertha's church of St. Martin's that Augustine and his monks worshiped and preached; and it was there in all likelihood that King Ethelbert was baptized in 597.

A few years later, Pope Gregory wrote to Bertha, stating that the fame of her learning and good words had spread as far as Rome and even Constantinople. While urging her to make still greater efforts to strengthen her husband's faith, he declared that she, more than anyone else, was responsible for the conversion of the English.

Bertha bore Ethelbert a son, who succeeded in time as king of Kent, and a daughter, Ethelberga, who was wed to a pagan king, Edwin of Northumbria. In important respects the marriage of Ethelberga and Edwin is a case of new actors playing a familiar script. The king permitted Ethelberga to practice her Christian faith in pagan Northumbria and to bring a bishop with her to serve as her chaplain. The pope wrote to King Edwin expressing

hope for his conversion, "most especially as we understand that your gra-
cious queen and true partner is already
endowed with the gift of eternal life
through Holy Baptism." And to Queen
Ethelberga the pope wrote, "We have
been much encouraged by God's goodness in granting you an opportunity to
kindle a spark of the true religion in
your husband. . . . Persist, illustrious
daughter, in using every effort to melt
the coldness of his heart by teaching
him about the Holy Spirit, so that the
warmth of divine faith may enlighten
his mind through your constant
encouragement."

Persuaded by Queen Ethelberga
and her chaplain, Edwin became
Northumbria's first Christian king. He
received baptism, along with all his
nobles and many of his lesser subjects,
on Easter Sunday, 627.

Augustine was assured a friendly reception by the fact that Queen Bertha, wife
of King Ethelbert of Kent, was a Frankish Christian. With Bertha's support, the
conversion proceeded swiftly, and on Whitsunday, 597, King Ethelbert and thousands of his subjects were baptized. The chief town of the realm, Canterbury,
became the headquarters of the new Church, and Augustine himself became
Canterbury's first archbishop. Under his influence Ethelbert issued the first written laws in the Anglo-Saxon language.

During the decades that followed, the fortunes of English Christianity rose
and fell with the varying fortunes of the Anglo-Saxon kingdoms. Kent declined
after King Ethelbert's death, and by the mid-600s political power had shifted to
the northernmost of the Anglo-Saxon states, Northumbria. This remote outpost
became the scene of a deeply significant encounter between the two great creative forces of the age: Irish-Celtic Christianity moving southward from its
monasteries in Scotland, and Roman Christianity moving northward from Kent
and influenced increasingly by the Benedictine Rule.

Although the two movements shared a common faith, they had different
cultural backgrounds, different notions of monastic life and ecclesiastical organization, and different systems for calculating the date of Easter. The Roman
Easter date won official recognition at a synod convened in 664 at the nunnery
of Whitby, situated atop a windy bluff high above the North Sea. At Whitby the
king of Northumbria decided in favor of Roman-Benedictine Christianity, and
papal influence in England was assured. Five years later, in 669, the papacy sent
the scholarly Theodore of Tarsus to assume the archbishopric of Canterbury
and reorganize the English Church into a coherent system of bishops and dioceses. As a consequence of Northumbria's conversion and Archbishop
Theodore's tireless efforts, England, only a century out of paganism, became
Europe's most vigorous and creative Christian society.

But in England, as elsewhere, old pagan customs lingered on for centuries
among the common people, blending into Christianity in interesting ways.
Here, for example, are some of the charms that were performed in Anglo-Saxon
England long after its conversion, in which Christian and pre-Christian reme-
dies are strangely mixed:

Against the Elfin Race: Make a salve [of various herbs, including] wormwood, bishopswort, lupine, viper's bugloss, crow leek, and garlic. Put the herbs into a vessel, place them under the altar, sing nine masses over them, then boil them in butter and sheep's grease . . . [etc].

To drive away a dwarf: pound the dung of a white dog into dust, mix it with flour, and bake it into a cake; give it to the afflicted person to eat before the time of the dwarf's arrival.

If someone is demented, take the skin of a porpoise, make it into a whip, and flog him with it: he will soon be well. Amen.

The Northumbrian Renaissance

The encounter between Celtic and Roman Christianity in seventh-century Northumbria produced a notable cultural awakening known as the "Northumbrian Renaissance." The two traditions influenced and energized one another to such an extent that the evolving civilization of the Christian West reached a pinnacle in this remote land. Boldly executed illuminated manuscripts in a curvilinear style both Celtic and Germanic in inspiration, a new script, a vigorous vernacular epic poetry, an impressive architecture—all contributed to the luster of Northumbrian culture in the late 600s and early 700s. The Northumbrian Renaissance centered on the great monasteries founded by Irish and continental missionaries at Lindisfarne, Wearmouth, Jarrow, and elsewhere. It was at the abbey of Jarrow (whose church still survives) that the supreme scholar of the age, St. Bede the Venerable, spent his life.

Bede entered Jarrow as a child and remained there until his death in 735. The greatest of his many works, the *Ecclesiastical History of England,* displays a critical sense far superior to that of Bede's medieval predecessors and contemporaries. The *Ecclesiastical History,* our chief source for early English history, is the first major historical work to employ the modern chronological framework based on the Christian era: AD, *Anno Domini,* the "year of the Lord." Bede's chronological scheme reflects his deep sense of historical unity and purpose: the transformation of the world, and particularly of England, through the spread of the Christian Gospel and the monastic life. The *Ecclesiastical History* reflects a remarkable cultural breadth and a penetrating mind; it establishes Bede as the foremost Christian intellect since Augustine of Hippo. And the progress of the Classical-Germanic synthesis is made clear by the fact that Bede, unlike the major scholars of the 500s and 600s, was not a well-born Roman but a man of Germanic roots.

By Bede's death in 735, the Northumbrian kings had lost their political hegemony, and Northumbrian culture was beginning to fade. But the tradition of learning was carried from England back to the Continent during the eighth century by a group of Anglo-Saxon Benedictine missionaries. In the 740s the English monk St. Boniface reformed the Church of Francia, infusing it with Benedictine idealism, systematizing its organization, and binding it more closely to the papacy. Pope Gregory had now been in his grave for 140 years, but his spirit was still at work. St. Boniface and other English missionaries founded new Benedictine monasteries among the Germans east of the Rhine and began the long, difficult task of Christianizing and civilizing Germany, just as Augustine and his monks had once Christianized Kent. By the later 700s the cultural center of Christendom had shifted southward again from England to the rising empire of the Frankish leader, Charlemagne.[2] Significantly, the leading scholar in Charlemagne's kingdom was Alcuin, a churchman from Northumbria, a student of one of Bede's own pupils.

The Church and Western Civilization

The West differed from the Byzantine East in innumerable ways, the most obvious being its lower level of civilization. But just as important is the fact that the Western Church was able to develop more or less independently of the state. Church and state often worked hand in hand in the Christian West, but religion and secular politics were never merged to the degree that they were in Constantinople and, indeed, in most ancient civilizations. Early Western Christendom was marked by a separation between cultural leadership, which was ecclesiastical and monastic, and political power, which was in the hands of the Germanic kings and Roman-Germanic aristocracies. This split contributed much to the fluidity and dynamism of Western culture. It produced a creative tension that tended toward change rather than crystallization. Like St. Augustine's two cities, the warrior culture of the Germanic kingdoms and the Classical-Christian culture of church and monastery remained always in the process of fusion, yet never completely fused. The interplay between them shaped the development of early medieval civilization.

[2]See pp. 93 ff.

CHAPTER 6

Carolingian Europe

THE CULTURAL, ECONOMIC, AND POLITICAL BACKGROUND

In the course of the eighth century, much of Western Christendom was united into a single dominion known to later historians as the Carolingian Empire. It was a vast constellation of territories welded together by the Frankish king Charlemagne and his warlike predecessors. In Charlemagne's realm the various cultural ingredients—Classical, Christian, and Germanic—that contributed to the making of European civilization achieved a degree of synthesis. Charlemagne was a Germanic king who surrounded himself with Germanic warrior-aristocrats. But he also consorted with well-educated churchmen who were trained in classical scholarship, and he took very seriously his role as protector and sustainer of the Western Church. Although his regime was modeled on traditional Germanic kingship, its intellectual life, limited though it was, drew heavily from the Classical-Christian tradition. The fusion of these ingredients was evident in the life of the Carolingian court, in the increasing effectiveness of the Carolingian Church, and in the person of Charlemagne himself.

Charlemagne's Francia stood in sharp contrast to contemporary Byzantium and the Abbasid Empire of Islam. Baghdad and Constantinople were great cities and centers of far-flung commerce. Charlemagne's kingdom had no cities worth the name, and his subjects were overwhelmingly an agrarian people. But it was beginning to dawn on a few of them that they were a people apart, *Europeans*, agents of a new, distinctive civilization rooted in Athens and Jerusalem, Germany and Rome, and bound together—much as the Byzantines and Muslims were—by a common faith, a common scholarly language, and a common heritage.

The new Europe was spiritually and intellectually enlivened by the wide-ranging Benedictines, who disseminated a cultural tradition based on the Bible, the writings of the Latin Doctors and their contemporaries, and the surviving masterpieces of Latin literature. This evolving culture was bound together politically by a new dynasty of Frankish monarchs, the Carolingians.[1]

---

[1]The Carolingians were named after their early leader Charles Martel, or Carolus (714–741).

Carolingian Europe differed profoundly from the Western Roman Empire of old. It was thoroughly agrarian in its economic organization, with its culture centered on the monastery, the cathedral, and the royal and noble courts instead of the urban marketplace. And although Charlemagne extended his authority into Italy, the center of his activities and interests remained northern Francia. In a word, the new Europe no longer faced the Mediterranean; its axis had shifted northward.

The Rise of the Carolingians

The Merovingian dynasty, founded by Clovis, had grown weak during its final century. A fundamental problem that the Merovingians shared with other early medieval monarchs was the necessity of giving away portions of their crown lands, generation after generation, in order to attract loyal followers. By the later 600s the Merovingians were impoverished, and power had passed to the landed aristocracy. Meanwhile, as a consequence of generations of civil strife among the kinsmen of deceased Merovingian kings, with their profusion of wives and sons, Francia had split into several distinct districts, the most important of which were Neustria (Paris and northwestern France), Austrasia (the heavily Germanized northeast including the Rhinelands), and Burgundy in the southeast (see map, p. 97).

The Early Carolingians

During the seventh century a dominating family, known to later historians as the Carolingians, emerged from the landholding aristocracy of Austrasia. Supported by a handful of allied and related families, the Carolingians managed to eliminate or assimilate rival aristocratic clans until they had achieved supremacy throughout Austrasia. Their family charisma was enhanced by the fact that they could claim a saint in their ancestry (Gertrude of Nivelles) and another "possible" saint (Arnulf, bishop of Metz).[2] The Carolingians became "mayors" of the Austrasian royal household—that is, they held the chief administrative office in the itinerant court of Austrasia and made the post hereditary. As the Merovingians became increasingly land-poor and powerless, the Carolingians became the real masters of Austrasia. Carolingian mayors built up their power by gathering around them considerable numbers of trained warriors, in the tradition of the old Germanic comitatus. These men became "vassals" of the Carolingians, placing themselves under the mayor's protection, accepting his food, shelter, and support, and pledging him their loyalty. Other aristocrats also had private armies of vassals, but the Carolingians, with far the greatest number of followers, dominated the scene.

---

[2]During the early Middle Ages, any person of conspicuous holiness could be popularly recognized as a saint; by the later twelfth century, however, sainthood was granted only through formal investigative proceedings at the papal court.

In 687 a Carolingian mayor named Pepin of Heristal led his Austrasian army to a decisive victory over the Neustrians at the battle of Tertry, and the Carolingians thenceforth controlled both districts. With Neustria in their grip they were able to dominate Burgundy, and when the Muslims moved into Gaul in the early 730s, the Franks stood united against them under the Carolingian mayor Charles Martel, Pepin of Heristal's bastard son.

Charles Martel (714–741)

Charles Martel, "the Hammer," was a skillful, ruthless military chieftain. Not only did he turn back the Muslims at the battle of Tours (732), he also won victory after victory over Muslims and Christians alike, consolidating his power over the Franks and extending the boundaries of the Frankish state. Charles Martel rewarded his military followers with estates in the conquered lands and with further estates that he confiscated from the Frankish Church. Although churchmen complained loudly, there was little they could do to oppose the hero of Tours and master of the Franks.

The Carolingians followed the same practice of divided succession among male heirs that had weakened the Merovingians. But, as it happened, the Carolingian rulers over several generations had only one long-surviving heir. Frankish unity was maintained not by policy but by luck. When Charles Martel died in 741, his lands and authority were divided between his two sons, Carloman and Pepin the Short. But Carloman ruled only six years, retiring in 747 to the Benedictine monastery of Monte Cassino (voluntarily, so it appears), leaving the field to his brother, Pepin. Carloman represented a new kind of Germanic ruler, deeply affected by the spiritual currents of his age, whose piety foreshadowed that of numerous saint-kings of later centuries. Christian culture and Germanic political leadership were beginning to converge.

Carolingian Chronology

687	Pepin of Heristal, Carolingian mayor of Austrasia, defeats Neustria; Carolingian hegemony established
714–741	Rule of Charles Martel
732	Arabs defeated at Tours
741–768	Rule of Pepin the Short
751	Pepin crowned king of the Franks; Merovingian dynasty ends
754	Death of St. Boniface
768–814	Reign of Charlemagne
772–804	Charlemagne's Saxon wars
800	Charlemagne crowned Roman emperor
814–840	Reign of Louis the Pious
842	Oaths of Strasbourg
843	Treaty of Verdun

Missions from England

At the time of Charles Martel's death in 741, English monks had long been engaged in evangelical work among the Germanic peoples east of the Rhine. The earliest of these missions were directed at the Frisians, a maritime people who were settled along the coast of the Netherlands. The first of the evangelists were monks from Northumbria. They brought to the Continent not only the organizational discipline and devotion to the papacy that had been characteristic of the Northumbrian Benedictines but also the venturesome missionary fervor the Celtic monks had contributed to the Northumbrian revival. So it was that Benedictine monks such as Wilfrid of Ripon and Willibrord left their Northumbrian homeland during the later 600s to evangelize the Frisians. The course of Western civilization was deeply affected by the transfer to Francia and Germany of the vibrant culture and Roman-Benedictine discipline of Northumbrian Christianity. Wilfrid of Ripon, Willibrord, and their devoted followers represent the first wave of a movement that was ultimately to infuse the Frankish empire of Charlemagne with the spiritual life that had developed in Anglo-Saxon England during the century following St. Augustine's mission to Kent.

The key figure in this cultural movement was the English Benedictine, St. Boniface. Reared in monasteries of southern England, Boniface left his native Wessex in 716 to do missionary work among the Frisians. From then until his death in 754 he devoted himself above all other tasks to Christianizing the Germanic peoples. He became famous among them by publicly chopping down one of their sacred oak trees. Boniface was a person of commanding presence and, by contemporary standards, a giant of a man—well over six feet tall. He was also renowned for his learning and wisdom. A great number of his letters survive, many of which request support from his compatriots in Wessex and advice from Rome. On three occasions he visited the papal court, and from the beginning his work among the Germans was performed under papal commission. In 732 the papacy appointed him archbishop in Germany, and some years later he was given the episcopal see at Mainz as his headquarters. Throughout his career he was a devoted representative of the Anglo-Saxon Church, the Benedictine Rule, and the papacy. As he put it, he strove "to hold fast the Catholic faith and unity, and to yield submission to the Church of Rome as long as life shall last for us."

Boniface also worked with the backing of the Carolingian mayors—Charles Martel and his sons, Carloman and Pepin the Short. Armed with the Christian faith and the Benedictine Rule, and supported by England, Francia, and Rome, Boniface labored among the Germanic peoples in Frisia, Thuringia, Hesse, and Bavaria. There he won converts, founded new Benedictine monasteries in the German wilderness, and erected the organizational framework of a disciplined German Church. He suffered moments of discouragement, as when he wrote to an English abbot, "Have pity upon an old man tried and tossed on all sides by the waves of a German sea." Yet Boniface accomplished much, and the monasteries that he established—particularly the great house of Fulda in Hesse—were to become centers of learning and evangelism that played a great role in converting and civilizing the peoples of Germany.

During the decade following Charles Martel's death in 741, Boniface devoted much of his energy to Francia. Well before his arrival, a monastic reform movement was flourishing in Francia independent of the English missionaries. Nevertheless, the Frankish Church as a whole stood in urgent need of reform. Many areas had no priests at all; numerous peasants were scarcely removed from paganism; and priests themselves are reported to have hedged their bets by sacrificing animals to Germanic gods. Charles Martel, although willing enough to support Boniface's missionary endeavors among the Germanic pagans, did not want reformers interfering with his own Frankish Church and perhaps raising awkward questions about his policy toward Church lands. Carloman and Pepin, however, encouraged Boniface to reform the Frankish Church, and beginning in 742 he held a series of synods (church councils) for that purpose. Working closely with the papacy, he remodeled the Frankish ecclesiastical organization on the disciplined pattern of England and papal Rome. He reformed Frankish monasteries along the lines of the Benedictine Rule, saw to the establishment of monastic schools, encouraged the appointment of dedicated bishops and abbots, and worked toward the development of an adequate system of local parishes and parish churches to bring the Gospel to the countryside. Thus Boniface laid the groundwork for both the new Church in Germany and the reformed Church in Francia. In doing so, he served as one of the chief architects of the Carolingian cultural revival. And the bishops and abbots of his reformed Frankish Church became valuable supporters and servants of the Carolingian regime.

The Franco-Papal Alliance

Boniface's introduction of Roman discipline and organization into the Frankish Church was followed almost immediately by the consummation of a political alliance between Rome and Francia. It may well have been at Boniface's prompting that the Carolingian mayor, Pepin the Short (741–768), sought papal support for his seizure of the Frankish crown. Although the Merovingian monarchs had become impoverished puppet-kings, they retained the enormous prestige of having ruled the greatest of the Germanic kingdoms for 250 years. If the Carolingians hoped to replace the Merovingians on the Frankish throne, they would have to call on the most potent spiritual sanction available to their age: papal consecration. In supporting Boniface and his fellow Benedictines, the Carolingian mayors had fostered papal influence in the Frankish Church. Now, seeking papal support for a dynastic revolution, Pepin the Short could reasonably expect a favorable response from Rome.

The popes, for their part, were seeking a strong, loyal ally against the Byzantines and Lombards who had long been contending for political supremacy in Italy. The Carolingians, with their policy of aid to the Benedictine missionaries and their support of Boniface's reforms, must have seemed strong candidates for the role of papal champion. And by the mid-eighth century a champion was badly needed. For many years the papacy had been trying to establish its own autonomous state in central Italy, the "Republic of St. Peter."

In pursuing this goal, the popes had often turned to Byzantium for protection against the Lombards, who, although Christian, remained an ominous threat to papal independence. By 750 the popes could no longer depend on Byzantine protection for two reasons: (1) the Byzantine emperors had recently embraced a doctrine known as "iconoclasm," which the papacy regarded as heretical, and (2) Lombard aggression was rapidly becoming so effective that the Byzantine army could no longer be counted on to defend the papacy.

The iconoclastic controversy was the chief religious dispute of the Christian world in the eighth century. It was a conflict over the use of statutes and pictures of Christ and the saints. These icons had gradually come to assume an important role in Christian worship, particularly in East Roman monastic communities. Strictly speaking, Christians might venerate them as symbols of the holy persons whom they represented, but in fact there was a tendency among the uneducated to worship the objects themselves. A line of reform emperors in Constantinople, beginning with Leo the Isaurian (717–741), sought to end the practice of worshiping images—vigorously fostered by the numerous monks of the Eastern Empire—by banning icons altogether. This new policy, iconoclasm, served the interests of the Byzantine emperors by weakening the power of the Eastern monasteries, which controlled far more land than the emperors would have wished. But the iconoclastic decrees offended a great many Byzantines, image worshippers and intelligent traditionalists alike. In the West little support was to be found for the policy of banning images. The papacy in particular opposed iconoclasm as heretical and contrary to the Christian tradition. Although it ultimately failed in the Byzantine Church, iconoclasm in the 750s was a center of controversy that aroused intense enmity between Rome and Constantinople. The papacy was deeply apprehensive of depending on the troops of a heretical emperor for its defense.

Even without the iconoclastic controversy it was becoming increasingly doubtful that the papacy could count on the military power of Byzantium in Italy. By 750 the Lombards were on the march once again, threatening not only Byzantine holdings but also the territories of the pope himself. In 751 the Lombards captured Ravenna, which had long served as the Byzantines' Italian capital and was believed to be impregnable. With the fall of Ravenna, the papal position in Italy became more precarious than ever.

Accordingly, the alliance was struck. Pepin sent messengers to Rome with the far from theoretical query, "Is it right that a powerless ruler should continue to bear the title of king?" The pope answered that by the authority of the Apostle Peter, Pepin was henceforth to be king of the Franks, and ordered that he should be anointed into his royal office by a papal representative. The anointing ceremony was duly performed at Soissons in 751. It had the purpose of buttressing the new Carolingian dynasty with the strongest of spiritual sanctions. Not by force alone, but by the supernatural potency of the royal anointing was the new dynasty established on the Frankish throne. Appropriately, this ceremony—the symbolic junction of the power of Rome and Francia—was performed by the aged Boniface.

With Pepin's anointment, the last of the Merovingians were shorn of their long hair (a symbol of their royalty) and packed off to a monastery. Three years thereafter, in 754, Boniface, now nearing eighty, returned to his missionary work in Frisia and met a martyr's death. In the same year, the pope himself traveled northward to Francia where he personally anointed and crowned Pepin at the royal monastery of St. Denis, thereby conferring every spiritual sanction at his disposal on the upstart Carolingian monarchy. At the same time he sought Pepin's military support against the Lombards.

Pepin obliged, leading his army into Italy, defeating the Lombards, and granting a large portion of central Italy to the papacy. This "Donation of Pepin" was of lasting historical significance. It had the immediate effect of relieving the popes of the ominous Lombard pressure. In the long run, it became the nucleus of the Papal States, the "Patrimony of St. Peter," which would remain a characteristic feature of Italian politics until the later nineteenth century. For the moment, the papacy had been rescued from its peril. It remained to be seen whether the popes could prevent their new champion from becoming their master.

Pepin the Short, like all successful monarchs of the early Middle Ages, was an able war leader. As the first Carolingian king, he followed in the warlike tradition of his father, Charles Martel. Besides defeating the Lombards in Italy, he drove the Muslims from Aquitaine and maintained domestic peace. He died in 768, leaving Francia larger, more powerful, and better organized then he had found it. But perhaps his most significant contribution to his kingdom was his alliance with papal Rome, which affected Carolingian kingship for many generations to come.

Charlemagne (768–814)

Pepin was a remarkably successful monarch, but he was overshadowed by his son. Charlemagne was a talented military commander, a statesman of rare ability, a friend of learning. And he exhibited a strong sense of responsibility for the welfare of the society over which he ruled. In this last respect he contributed much to the developing conception of Christian monarchy.

Charlemagne towered over his contemporaries both figuratively and literally. He was six feet, three and a half inches tall, thick-necked, and potbellied, yet imposing in appearance for all that. Thanks to his able biographer, Einhard, whose *Life of Charlemagne* was written a few years after the emperor's death, Charlemagne has come down to posterity as a three-dimensional figure. Einhard, who was dwarfish in stature, wrote enthusiastically of his oversized hero. The Roman historian Suetonius was Einhard's model, and he lifted whole passages from the biography of the emperor Augustus in Suetonius's *Lives of the Twelve Caesars*, adapting many other phrases from the work to his own purposes. Yet there is much in Einhard's *Life* that represents his own appraisal of Charlemagne's deeds and character. Reared at St. Boniface's monastery of Fulda, Einhard served for many years in Charlemagne's court and thereby

Charlemagne on horseback: a later depiction from the treasury of the Cathedral of Metz, now at the Louvre Museum, Paris.

gained an intimate knowledge of the emperor. Einhard's warm admiration of Charlemagne emerges clearly from the biography, yet the author was able to see Charlemagne's faults as well as his virtues:

> Temperate in both eating and drinking, he hated drunkenness in anybody, particularly in himself and those of his household. But he found it difficult to abstain from food and often complained that fasts injured his health. . . . His meals usually consisted of four courses, not counting the roast, which his huntsmen used to bring in on the spit. He was fonder of this than of any other dish. While at the table he listened to reading or music. The readings were stories and deeds of olden times; he was also fond of St. Augustine's books, especially of the one entitled *The City of God*. So moderate was he in the use of wine and all sorts of drink that he rarely allowed himself more than three cups in the course of a meal.[3]

Charlemagne could be warm and talkative, but he could also be hard and cruel, and his subjects came to regard him with both admiration and fear. The most fascinating passages in Einhard's biography, however, bear on the emperor's way of life and personal idiosyncrasies that disclose him as a human being rather than as a shadowy hero of legend:

[3]The size of the cup is not provided.

While he was dressing and putting on his shoes, he not only gave audience to his friends, but if the Count of the Household told him of any lawsuit in which his judgment was necessary, he had the parties brought before him then and there, considered the case, and gave his decision, just as if he were sitting on the judgment seat.

Einhard was also eager to show Charlemagne's thirst for learning. He portrayed the emperor as a fluent master of Latin, a student of Greek, a speaker of such skill that he might have passed for a teacher of rhetoric, a devotee of the liberal arts, and in particular a student of astronomy who learned to calculate the motions of the heavenly bodies. Einhard concluded this impressive discussion of Charlemagne's scholarship with a final tribute that unwittingly discloses the emperor's limitations:

> He also tried to write, and used to keep tablets and blank pages in bed under his pillow so that in his leisure hours he might accustom his hand to form the letters; but as he did not begin his efforts at an early age but late in life, they met with poor success.

He possessed a strong, if superficial, piety that prompted him to build churches, collect relics, and struggle for a Christian cultural revival in Francia. In keeping with the views of his papal ally, he issued laws forbidding the practice of polygamy (which had characterized the society of Merovingian Francia) and commanded that marriages among his aristocracy and, indeed, all his subjects, be monogamous. In time, this insistence on monogamy altered and simplified inheritance patterns drastically, creating an important legal distinction between legitimate children (who could inherit) and illegitimate children (who often could not). But the laws against polygamy did not prevent Charlemagne from sharing his royal bed with mistresses and filling his court with concubines.

The Expansion of the Empire

Above all else Charlemagne was a warrior-king. He led his armies on yearly campaigns as a matter of course. When his magnates and their retainers assembled around him annually on the May Field, the question was not whether to go to war but whom to fight. It was only gradually, however, that Charlemagne developed a coherent scheme of conquest built on a notion of Christian mission and addressed to the goal of unifying and systematically expanding the Christian West. At the behest of the papacy, he followed his father's footsteps into Italy. There he conquered the Lombards completely in 774, incorporated them into his growing state, and assumed for himself the Lombard crown. Thenceforth he employed the title "King of the Franks and the Lombards."

In 778 Charlemagne launched a campaign against the Spanish Muslims that met with little success. He did manage subsequently to establish a border district on the Spanish side of the Pyrenees Mountains known as the "Spanish March" (march = frontier). In later generations the southern portion of Charlemagne's Spanish March evolved into the county of Barcelona, which remained more receptive to the influence of French institutions and customs than any other district in Spain.

A relatively minor military episode in Charlemagne's Spanish campaign of 778—an attack by a band of Christian Basques against the rear guard of Charlemagne's army as it was withdrawing across the Pyrenees into Francia—became the inspiration for one of the great epic poems of the eleventh and twelfth centuries: the *Song of Roland*. The unknown author or authors of the poem transformed the Christian Basques into Muslims and made the battle a heroic struggle between the rival faiths. (The struggle is superbly portrayed on one of the great thirteenth-century stained-glass windows of Chartres Cathedral.) The *Song of Roland* describes Charlemagne as a godlike conqueror, 200 years old, while providing his heroic vassal Roland, the warden of the Breton March and commander of the rear guard, with a fictional reputation far out of proportion to his actual historical importance.

Charlemagne devoted much of his strength to the expansion of his eastern frontier. In 787 he conquered and absorbed Bavaria, organizing its easternmost district into a forward defensive barrier against the Slavs. This East March, or *Ostmark*, became the nucleus of a new state later to be called Austria. In the 790s Charlemagne pushed still farther to the southeast, destroying the rich and predatory Avar state, which had long tormented Eastern Europe. For many generations the nomadic Avars had been enriching themselves on the plunder of their victims and on heavy tribute payments from Byzantium and elsewhere. Charlemagne had the good fortune to seize a substantial portion of the Avar treasure; it is reported that fifteen four-ox wagons were required to transport the hoard of gold, silver, and precious garments back to Francia. The loot of the Avars contributed significantly to the resources of Charlemagne's treasury and broadened the scope of his subsequent building program and patronage to scholars and churches.

Charlemagne directed his most prolonged military effort against the pagan Saxons of northern Germany. With the twin goals of protecting the Frankish Rhinelands and bringing new souls into the Church, he campaigned for some thirty-two years, conquering the Saxons repeatedly and baptizing them by force, only to have them rebel when his armies withdrew. In a fit of savage exasperation he ordered the execution of forty-five hundred unfaithful Saxons in a single day in 782. At length Saxony submitted to the remorseless pressure of Charlemagne's soldiers and the monks who followed in their wake. By 804 Frankish control of Saxony was well established, and in subsequent decades Christianity seeped gradually into the Saxon soul. A century and a half later, Christian Saxons were governing the most powerful state in Europe and were fostering a significant artistic and intellectual revival that was to enrich the culture of tenth-century Christendom.

The Imperial Coronation of AD 800

Charlemagne's armies, by incorporating central Germany into the new civilization, had succeeded where the legions of ancient Rome had failed. No longer a mere Frankish king, Charlemagne, by 800, was the master of the West. A few small Christian states remained outside his jurisdiction—the principalities of

THE CAROLINGIAN EMPIRE

Carolingian Empire

Byzantine Empire

PICTS

SCOTS

SWEDES

DANISH KINGDOM

North Sea

ANGLO-SAXON KINGDOMS

SAXONY

SLAVS

Cologne

Aachen

Fulda

Elbe

Rouen

AUSTRASIA

BRITTANY

NEUSTRIA

Paris   Rheims

Rhine

Angers   Orleans

Loire

Danube

Tours

Poitiers

St. Gall

BAVARIA

AVARS

EAST MARCH

AQUITAINE

BURGUNDY

LOMBARDY

Pavia

Venice

SLAVS

Rhone

Po

Ravenna

Pyrenees Mts.

SPANISH MARCH

Corsica

Rome

Balearic Is.

Sardinia

Monte Cassino

0   125   250 miles

0   125   250 kilometers

Sicily

southern Italy, the kingdoms of Anglo-Saxon England. But with a handful of exceptions such as these, Charlemagne's political sway extended throughout Western Christendom. On Christmas Day, 800, his immense accomplishment was given formal recognition when Pope Leo III placed the imperial crown on his head and acclaimed him "Emperor of the Romans." From the standpoint of legal theory, this dramatic act reconstituted the Roman Empire in the West after a 324-year intermission. In another sense it was the ultimate consummation of the Franco-papal alliance of 751.

Charlemagne's imperial coronation has evoked heated controversy among historians. According to Einhard, Pope Leo III took Charlemagne by surprise and bestowed on him an unwanted dignity. Charlemagne had such an aversion to the title of "emperor," so Einhard reported, "that he declared he would not have set foot in the church the day that it was conferred, although it was a great feast day, if he could have foreseen the pope's design."

Many modern historians have tended to be skeptical, arguing that Charlemagne was too powerful—too firmly in control of events—to permit a coronation that he did not wish. It has been pointed out that scholars in Charlemagne's court, beguiled by the dream of empire, may well have urged him on. Some historians have stressed the fact that Byzantium lacked an emperor in 800 and that Charlemagne disclosed his interest in the Roman imperial crown by engaging unsuccessfully in marriage negotiations with the Byzantine empress Irene. Conversely, it has been suggested that the coronation was largely a product of internal Roman politics during the years 799–800. In any event, the acclamation that Charlemagne received from the people of Rome immediately after his coronation had obviously been well rehearsed, and it is hard to believe that Charlemagne did not know what was afoot.

Most likely Charlemagne's imperial coronation of 800, like the royal coronation of Pepin the Short in 751, represented a blend of papal and Carolingian interests. For some years Charlemagne had been attempting to attain a status comparable to that of the Byzantine emperors. To take one example, he modified the practice, traditional among Germanic kings and aristocrats, of traveling constantly with his court, consuming the surplus food of one estate and moving on to the next. In 794 he established a permanent capital at Aachen in Austrasia, where he sought, though vainly, to create a Constantinople of his own. Aachen was called "New Rome," and an impressive palace-church was built in the Byzantine style—almost literally a poor man's Hagia Sophia. Even though Charlemagne's "Mary Church" at Aachen was a far cry from Justinian's masterpiece, it was a marvel for its time and place. It made a powerful impact on contemporaries, and it remains impressive to this day. Einhard described it as a beautiful basilica adorned with gold and silver lamps, with rails and doors of solid brass, and with columns and marbles from Rome and Ravenna. It was the product of a major effort on Charlemagne's part—an effort not only to create a beautiful church but also to ape the Byzantines. The coronation of 800 may well have been an expression of this same imitative policy.

The papacy, on the other hand, may well have regarded the coronation as an opportunity to regain some of the initiative it had lost to the all-powerful

Charlemagne's Mary Church, Aachen.

Charlemagne. To be sure, the Carolingians had been promoted from kings to emperors, but their empire thenceforth bore the stamp "Made in Rome." In later years the popes would insist that what they gave they could also take away. If the papacy could make emperors, it also could depose them. Indeed, it was only shortly before that the papal chancery had produced a famous forged document called the "Donation of Constantine"[4] in which the first Christian emperor allegedly gave to the pope the imperial diadem and governance over Rome, Italy, and all the West. The pope is alleged to have returned the diadem but kept the power of governance. Later popes, drawing on the "Donation of Constantine," regarded Charlemagne's imperial successors as stewards exercising political authority by delegation from the papacy, wielding their power in the interests of the Roman Church.

[4]Probably sometime in the 740s.

So convincing was this theory of papal supremacy in the eyes of the popes that it justified the use of a forgery to support the case. The "Donation of Constantine" was not an effort to rewrite history but an attempt to buttress the papal position by manufacturing evidence for an event that had actually occurred, so the papacy supposed, but for which the documentation had unfortunately perished.

But although Charlemagne respected the papacy, he was unwilling to cast himself in the subordinate role papal theory demanded of him. He was careful to retain the title "King of the Franks and the Lombards" alongside his new imperial title. When the time came to crown his son emperor, Charlemagne excluded the pope from the ceremony and did the honors himself. These maneuvers represent the prologue to a long, bitter struggle over the correct relationship between empire and papacy—a struggle that reached its crescendo in the eleventh, twelfth, and thirteenth centuries. For the present, however, Charlemagne's power was unrivaled and the popes were much too weak to resist him. The warm Carolingian-papal relations of Pepin's day continued, and the papacy was nearly smothered in Charlemagne's affectionate embrace.

Carolingian Theocracy

At no time since has Europe been so nearly united as under Charlemagne. And never again would Western Christendom flirt so seriously with theocracy. The papal anointing of Pepin and Charlemagne gave the Carolingian monarchy a sacred, almost priestly quality. Charlemagne used his immense authority to govern not only the body politic but the imperial Church as well. The laws and regulations of his reign, known as "capitularies," dealt with both ecclesiastical and secular matters. At his Synod of Frankfurt in 796, he issued legislation on Christian doctrine. Driven by a sense of responsibility for systematizing Church discipline, and by the need to incorporate dependable educated churchmen into the structure of Carolingian government, he was a far greater force in the Carolingian Church than was the pope. Indeed, the significant intellectual revival known as the "Carolingian Renaissance" grew out of Charlemagne's concern for the welfare of the Church and the perpetuation of ecclesiastical culture as essential buttresses of the Carolingian state.

CAROLINGIAN CIVILIZATION

The Carolingian Renaissance

The term "Carolingian Renaissance" can be misleading. Charlemagne's age produced no serious abstract thought and little original philosophical or theological work. It produced no Thomas Aquinas or Leonardo da Vinci. If we look for a "renaissance" in the ordinary sense of the word, we will be disappointed. The intellectual task of the Carolingian age was less exalted: to rescue Continental culture from the pit of ignorance into which it was sinking. Nevertheless, it would be pointless to abandon the tradition of calling the Carolingian revival a "renaissance." As the perceptive historian Sir Richard Southern once wrote, " 'Renaissance' is no more misleading than any other word. It achieves indeed the sort of sublime meaninglessness which is required in words of high but uncertain import."

As with so many other aspects of the era, the Carolingian Renaissance bears the stamp of Charlemagne's will and initiative. It was he who saw the desperate need for schools in his kingdom and sought to provide them. There could be no question of establishing institutions of higher learning. None existed north of the Alps, and none would emerge until the High Middle Ages. All that the Carolingians could do was to promote primary and secondary education, and this itself was an immensely difficult task. Francia had no professional class of teachers, either lay or clerical. The only hope for educational reform lay with the Church, which had an almost complete monopoly on literacy. So Charlemagne tried to force the cathedrals and monasteries of his realm to operate schools that would preserve and disseminate the rudiments of Classical-Christian culture. A capitulary of 789 commands that "In every episcopal see and in every monastery, instruction shall be given in the psalms, musical notation, chant, the computation of years and seasons, and grammar, and all books used shall be carefully corrected."

A curriculum of the sort proposed in this capitulary can hardly be described as sophisticated or demanding, yet many Carolingian monasteries and cathedrals fell considerably short of the modest standards that it sought to establish. Still, Charlemagne succeeded in improving vastly the quantity and quality of schooling in his empire. There was even an attempt to make village priests provide free instruction in reading and writing (on the frail hope that the priests could themselves read and write). Only a fraction of Charlemagne's subjects acquired literacy. But those few provided an all-important learned nucleus that kept knowledge alive and transmitted it to future generations. It was above all in the monastic schools that learning flourished—in houses such as Fulda, Tours, and Reichenau. During the turbulent generations following Charlemagne's death, many of these monastic schools survived to become seedbeds of the much greater intellectual awakening of the eleventh and twelfth centuries.

As an integral part of his effort to raise the intellectual standards of his realm and sustain Christian culture, Charlemagne assembled scholars at his court from all over Europe. One such scholar was the emperor's biographer, Einhard, from eastern Francia. Another was the poet-historian Paul the Deacon, of the great Italian Benedictine house of Monte Cassino. Paul the Deacon's *History of the Lombards* provides an invaluable account of that Germanic tribe and its settlement in Italy. From Spain came Theodulf, later bishop of Orléans and abbot of Fleury, a tireless supporter of Charlemagne's educational reforms and a poet of considerable talent. The most important of these Carolingian scholars was Alcuin of York, the last significant mind to be produced by the Northumbrian Renaissance. Alcuin, along with his countrymen of an earlier generation— Wilfrid of Ripon, Willibrord, and Boniface—represents a vital connecting link between the Christian cultural life of seventh- and eighth-century England and the intellectual upsurge of Carolingian Francia.

Alcuin performed the essential task of preparing an accurate new edition of the Bible. He purged it of the scribal errors that had crept into it over the centuries, thereby saving Christian culture from the confusion arising from the corruption of its most fundamental text. For many years the chief scholar in Charlemagne's court school, Alcuin spent his final years as abbot of the wealthy and venerable monastery of St. Martin of Tours. He was extraordinarily well educated for his period, and his approach to learning typified the whole philosophy of the Carolingian Renaissance: to produce accurate copies of important traditional texts, to encourage the establishment of schools, and in every way possible to cherish and transmit the Classical-Christian cultural tradition, without, however, adding to it in any significant way. "There is nothing better for us," Alcuin wrote, "than to follow the teachings of the Apostles and the Gospels. We must follow these precepts instead of inventing new ones or propounding new doctrine or vainly seeking to increase our own fame by the discovery of newfangled ideas."

Alcuin and his fellow scholars were neither intellectual innovators nor people of conspicuous holiness. Drawn by Charlemagne's wealth and power and enriched by his patronage, they struggled to improve the scholarly level of the Carolingian Church, but they showed little concern for deepening its devotional life or exploring uncharted regions of speculative thought. They had the talents and inclinations—and the limitations—of schoolteachers. At best they were scholars and Christian humanists; in no sense could they be described as philosophers or mystics.

Accordingly, Alcuin, Theodulf, Einhard, Paul the Deacon, and others like them regularized the liturgy of the Church and encouraged the preaching of sermons. Carrying forward some of the monastic reforms begun by Boniface, they persuaded Charlemagne to command that all monasteries establish schools and follow the Benedictine Rule (an accurate and official copy of which was obtained at Monte Cassino). Although these commands were not everywhere obeyed, they did contribute to the standardization of monastic life and the preservation of literacy. A new official script was developed—the Carolingian minuscule—that derived in part from the Irish and Northumbrian scripts of the previous century and from the scripts of certain Merovingian abbeys. Thenceforth the Carolingian minuscule superseded the often illegible scripts earlier employed on the Continent. Its letters were clearly and separately formed (rather like modern printing, which derives from it), and individual words were separated by spaces, unlike the practice that was common among earlier scribes of runningtheirwordstogether. As a result, reading became much easier than before and gradually more widespread. Throughout the realm monks set about copying manuscripts on an unprecedented scale. If Classical-Christian culture was advanced very little by these activities, it was at least preserved. Above all, its base was broadened. In the task they set themselves, the Carolingian scholars were eminently successful.

The Renaissance after Charlemagne

It was characteristic of the powerful theocratic tendencies of the age that this educational achievement was accomplished through royal rather than papal initiative. Germanic kingship and Classical-Christian culture had joined hands at last. With the breakdown of European unity after Charlemagne's death, the momentary fusion of political and cultural energies dissolved, yet the intellectual revival continued. A deeply spiritual movement of monastic reform and moral regeneration began in Aquitaine under the leadership of the saintly Benedict of Aniane. Soon the influence of this movement took hold at the court of Charlemagne's son and successor, Louis the Pious (814–840). Louis gave St. Benedict of Aniane the privilege of visiting any monastery in the Empire and tightening its discipline in whatever way he chose, to the chagrin of numerous abbots and monks anxious to protect their prerogatives. And in 817 a significantly expanded version of the Benedictine Rule, based on the strict monastic regulations of Benedict of Aniane, was promulgated for all the monasteries of the Empire and given the weight of imperial law. Benedict of Aniane's reform represents a marked shift from the spiritually superficial monastic regulations of Charlemagne's day to a deep concern for the Christ-centered life. The elaborated Benedictine Rule of 817 lost its status as imperial law in 840, with the death of Louis the Pious, but it remained an inspiration to subsequent monastic reform movements in the centuries that followed.

While Carolingian spiritual life was deepening in the years after Charlemagne's death, Carolingian scholarship continued to flourish in the cathedral and monastic schools. In keeping with the Carolingian intellectual program of preserving the Classical-Christian tradition, learned churchmen of the Carolingian Renaissance's second generation devoted themselves to preparing encyclopedic accounts of existing knowledge. Although unoriginal, these works contributed significantly to the process of cultural transmission. For example, Raban Maur (d. 856), abbot of Fulda, produced a learned collection of all information available to him on all subjects that occurred to him—on the pattern of Isidore of Seville's *Etymologies*. Raban Maur also carried forward the Carolingian educational tradition by writing a handbook on the instruction of the clergy that had a great impact on the operation of monastic schools.

The one original scholar in this second generation was the Irishman John Scotus Erigena, or John the Scot (the Scots in his day were inhabitants of Ireland rather than Scotland). He served for years in the court of Charlemagne's grandson, King Charles the Bald, himself a man of learning. John the Scot was not only a philosopher but a wit as well, at least if we can believe the legend of a dinner table conversation between John and King Charles. The king, intending to needle his court scholar, asked him whether there was anything separating a Scot from a sot. "Only the dinner table" was John's reply.

John Scotus was a student of Neoplatonism and the only Western European scholar of his age known to have mastered the Greek tongue. He translated into Latin an important Greek philosophical treatise, *On the Celestial Hierarchy*, written by an anonymous late-fifth-century Christian Neoplatonist known as "the

Walafrid Strabo

Although the Carolingian Renaissance could boast no thinkers of great originality, it did produce a considerable number of intelligent and productive scholars who merit respect, at least from those of us who lack universal genius. Among the most attractive of them was Walafrid Strabo, or "Walafrid the squint-eyed," as he cheerfully called himself.

Born in southern Germany, about 808, of impoverished parents, Walafrid was sent as an illiterate boy of eight to the nearby Benedictine monastery of Reichenau, an important center of Carolingian learning set on an island in the Rhine. An apt and enthusiastic pupil in the abbey school, he quickly learned to read and write in Latin and then proceeded to master the Bible, the writings of the Latin Doctors, and the principles of the liberal arts. Like many well-educated men of his era, Walafrid enjoyed writing Latin poetry; unlike most of them, he did it well.

Walafrid had entered Reichenau as an oblate—a child whose parents had dedicated him for lifelong service as a monk. As was expected of him, therefore, Walafrid took lifetime monastic vows on coming of age. He did so happily, because he had by then developed a deep religious faith and a devotion to Benedictine monasticism. Perhaps because he was genial by nature, or perhaps because he took very seriously Christ's injunction to "love your neighbor," Walafrid was the kindest and most loving of the Carolingian writers. In an age of keen intellectual and political rivalries and theological controversies, he muted his criticisms and looked for the best in everyone.

Because Reichenau was in close communication with other centers of Carolingian learning, news of Walafrid's intellectual precocity spread quickly. By the age of fifteen, at the urging of a teacher, he was sending his verses to imperial bishops, but always with characteristic Benedictine humility. He addressed a verse to one bishop "as a mouse to a giant" and identified himself thus: "It's the boy with the squinty eye, Father, who writes these words to you."

Walafrid also began writing lives of the saints, one of the most popular literary genres of the early Middle Ages. By the time he was eighteen he had written two such lives, both in verse. The second—a portent of disasters to come—was the life of an Irish saint who had been killed by Vikings on the isle of Iona just a year earlier.

Walafrid's abbot at Reichenau sent him at eighteen to study under one of the most eminent scholars of the age, Raban Maur, abbot of the great German monastery of Fulda, which St. Boniface had founded a century before. Raban Maur (or "Robin Moore," as a professor of mine playfully called him) was in the midst of the immense and typically Carolingian labor of compiling Biblical commentaries excerpted from the writings of the Latin Fathers. Walafrid was fascinated by Raban Maur's project and enthusiastically joined him in it. And Raban, who was himself a poet (to put it charitably), encouraged Walafrid's poetic gift. The two became lifelong friends.

Walafrid remained at Fulda for only three years. At twenty-one, he was summoned by Emperor Louis the Pious to his court at Aachen to tutor the emperor's youngest son, Charles, who, being only five years old, had not yet won his nickname, "the Bald." Walafrid remained at court for nine years (829–838), tutoring, studying, writing (poetry, Biblical commentaries, and more saints' lives), and, as always, winning friends. These were tumultuous years for the Empire; from 829 onward, Charles's two older brothers, Lothar and Louis the German, were engaged intermittently in civil war against their father, who was virtually imprisoned at Aachen in 832 and was forced by hostile bishops to abdicate temporarily in 833. Walafrid wrote, in a letter to a friend, of the evils rife throughout the realm: "Alas, how plainly is Satan's honor served! Peace is driven far from earth."

Throughout these upheavals Walafrid remained faithful to his duties as tutor, with the result that Charles the Bald turned out to be the best educated of the Carolingian monarchs. In 838 Walafrid, now thirty, was rewarded by being appointed abbot of Reichenau, the abbey that he had entered as a child. At the death of Louis the Pious in 840, the civil war between his sons intensified, with the consequence that Louis the German, who ruled in the east, removed Walafrid from his abbatial office and sent him into exile for two years. Walafrid wrote to Raban Maur complaining of being in dire poverty and need, in pain and anguish, lacking even sandals for his feet. Even so, he continued to write and study, and in 842 changing political winds prompted Louis the German to restore Walafrid to his abbey and to the royal favor.

Walafrid looked regretfully on the division of the Empire between Lothar, Louis the German, and Charles the Bald, yet he now enjoyed the trust and favor of all three royal brothers and was welcomed at their courts. At Reichenau he restored with his own labor an abandoned herb and vegetable garden and wrote a set of touching poems about the various plants, under the title, *The Little Garden*. And to an absent friend he wrote in eloquent affection:

When from on high the moon's pure splen-
    dor shines,
Stand then beneath the sky and think,
    enthralled,
Upon that glory's far-flung radiance;
How its pure splendor holds encircled those
In body far apart, in love fast bound.
If face can see no more the face that cares,
At least this light shall tell us of our love.
Abiding friendship sends these little lines;
If, too, in you the chain of faith stands firm,
For you I pray forever happiness.*

In 848, at about the age of forty, Walafrid traveled to the court of his former pupil Charles the Bald, now king of the West Franks, to represent Louis the German on a diplomatic mission. As he was about to return, he was killed in a boating accident while crossing the River Loire in summer, 849. His body was carried back to Reichenau and buried on his beloved island. His former teacher and grieving friend, Raban Maur, wrote his epitaph.

*Adapted from the translation of Eleanor Shipley Duckett, *Carolingian Portraits: A Study in the Ninth Century* (Ann Arbor, 1962), p. 160.

Pseudo-Dionysius." This author was incorrectly identified in the Middle Ages as Dionysius the Areopagite, a first-century Athenian philosopher who is described in the *Acts of the Apostles* as being converted to Christianity by St. Paul. He was further misidentified as St. Denis, evangelist of the Gauls and first bishop of Paris, who was beheaded by pagans in the third century and in whose honor the great royal monastery of St. Denis was built. ("Denis" is the French equivalent of "Dionysius.") Accordingly, the writings of the Pseudo-Dionysius passed into the Middle Ages with the commanding credentials of an early Christian author, a Pauline convert, and a martyred missionary who brought Christianity to Gaul. In reality, the importance of the Pseudo-Dionysius lay in his providing a Christian dimension to the philosophical scheme of Plotinus and other pagan Neoplatonists. The unknowable and indescribable Neoplatonic god—the center and source of the concentric circles of reality—was identified as the God of the Christians. Such a god could not be approached intellectually but only by means of a mystical experience; hence the Pseudo-Dionysius became an important source of inspiration to later Christian mystics.

Stimulated by the work of the Pseudo-Dionysius, which he translated from Greek into Latin, John Scotus went on to write a highly original Neoplatonic treatise of his own, *On the Divisions of Nature*. In its blurred distinction between God and the created world, the treatise reflected the Neoplatonic tendency toward pantheism. It was controversial in its own time and even more so in later centuries.

The intellectual revival instigated by Charlemagne echoed through subsequent generations. In the monasteries and cathedrals of the ninth and tenth centuries, particularly in the German districts of Charlemagne's old Empire, documents continued to be copied, schools continued to operate, and commentaries and summaries of ancient texts continued to appear. By the eleventh century, Europe was ready to build on its sturdy Carolingian foundations.

THE DYNAMICS OF CAROLINGIAN EXPANSION AND DECLINE

Expansion

The Carolingian Empire was ephemeral. Rising out of a chaotic past, it disintegrated in the turbulent era that followed. The Carolingians had achieved their early successes, under Pepin of Heristal and Charles Martel, not only through strong leadership but also because of the sizable landed resources that the family came to control and the loyal, well-armed vassals and aristocratic supporters whom these resources could attract. Carolingian armies were better organized and better disciplined than those of most neighboring powers. No rival principality made such effective use of armored horsemen as did the Carolingians. And once Carolingian expansion was under way, it fed on its own momentum. Conquests brought plunder and new lands with which the Carolingians could enrich themselves and reward their supporters. Indeed, it became Carolingian policy to install loyal Franks, mostly Austrasians, as counts and dukes of the conquered provinces. Accordingly, the interests of the Frankish landholding aristocracy became ever more closely tied to the political and military fortunes of the ruling family. As long as the Carolingians could bring in profits from military campaigns, they commanded the enthusiastic obedience of disciplined followers. A Frank would gladly obey Charlemagne if it meant a cut of the Avar treasure or a lordship in Italy or Saxony. In short, Carolingian expansion was like a snowball, growing as it rolled, rolling as it grew.

This process typified the entire early medieval economy, in which lords and kings sought to enrich themselves not only through trade but also through plunder. Such wealth, resulting chiefly from successful warfare, gave rise to one of the primary economic transactions between a lord and his neighbors or followers: the exchange of gifts. Among aristocratic peers, the giving of gifts was a means of impressing rivals and gaining prestige; it was also the motivation for the followers of a lord to serve him faithfully. At the highest level, in the relationships between the Carolingian kings and their counts and vassals, the flow of gifts from the plunder of conquests bound the upper aristocracy to the Carolingian monarch.

Limitations

But despite the conquests and plunder, Charlemagne's regime remained economically primitive and undergoverned. Towns were small and scattered, and the roads that linked settled areas were miserably bad. There was some trade, most of it dependent on the river network. Carolingian villages often had to obtain their iron, salt, and wine from outside sources, and the great lay and ecclesiastical landholders imported luxury goods such as jewelry and precious fabrics from afar. Charlemagne did what he could to encourage such trade: he maintained a silver coinage of good quality (though most ordinary transactions continued to be based on barter or food rents); he concluded a reciprocal agreement with an English king guaranteeing the safety of merchants; he encouraged the construction of roads, bridges, and lighthouses; he even contemplated building a canal to link the Rhine and Danube rivers (although he never quite managed it). But by Byzantine or Islamic standards, Carolingian commerce trickled rather than gushed.

Despite the plunder of conquests, Charlemagne had nowhere near the funds sufficient to support a salaried bureaucracy. Like his predecessors, he had to depend on the competence and loyalty of landholding regional officials: dukes, lords of the marches (margraves), and, most commonly, counts of the nearly three hundred counties of the Empire. These men were oath-bound to obey the king-emperor. But oaths are frail threads, and the Carolingian counts were in a position to act on their own when loyalty no longer suited their interests. Many were drawn, of necessity, from aristocratic Frankish families with landed power bases of their own. Moreover, in place of the salaries that the central government could not afford to pay, regional officials were granted the use of extensive royal lands from which they could not easily be dislodged. And because of the vast distances and poor communications, they had to be entrusted with broad powers over the royal tribunals, taxation systems, and military recruiting arrangements in their counties.

Even under the overarching authority of Charlemagne, the Empire was afflicted by widespread local and regional violence: blood feuds between aristocratic families, private warfare over disputed lands, plundering raids, highway robberies. Sources of the period also speak of widespread judicial corruption and gross favoritism in the local courts. The imperial government was much too weak to contend effectively with well-entrenched regional aristocratic elites as long as they were not too blatantly conspicuous in pursuing their self-interests. Charlemagne kept track of his regional administrators after a fashion by sending out pairs of inspectors known as *missi dominici* (envoys of the lord) to see that his orders were being obeyed and his revenues were not being pocketed. The missi dominici, consisting usually of one churchman and one layman, typified the theocratic trend of Charlemagne's reign. But they were only moderately effective, and they would become less so under subsequent monarchs who lacked Charlemagne's power to punish and reward. A count who owed his office to Charlemagne and whose authority over potentially troublesome provincials depended on Charlemagne's continued backing would receive the missi dominici with respect. Provincial officials obeyed royal commands and capitularies not out of patriotic allegiance to the Carolingian state but because of their loyalty to Charlemagne himself—a loyalty based on the bonds of common interest that linked the conquering monarch and his highly favored aristocracy.

Disintegration

These bonds had always been fragile. And when the Carolingian Empire ceased expanding, as it did after the final submission of Saxony in 804, they began to loosen. As the flow of lands and plunder dried up, aristocratic loyalty diminished and the Empire started to disintegrate. Disaffection and rebellion clouded the final decade of Charlemagne's life and brought political chaos to the reign of his son and heir, Louis the Pious. Once the snowball stopped rolling, it began to melt.

Carolingian Europe: An Overview

The Carolingian Empire, impressive though it was, lacked a vigorous commercial life and other necessary ingredients of a flourishing civilization. Its revenues were small and its administrative institutions grossly inadequate to the needs of a great state.

But even though Charlemagne's "Roman Empire" was merely a shadow of its ancient namesake, one cannot help respecting its founder for dong so much with so little, for making such an effort to transcend his own primitive past. The historian Karl Ferdinand Werner caught the spirit of Charlemagne's policy when he described it as a "grand design"—not simply a royal-aristocratic partnership in pursuit of conquest and loot, but a new conception of the ruler and the state. Werner was well aware of the Carolingians' greed and brutality and the flimsiness of their administration. But that is not the whole story:

> Their willingness to use all the help available—for example, the Anglo-Saxon missionaries and the papacy; their eagerness to discover and take over whatever they believed to be good, reliable and authentic, and to spread it; these Carolingian qualities, which reached their peak under Charlemagne, were not only an achievement that will always be remarkable; they helped refashion the high nobility and exercised an immeasurable influence on the future development of Europe, long after their dynasty had vanished.

The new invasions evolved into a campaign of conquest directed by the Danish monarchy. The English defense was plagued by incompetence, treason, and panic. In 991 Ethelred began paying a tribute to the Danes, known thereafter as *danegeld*, which was raised by levying a tax on all English lands. In later years when the Danes departed, the tax continued as a lucrative source of revenue for the English monarchy. But in Ethelred's time it was a sign of desperation and resulted in a massive outflow of English wealth. In 1016 Ethelred died, and in the following year King Canute of Denmark became the ruler of the English.

King Canute (1017–1035) was known to later generations as Canute the Great, and appropriately so. He conquered Norway as well as England, and joining these two lands to his kingdom of Denmark, he became the master of a huge empire centering on the North Sea, held together by the wealth of England. A product of the new civilizing forces at work in eleventh-century Scandinavia, Canute was no footloose Viking. He issued law codes, practiced Christianity, and kept the peace. Devoting much of his time to England, he cast himself as an Anglo-Saxon king in the old West Saxon tradition. After commencing his reign with an appallingly bloody purge of potential troublemakers, he afterward respected and upheld the ancient customs of the land and gave generously to monasteries: "Merry sang the monks of Ely," we are told, "as Canute the king rowed by."

But Canute's Danish-Norwegian-English empire was hopelessly disunited and failed to survive his death in 1035. When the last of his two sons died in 1042, the English realm fell peacefully to Edward the Confessor, a member of the old Wessex dynasty who had grown up in exile in Normandy.

The Aftermath

King Edward the Confessor ruled England in relative peace. But his childless marriage ensured a disputed succession on his death in 1066 and set the stage for the Norman Conquest. When William the Conqueror, duke of Normandy, invaded England and won its crown on the field of Hastings in 1066, he inherited a prosperous kingdom with well-established political and legal traditions—a kingdom still divided by differences in custom but with a deep-seated respect for royal authority. With the timber that Alfred collected, his successors had built an ample and sturdy edifice.

FRANCE: FRAGMENTATION

In England the invasions resulted in royal unification; in France they encouraged a breakdown of political authority into regional and local units. This difference can be explained in part by the fact that France, unlike England, was too large for the Vikings to hope to conquer. Although many of them settled in Normandy, the chief Norse threat to France came in the form of plundering expeditions rather than conquering armies. Distances were too great, communications too primitive, the aristocracy too firmly entrenched, and the kingdom-wide army too unwieldy for the monarchy to assume strong leadership in defending the realm. Military responsibility descended more and more to dukes, counts, and local nobles, who were better able to protect their regions from sudden Viking assaults.

As the monarchy waned, the dukes and counts evolved from Carolingian royal officials into territorial princes only loosely tied to the king. Their former custody of royal lands, tribunals, tax revenues, and military conscription ripened into hereditary authority. Lands and powers that they had once administered for the king they now administered for themselves, transforming France into a mosaic of largely independent duchies and counties.

The Carolingian kings of France became increasingly powerless until at length, in 987, the crown passed permanently from the Carolingian dynasty to the Capetian dynasty (in the person of an important territorial lord named Hugh Capet). Much later on, during the twelfth and thirteenth centuries, the Capetian family would produce some of France's most celebrated kings, but for the time being the new dynasty was nearly as feeble as its predecessor. The Capetian power base was the region around Paris and Orléans in north-central France—an area known as the "Ile de France," which was no greater in size and wealth than any of a number of French principalities of the period. In theory the Capetian monarch was king of the French, but on the basis of his limited jurisdiction and revenues, he was merely one prince among many.

Nobles, Knights, and Castles

The process of disintegration did not stop at the duchy-county level. Within these principalities, and often between them, lay clusters of estates ruled by important lords who lacked such titles as "duke" or "count" but nevertheless exercised considerable authority and commanded large resources. These lords might or might not support their regional princes, depending on the lord's interests and the prince's strength. Contemporary observers tended to regard the great landholders, whether dukes, counts, or untitled lords, as constituting a single class known as "nobles." Descended for the most part from powerful families of the Carolingian era and before, the nobles had the responsibility for maintaining peace and public order—and the capacity to wage war against Viking invaders and against each other.

Within each noble household was a group of military retainers—vassals—who by the late tenth century had come to be known as "knights." Midway in status between the great noble families and the peasantry, the knights constituted the lower level of a two-tiered warrior aristocracy. Both nobles and knights were trained in the techniques of mounted combat. They shared a common military vocation, were similarly equipped with arms, armor, and warhorses, and of course were exempt from agricultural labor. Indeed, great aristocrats came increasingly to describe themselves as "knight-nobles," higher in status than common knights, yet knights nonetheless. But whereas nobles possessed large estates, many knights had little or no land, and whereas nobles led armies into battle, knights followed and obeyed. Only later did it become common for knights to hold land and to marry into noble families.

The trend toward local centers of power gave rise, during the tenth century, to a military innovation of surpassing importance: the castle. The earliest castles bore little resemblance to the great turreted fortresses of the later Middle Ages; many were nothing more than small, square towers, usually of wood, planted on hilltops or artificial mounds and encircled by wooden stockades. But when effectively garrisoned, they could be powerful instruments not only of defense but of territorial control as well. Many castles were built by nobles. Others were built (or seized) by ambitious men of less exalted status known as "castellans," who assembled knightly retinues of their own, subjected surrounding territories to their control, and ascended in time into the old nobility.

Bridgenorth Castle, Shropshire, England. Built by the rebellious earl of Shropshire c. 1101, this dramatic stronghold, situated at the summit of the hilltop town of Bridgenorth overlooking the River Severn, is now surrounded by a public park. It was successfully besieged by King Henry I of England in 1102, was used as a headquarters by sheriffs of Shropshire long thereafter, and was blown up in 1646 during the English Civil War. Photo by C. Warren Hollister.

The coming of castles changed the character of the aristocracy by giving great families, old and new, a specifically located center of power. Soon many of them began identifying themselves by the name of their chief castle, their "family seat." Nobles previously known simply by their first names—Amaury, Geoffrey, Roger—became Amaury de Montfort, Geoffrey de Mandeville, Roger de Beaumont, hereditary lords of the castles of Montford, Mandeville, and Beaumont. Castles thus fostered a new sense of family identity among the nobility. And as the castle and lordship passed over generations from father to eldest son, the family tended increasingly to regard itself not simply as a group of relatives but as members of a hereditary line of descent. The result was a much clearer idea of family ancestry and (as one historian has expressed it) "a strengthening of family solidarity within the framework of lineage." When in time members of the knightly class began settling on estates, they too took the name of their estate as their family name and, like the nobility, evolved into a class of hereditary landholders.

Feudalism

During the era of invasions and unrest, many knights and nobles of northern France came to hold estates conditionally, in return for military and other service to a greater lord. An estate held on these terms was often called a "fief" (rhyming with "beef"), and the relationship of landholding to service has come to be known as "feudalism" (after *feudum,* Latin for fief). Typically, the holder of a fief became the vassal of his lord, rendering him loyalty and service in a solemn ceremony of homage. The granting of estates in exchange for loyalty and service was a convenient way for a lord to support a retinue of warriors in an age in which money was scarce and land abundant.

Often such feudal arrangements would extend down through several levels of lordship. In theory at least, the great territorial princes held their duchies and counties as fiefs of the king of France (though they did not always bother to render him homage, and they were as apt to fight against him as for him). Lesser nobles, in turn, might hold estates as vassals of counts or dukes, while granting smaller fiefs to vassals of their own. A single person might thus be both the vassal of a greater lord and the lord of lesser vassals.

The feudal concepts of vassalage and conditional land tenure were deeply rooted in the European past. One such root was the oath of fidelity and service that bound a warrior to his lord in Carolingian and Merovingian times. Another root was the late Roman and early medieval concept of granting an estate—a *benefice*—in return for certain services. Charlemagne, as we have seen, permitted his counts and dukes the use of royal estates in return for their military and administrative service to his regime, and the entire Carolingian political structure had been bound together by oaths of personal loyalty—rendered to the king by his great magnates and to the magnates by their own followers.

Only in the tenth and eleventh centuries, and only in portions of France, did these elements coalesce into the pattern of fiefs, lords, and vassals known to historians as "feudalism." The term "feudal system," widely used in textbooks, conveys a misleading impression of order and universality. In reality feudal relationships coexisted with entirely different arrangements: lands held unconditionally, landless knights supported in noble households (a very common practice), political power based on public sovereign authority rather than on personal lordship over vassals, and loyalties based on kinship, friendship, or wages rather than on a fief. Even when relationships were "feudal," they were not necessarily systematic. A single vassal, for example, might acquire several estates by swearing homage to several lords. The resulting confusion of loyalties is suggested in this twelfth-century document:

> I, John of Toul, affirm that I am the vassal of the Lady Beatrice, countess of Troyes, and of her son Theobald, count of Champagne, against every creature living or dead, excepting my allegiance to Lord Enjourand of Coucy, Lord John of Arcis, and the count of Grandpré. If it should happen that the count of Grandpré should be at war with the countess and count of Champagne in his own quarrel, I will aid the count of Grandpré in my own person, and will aid the count and countess of Champagne by sending them the knights whose services I owe them from the fief which I hold of them.

Like much historical evidence, this document can be interpreted in more than one way. It suggests that feudal arrangements could be hideously complex, but it also represents an effort to bring order out of the chaos of multiple allegiances. In this last respect it typifies the tendency, beginning in the eleventh century and growing in the twelfth, to systematize feudal practices that had originally sprouted like dandelions in an ill-kept lawn.

Even today, feudalism is heartbreakingly difficult to define. Some scholars reject the word altogether;[2] others prefer the term "feudalisms" to "feudalism." I continue to find feudalism a useful word if employed with caution—no more misleading then humanism, democracy, communism, capitalism, classicism, or renaissance (all of which some scholars would also like to abolish). If feudalism cannot be precisely defined, it can at least be described. The great French historian Marc Bloch described it well:

> A subject peasantry; widespread use of the service tenement (that is, the fief) instead of a salary, which was out of the question; the supremacy of a class of specialized warriors; ties of obedience and protection which bind man to man and, within the warrior class, assume the distinctive form called vassalage; fragmentation of authority—leading inevitably to disorder; and in the midst of all this, the survival of other forms of association, family and state. . . . Such then seem to be the fundamental features of European feudalism.

Political Breakdown and the Rise of Principalities

We have seen how Carolingian royal authority disintegrated, first into regional principalities and eventually, in many cases, into still smaller units such as

---

[2]David Bates, in his *William the Conqueror* (London, 1989, p. 14), described "feudalism" and "feudal society" (tongue in cheek) as "terms which have been invented in modern times to make the study of the Middle Ages more difficult!"

castleries dominated by some local lord whose castle controlled the neighbor-hood. As one historian expressed it, "Dirty, bloodstained, and exhausted lords surrounded by brutal warriors, making their way from primitive wooden cas-tles to austere monastic refuges, must have been common sights on the West Frankish roads."[3]

The breakdown of authority—from Carolingian kings to regional princes (dukes, counts) and finally to local castellans—has given rise to a fierce interna-tional debate among historians as to how these changes affected living condi-tions and levels of domestic violence. A school of French medievalists argues that the consequences of the breakdown—from public authority exercised by counts to private authority usurped by castellans—were disastrous for medieval French society. They maintain that in the decades around AD 1000 France expe-rienced a "feudal transformation" or "feudal revolution"—an explosive upsurge of violence and a brutalization of the peasantry resulting from the unauthorized seizure of power by local strong men. Other historians disagree, contending that although lordship became more localized it did not undergo any significant change in its nature—that the distinction between public and pri-vate authority is more theoretical than real, and that even under Charlemagne the autonomy of local and regional officials was great, private warfare was not uncommon, and domestic violence was widespread. They further point out, quite correctly, that even under a regime of independent and contentious castel-lans, it was not unusual to settle disputes through compromises and voluntary adjudication. And, finally, they find little reliable evidence that castellans treated their peasants more brutally than did Carolingian counts. They argue that living conditions in the French countryside underwent no catastrophic decline between the age of Charlemagne and the tenth and eleventh centuries.[4]

Whatever the case, as time went on the process of political disintegration was gradually reversed. New principalities emerged as ambitious noble families succeeded in combining groups of counties, through marriages and conquests, into larger territorial blocs. By the early twelfth century the French principalities, old and new, were growing steadily in wealth and power. The dukes of Aquitaine and Normandy and the counts of Flanders, Anjou, Blois, Champagne, and Burgundy were in most practical respects the equals of the king of France.

These great princes continued to base their power on the control of lands, tribunals, and public taxes and services that had formerly pertained to the Car-olingian monarchy. The Carolingian system of government was not demol-ished but merely fragmented. Indeed, in some important respects it was improved. A number of territorial princes generated sufficient revenues to administer their dominions not through powerful regional landholders but

---

[3]Jean Dunbabin, *France in the Making, 843–1180* (Oxford, 1985), p. 241.
[4]The issue of the "feudal transformation" is far too complex to discuss adequately here. For differ-ent points of view see Thomas N. Bisson, "The 'Feudal Revolution,'" *Past and Present* 142 (1994), pp. 6–42; and Dominique Barthelemy and Stephen D. White, "Debate: The 'Feudal Revolution,'" *Past and Present* 152 (1996), pp. 196–223. A rejoinder by Thomas N. Bisson will appear in a forth-coming issue of *Past and Present*.

through salaried officials who could be transferred or removed at will. The princes ruled not only as lords of fief-holding vassals but also through the exercise of public authority such as Carolingian kings had once delegated to their counts, and through the control of increasingly efficient and flexible administrations. In time their governance became more intensive and effective than that of the old Carolingian Empire. They had the advantage of ruling compact territorial units and the further advantage of controlling a growing number of castles (increasingly built of stone), which served as military and political power centers throughout their principalities. And as the eleventh century progressed, they benefited from an accelerating commercial revival.

The princes themselves contributed to this revival in a variety of ways. They established new agricultural settlements on depopulated lands. They supported monastic reform (which usually brought marked improvement to the management of monastic estates) and encouraged the construction of water mills. They founded hundreds of new abbeys and smaller priories as centers of princely influence and agrarian development. And they opened up new lands for cultivation by clearing forests and draining bogs. The counts of Flanders organized and encouraged an elaborate program of dike building to reclaim land from the sea and convert it to sheep farming. The counts of Champagne sponsored a series of annual fairs for long-distance merchants and—for a price—guaranteed them safe passage through the county.

The growth of agricultural productivity and vitalization of commerce increased the revenues of the princes. With their new wealth they enlarged their administrations, armies, and networks of castles to the point where they could overawe their vassals and bring relative peace to their principalities, protecting the more helpless of their inhabitants from terror, robbery, and slaughter. In late-eleventh-century Normandy and Flanders, no magnate could build a castle without ducal or comital permission, and the dukes of Normandy claimed the right to occupy a vassal's stronghold on demand.

The rise of strong principalities by no means put an end to military violence. Warfare was almost incessant—between rival princes and between lesser magnates within principalities or in the turbulent regions between them. Territorial princes in the south of France proved much less successful than those elsewhere in bringing order to their lands. But in central and northern France, for the first time since Roman antiquity, princely regimes were acquiring the administrative, military, and financial resources necessary for effective governance. As such, they mark a crucial stage in the development of political cohesion from the loosely governed Carolingian Empire to the beginnings of the modern European state.

GERMANY: FRAGMENTATION AND REUNIFICATION

The invasions gave birth to unified monarchy in England while undermining it in France. Germany's response was different still: first the emergence of powerful semi-independent duchies; then a resurgence of royal power.

Although East Francia (Germany) was subject to Viking attacks, the greater threat came from mounted Hungarian warriors from the southeast. When the late-Carolingian kings of Germany proved unable to cope with the Hungarian raids, authority descended, as in France, to the great regional officials of the realm—the dukes, who had formerly administered their duchies as agents of the monarchy.

Following their accustomed policy, the Carolingians had patterned their German duchies on earlier tribal divisions. During the turbulent years of the ninth century, these "tribal duchies" became virtually autonomous. Their dukes took direct control of royal lands and powers and dominated the churches within their districts. The process should by now be all too familiar.

In the early tenth century Germany was dominated by five duchies: Saxony, Swabia, Bavaria, Franconia, and Lorraine. The first three had been incorporated only quite recently into the Carolingian state, whereas the western duchies of Franconia and Lorraine were much more strongly Frankish in outlook and organization. The five tribal dukes might well have become the masters of Germany. Their ambitions were frustrated by two related factors: (1) their failure to curb the Hungarians and (2) the reinvigoration of the German monarchy under an able, new dynasty. The Carolingian line came to an end in Germany in 911 with the death of King Louis the Child. He was succeeded first by the duke of Franconia and then, in 919, by the duke of Saxony—the first of an illustrious line of kings whose power was based on their domination of the powerful Saxon duchy.

Otto I, "the Great" (936–973)

The Saxon monarchy struggled vigorously to assert its authority over the tribal duchies. With the duchy of Saxony under their power, the Saxon kings quickly won direct control over Franconia and Lorraine as well, and a protectorate over the kingdom of Burgundy. But the semi-independent dukes of the two southern duchies, Swabia and Bavaria, presented greater problems. The real victory of the monarchy occurred in the reign of the second and ablest of the Saxon kings, Otto I (936–973).

Otto I, "the Great," directed his considerable talents toward three goals and achieved them all: (1) the defense of Germany against the Hungarian invasions, (2) the recovery of royal lands and powers within the remaining tribal duchies, and (3) the extension of German royal control to the crumbling, unstable Middle Kingdom that the Treaty of Verdun had assigned to Emperor Lothar back in 843. We have already seen how this Middle Kingdom began to fall to pieces after Lothar's death. By the mid-tenth century it had become a political shambles. Parts of it had been taken over by Germany and France, but its southern districts—Burgundy and Italy—retained a chaotic independence. The dukes of Swabia and Bavaria both had notions of seizing these territories. Otto the Great, in order to forestall the development of an unmanageable rival power to his south, led his armies into Italy in 951 and assumed the title "King of Italy."

Otto the Great and his imperial successors ruled northern Italy from a distance. Except on the rare occasions when they led their armies southward across the Alps, they based their authority on the support of the urban bishops, whose powers endured and grew under German rule. In this respect, Otto's conquest changed nothing, but it did furnish Italy the vitally important benefits of relative peace and stability after a century of anarchy. The emperors helped relieve Italy of the Muslim menace, both by leading armies against Muslim enclaves and by providing a settled environment that encouraged urban growth and commercial revival. By the late 900s, the north Italian ports of Genoa and Pisa were developing a vigorous, widespread Mediterranean trade and a growing merchant class. In the course of the next century, Genoa and Pisa seized the offensive from the Muslims, expelling them from the important Mediterranean islands of Sardinia and Corsica and launching raids against Muslim ports in Spain and North Africa. Other Italian coastal cities, beyond the lands ruled by the German emperor, were taking to the sea as well: Amalfi, Salerno, and Naples in southern Italy and, above all, the republic of Venice on the northern shore of the Adriatic Sea.

Long a Byzantine dependency, Venice had achieved virtual independence by the ninth century and yet continued to send fleets to assist Byzantium in its wars. By carefully cultivating its relations with both Constantinople and Islamic North Africa, Venice developed a flourishing triangular trade. And during the 900s Venice evolved into the foremost commercial center in Western Christendom. In a Europe that was overwhelmingly agrarian, the Venetians developed the first state to live by trade alone. Enriched by the exporting of salt from their lagoons and glass from their furnaces, and by the profits of commerce, they produced very little food but purchased it instead in the markets of other north Italian towns. A Lombard writer remarked with astonishment that "These people neither plow nor sow nor gather grapes," but "buy grain and wine in every marketplace."

In this respect Venice was unique, but other Italian ports—Genoa, Pisa, Amalfi—were following it into the lucrative Mediterranean trade. And their bustling commercial life stimulated the growth of inland cities such as Milan, Bologna, and Florence. Milan's population in AD 1000, although probably no more than about twenty thousand, made it the largest city in Lombardy and one of the most populous in Western Christendom. With the closing of the age of invasions, Italy had thus achieved the reversal of two age-long historical trends: its cities were growing once more, and its well-armed fleets were at last challenging the Byzantine and Muslim domination of Mediterranean commerce.

VILLAGES, FIELDS, AND MANORS

During the tenth and eleventh centuries the commercial city remained a rarity in Western Christendom. Almost everywhere wealth and power were associated with the holding of land. And beneath the social layer of nobles and knights, the great majority of Europeans labored on the soil.

To discuss the typical medieval farm is as difficult as to discuss the typical American business, for medieval agriculture exhibited countless variations. Nevertheless some features of agrarian life recur throughout the more fertile and heavily populated portions of northwestern Europe. Certain generalizations can be made about medieval agrarian institutions, if we bear in mind that numerous exceptions to any of them can be found.

Any discussion of medieval husbandry must begin by distinguishing between two fundamental institutions: the village and the manor. The village, the basic unit of the agrarian economy, consisted of a population nucleus ranging from about a dozen to several hundred peasant families living in a cluster, encircled by their fields. In regions where the soil was poor, peasant families might live in separate farms or hamlets, but across the fertile lowlands of northern France, England, and Germany, village life was the norm.

The manor, on the other hand, was an artificial unit—a unit of jurisdiction and economic exploitation controlled by a single lord. The lord might be a king or a great nobleman or churchman with numerous manors under his control. Or he might be a simple knight with only one or two manors at his disposal. The manor—the unit of jurisdiction—was often geographically identical with the village, but some manors embraced two or more villages, and an occasional large village might be divided into two or more manors. In any case, the agrarian routine of plowing, planting, and harvesting was based on the village organization, whereas the peasants' dues, obligations, and legal and political subordination were based on the manor.

The Village

The peasants of the early Middle Ages, like the Romans and Celts before them, tended to live in agrarian settlements consisting of scattered individual farms or small clusters of them. The agricultural community, which had been an important element in the European landscape since prehistoric times, underwent fundamental changes between approximately the ninth and twelfth centuries, the chronology of this change varying from region to region. Before it occurred, rural communities were rootless, flimsy, and impermanent, consisting of ramshackle cottages that lasted no more than a lifetime (at most) and were easily abandoned if the villagers chose to relocate their village (as they often did). Around the turn of the millennium, these scattered, ephemeral settlements began to merge into villages of the later medieval and modern type, with their houses set close together, often centered on a village green, or a well or fish pond, and surrounded by great fields. Agrarian communities of this sort are known as "nucleated villages"—that is, a nucleus of houses encircled by fields. The causes of this process of village formation are not entirely clear. Perhaps a particularly large cluster of farms began to attract the inhabitants of the neighboring district through the power or initiative of a central lordship or through community consensus.

Village formation was stimulated by the emergence of castles or stone manor houses, which served as "anchors" to the agrarian community. Another stimulus was the development of "parishes," small ecclesiastical districts centering on a local church, which tended increasingly to be built of stone, thereby becoming a second "anchor." The social and religious life of villagers typically centered on their parish churches, which provided the village community a sense of permanence.[6]

At about this same period it became common for the village population to include a substantial group of artisans—wheelwrights, blacksmiths, carpenters, coopers, and joiners. With the help of these craftsmen, peasant families began building larger and better-constructed cottages. In short, the European village of high and late medieval and early modern times—with its church, its castle or manor house, its nucleus of sturdily built cottages surrounded by fields, and its organized community of artisans—was by about 1000 or 1050 a recent creation.

The lands surrounding these villages would normally be divided into either two or three large fields. Two had been the traditional number and remained so throughout southern Europe. But the agrarian economy had been shifting in some districts of northern Europe from a two-field to a three-field system of rotation. The peasants of a three-field village would plant one field in the spring for fall harvesting, plant the second field in the fall for early summer harvesting, and let the third field lie fallow throughout the year. The next year the fields would be rotated and the process repeated. Although three-field agriculture was becoming common in northern Europe, it was necessarily limited to areas where soil fertility was sufficient to sustain more intensive cultivation. Many villages continued to function with only two fields, while others might have four, five, or even more, all subject to complex rotation arrangements.

The arable lands surrounding the village were known as "open fields" and were normally divided into unfenced strips, each about 220 yards long. Typically, a single peasant family possessed several strips, scattered throughout the fields, from which it produced its own food for consumption, sale, or the rendering of manorial dues. But the village community pooled its plows, draught animals, and toil. Collective farming was necessary because plows were expensive and had to be shared, and because no one peasant owned sufficient oxen to make up the team of several beasts (often four) necessary to draw the heavy plow. The details of this collective process were usually worked out in the village council and guided by custom.

The necessity of cooperation in farming their open fields forced European villagers to learn how to regulate the inevitable disputes that would arise over field boundaries and plowing rights. Villagers were under strong practical pressure to develop skill at manipulating and resolving their conflicts, and they acquired the ability to carry on their agrarian routine without the constant intervention of manorial lords or their bailiffs and without destructive community violence. It has been suggested (though not all would agree) that these skills contributed to the later emergence of cooperative commercial enterprises and effective local government in the principalities of medieval Western Europe.

[6]Jean Chapelot and Robert Fossier, *The Village and the House in the Middle Ages* (Berkeley, 1985).

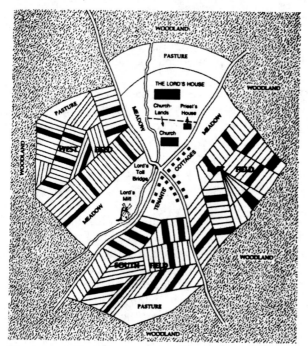

Diagram of a more-or-less typical three-field manor.

The shape, contour, and method of cultivation of the open fields varied from place to place, depending on the topography of the region and the fertility of the soil. The strips themselves were often determined by the heavy plow and the necessity of reversing the ox team as seldom as possible (though there are instances of strip fields cultivated by light plows). The length of the strips frequently depended on the distance a team could draw the plow without rest. A group of four strips, which constituted the normal day's work of a plow team, became the basis of our modern acre.

The open fields were fundamental to the village economy and, indeed, to the entire agrarian system of northern Europe. But there was more to the village community than the cluster of peasants' cottages and the encircling fields. Besides their scattered strips in the fields, peasants ordinarily had small gardens next to their cottages where vegetables and fruits could be raised and fowl kept to provide variety to their diet. The village also included a pasture where the plow animals grazed, and a meadow from which hay was cut to sustain the precious beasts over the winter. Some village communities kept sheep on their pasture as a source of cheese, milk, and wool. Certain districts, particularly in Flanders and northern England, took up sheep raising on a scale so large as almost to exclude the growing of grains.

Attached to most village communities was a wooded area from which fuel and building materials could be gathered. It also served as a forage for pigs, which provided most of the meat in the peasants' diet. There was commonly a stream or pond nearby that supplied the community with fish, a water mill for grinding grain, and a large oven that the community used for baking bread. By the eleventh century, as we have seen, some village communities were organized as parishes, with village churches and parish priests who were allotted lands of their own in the open fields. A single priest might frequently acquire the revenues of several village churches, living in style and delegating his priestly responsibilities to a local vicar, often of peasant birth.

The village community was economically self-sufficient only to a degree. There was always a certain amount of regional trade, and crucial items such as salt and metals often had to be imported from fairly distant sources. Thus, villagers had some incentive to produce food surpluses for trade. This incentive was intensified when the commercial revival of the eleventh and twelfth centuries vastly increased the market for grain.

The commercial revival was itself supported by the increased agricultural productivity brought about by early medieval innovations in agrarian organization and technology. Commercial expansion thus depended on food surpluses (as we have seen in the case of Venice) while at the same time encouraging further surpluses. As towns and commerce grew, the village economy was integrated more and more into region-wide trade networks, and enterprising peasants were provided a means of acquiring considerable wealth in exchange for surplus grain. The expanding grain market in turn encouraged the creation of new fields from forests and marshes. By the mid-eleventh century the limited horizons of the early medieval village were visibly widening.

The Manor

Superimposed on the economic structure of the village was the jurisdictional structure of the manor. In the eleventh century the manorial regime was only incompletely established in England and was scarcely evident at all in Scandinavia, Italy, and parts of northern Germany and southern France. But throughout much of northern France and, later, southern England and elsewhere, most peasant villagers were bound to manorial lords.

During the early Middle Ages many agrarian laborers were outright slaves. But slavery was declining in the eleventh century, and by 1100 it had become uncommon. Some peasants were of free status, owing rents to their lord but little or nothing more. A few were landless laborers working for a wage. But the great middle stratum of the peasantry came to consist of serfs—people of unfree status, bound to their lords and usually bound also to their land. In return for their strips in the open fields, serfs owed various dues to their manorial lords, chiefly in kind, and were normally expected to labor for a certain number of days each week—often three—on the lord's fields. The insecure conditions of the invasion era prompted many free peasants to relinquish their freedom in exchange for the protection of nearby lords, often bishops or abbots who could offer both military aid and the supernatural support of a local saint whose venerated relics they possessed. A monastic land survey of around AD 900 records "fourteen freemen who have handed over their property to the [abbey's] manor, the condition being that each shall do one day's work a week."

The lord drew his sustenance from the dues of his peasants and from the produce of his own fields. The lord's fields were strips scattered among the strips of the peasants and were known collectively as his *demesne*. Theoretically, the fields of the manor were divided into two categories: the lord's demesne (perhaps one-fourth to one-third of the total area) and the peasants' holdings. But in actuality the demesne strips were usually intermixed with the peasants' strips. The lord's demesne might be cultivated by slaves or hired hands. But in the eleventh century much of the demesne labor was performed by landed serfs who also paid their lord a percentage of the produce of their own fields and rendered him fees for the use of the pasture, the woods, and the lord's mill and oven. These at least were some of the more common peasant obligations.

The lord also enjoyed significant jurisdictional authority over his peasants. The administrative center of the manor was the manorial court, usually held in the lord's castle or manor house. Here a rough, custom-based justice was meted out, disputes settled, misdeeds punished, and obligations enforced. Since most lords possessed more than one manor, authority over individual manors was commonly exercised by an agent known as a "bailiff," or "steward," who supervised the manorial court, oversaw the farming of the demesne, and collected the peasants' dues. In addition to the peasants' demesne labor, the lord was entitled to certain payments deriving from his political and personal authority over his tenants. He might levy a *tallage,* a manorial tax that was theoretically unlimited in frequency and amount but was usually circumscribed by custom. He was normally entitled to payments when a peasant's son inherited the holdings of his father and when a peasant's daughter married outside the manor.

In theory, serfs had no standing before the law. But most lords were restrained from exploiting them arbitrarily by the force of custom. Some lords ignored this restraint and abused their serfs pitilessly. But custom was strong in the Middle Ages and could protect serfs in many ways. They were by no means chattel slaves: they could not normally be sold away from their lands or families, and after paying their manorial dues, they were entitled to the remaining produce of their fields. The serf's condition was hardly enviable, but it was better than the slavery of ancient times.

THE POST-CAROLINGIAN CHURCH

The existence of parish churches in eleventh-century villages illustrates the deeply significant fact that the long process of Christianizing Europe was by now well advanced. Whatever the intellectual and moral shortcomings of the village priests or vicars may have been, they were at least representatives of the international Church operating at the most immediate local levels throughout the European countryside.

At a rather more elevated level, Benedictine monasticism remained a potent force in European society. The Benedictines offered a continuous round of prayers for the welfare and salvation of their friends, neighbors, and benefactors. (They also sometimes prayed for the ruin and damnation of their enemies.) They copied manuscripts, supplied knights from their estates to secular armies, and served as counselors to princes. Perhaps even more than in Carolingian times, they played a major role in political life. This close association with secular politics sometimes resulted in abuses and corruption. Abbeys often found themselves under the direct "protection" of lay lords, who might pack monasteries or nunneries with their unmarriageable kinfolk, appoint cronies or younger siblings as abbots or abbesses, or even assume the abbatial function themselves, as "lay abbots." Aristocratic intervention in monastic affairs is understandable in view of the great wealth of the abbeys and the fact that many were founded by nobles as "family houses." But the results of such intervention on the Benedictine spiritual life were, at best, mixed.

Bishops and archbishops, too, were commonly appointed and controlled by lay lords. It was not unusual for a noble family to reserve a local bishopric, generation after generation, for its own junior members. Some bishops, on the other hand, wielded independent power over large districts, and there were times when bishops waged war against lay nobles. More often, however, bishops and nobles worked together in relative harmony, springing as they did from the same aristocratic milieu and sometimes the same family. All too frequently the interests and policies of such bishops were more worldly than spiritual and directed more toward the advancement of their families than toward the welfare of the Christian community. These problems affected the mid-eleventh-century episcopacy from bottom to top, extending even to the papacy, which itself had become the grand prize of contending noble families in the city of Rome.

Abuses of these sorts gave rise throughout Western Europe to powerful countermovements of Church reform, typical of which was the reform movement centered on the Burgundian abbey of Cluny. Founded in 909 by the duke

The abbey of Cluny, seventeenth-century engraving. The church (four spires) dates from the twelfth century, at which time it was the largest church in Christendom; the domestic buildings to the left are from the early modern period.

of Aquitaine, Cluny was free of local aristocratic and episcopal control and subject only to the pope, whose authority was feeble and remote, and it was blessed with a series of able and long-lived abbots. Cluny followed Benedict of Aniane's modifications of the original Benedictine Rule. Its monks devoted themselves to an elaborate sequence of daily prayers and liturgical services and a strict, godly life. Richly endowed, holy, and seemingly incorruptible, Cluny was widely admired. Gradually it began to acquire daughter houses until, in time, it became the nucleus of a great congregation of reform monasteries extending across Europe, each of them headed by a prior who was subject to the abbot of Cluny. In the mid-eleventh century the congregation of Cluny was both powerful and wealthy, the recipient of countless gifts from the landed nobility from near and far, and its new abbey church, completed in the early twelfth century, was the most splendid building of its time in all Western Europe.

As the lay world became more and more exposed to Christianity, as kings such as Edward the Confessor in England and Henry III in Germany demonstrated their concern for the welfare of their churches, the Church itself tended increasingly to come to terms with lay society. Through the ceremony of anointing, kings became virtual priest-kings. Indeed, contemporary political theory taught that the Church and the world were one—a single, God-oriented organism in which churchmen and lay lords each had appropriate roles to play.

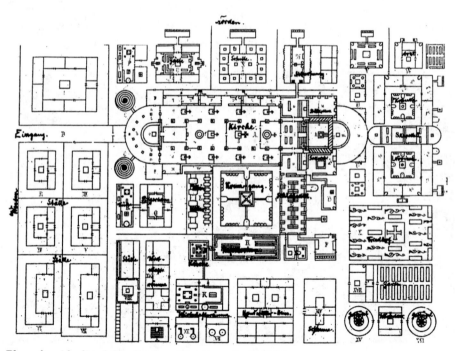

Plan of an idealized Carolingian monastery, St. Gall (reconstruction by Walter Horn). Although no such monastery was ever built, this was intended to be the perfect ground plan for a kind of monastic utopia.

EUROPE ON THE EVE OF THE HIGH MIDDLE AGES

During the centuries between the fall of the Roman Empire in the West and the great economic and cultural revival of the later eleventh century, the foundations were built on which Western civilization rose. Kingdoms emerged that would play dominant roles in the history of the modern world—England, Germany, France—and distinctive customs and institutions were developing that would define and vitalize Europe across the next millennium. A Classical-Christian cultural tradition was becoming absorbed, adapted, and fused with the customs of the Germanic peoples.

By the mid-eleventh century Europe's commerce was reviving, and the population was growing again. Indeed, the troubled era following the breakdown of Charlemagne's empire had a much livelier commerce than was once believed. Trade continued and even intensified during the post-Carolingian years along Europe's great river valleys—the Rhine, Seine, Po, Loire, Danube, Thames, and others. It was the growing wealth of the river valleys that had attracted Viking, Hungarian, and Saracen raiders, and as the invasions diminished, Europe's commerce surged. French princes, English kings, and German emperors alike encouraged markets and fairs and sought to control and systematize the minting of silver coins. The commerce of the Italian towns flourished under the Ottos and their successors, and when Otto the Great opened a rich silver mine in Rammelsberg in the 970s, a new wave of money flowed out across northern Europe.

By 1050 both England and Germany were comparatively stable, well-organized kingdoms. The Church was poised for a great movement of reform and centralization. The French monarchy was still weak, but by the end of the following century it would be on its way toward dominating France. Meanwhile, French principalities such as Champagne, Flanders, Normandy, and Anjou were well along the road to political coherence. Warfare was still commonplace, but it was beginning to lessen as Europe moved toward political stability. Above all, the invasions were over—the siege had ended. Hungary and the Scandinavian world were being absorbed into Western Christendom, and Islam was by now on the defensive. The return of prosperity, the increase in food production, the rise in population, the quickening of commerce, the intensification of intellectual activity—all betokened the coming of a new age. Western civilization was on the verge of a creative explosion.

THE HIGH MIDDLE AGES (C. 1050–1300): AN OVERVIEW

Part One of this book was organized more or less chronologically—except for our breathless sprints through Byzantium and Islam. Part Two shifts to a topical organization. We will explore the 250 years conventionally labeled the "High Middle Ages" from a variety of historical perspectives: economic and social change, territorial expansion, the deepening and broadening of religious life, the struggle between papacy and Empire, the evolution of England and France into coherent states, and concurrent developments in literature, art, and thought. Tying all these processes together is a multicolumned chronological chart near the end of this overview, to which readers can return if they get lost later on.

High medieval civilization rested on the material foundation of a somewhat earlier medieval commercial revival. Indeed, some historians would prefer to begin the High Middle Ages some years earlier than 1050, perhaps in 1000 or even 950. The process was gradual, commencing in the tenth century, gathering momentum in the eleventh, achieving full speed in the twelfth. Across these years devices such as the tandem harness and redesigned horse collar resulted not only in substituting animal for human labor but also in increasing the energy available for cultivation. The heavy plow, drawn by a team of oxen, was the machine most crucial to high medieval agriculture, but horses were important as well. As pullers of plows and carts, horses were of far greater significance in the High Middle Ages than they had been in Roman times. Additional energy was supplied by tens of thousands of water mills and, later, by windmills. Advances in agriculture produced food in greater abundance and greater variety than before: protein-rich peas and beans became for the first time an important element in the European diet, and there was greater consumption of cheese and eggs, fish and meat.

Consequently, Europe's population was not only much larger in 1300 than in 1050 but probably healthier, too, and more energetic. The best scholarly guesses put the population of Western Christendom at about thirty-five or forty million in the eleventh century and at twice that figure by 1300. To feed the millions of new mouths, the process of land clearing accelerated.

With the rise in population and food production came a decisive shift toward urbanization. Although society remained primarily agricultural throughout the Middle Ages and long thereafter, by 1300 cities had become a crucial factor in the European economy, culture, and social structure. Milan rose in population from about twenty thousand to something like a hundred thousand, and Venice, Florence, and Genoa reached comparable size. Urban populations north of the Alps tended to be lower, but by 1300 cities of twenty-five or fifty thousand were not uncommon, and Paris was approaching a hundred thousand.

Although small by present standards, the high medieval cities transformed Europe for all time to come. They were themselves the products of a tremendous intensification of commerce, centering on the twelfth century, which the historian Robert S. Lopez described as a commercial revolution. "For the first time in history," he wrote, "an underdeveloped society succeeded in developing itself, mostly by its own efforts." The great French medievalist Georges Duby referred to this process as Europe's economic takeoff. The awesome cathedrals of the high medieval cities have long been viewed as symbols of an "Age of Faith," but they could only have risen in a period that was also an age of commerce.

The economic transformation of the High Middle Ages was accompanied by far-reaching changes in political and social organization, as well as in mental attitudes. Europe evolved during these generations from a preliterate to a literate society. Although it is true that by the end of the period—by 1300—most Europeans could not read (or at least not very well), they had nevertheless come to depend on written records—deeds, letters, government surveys—to define their rights, property, and status. Whereas much had previously been left to memory and oral tradition, by 1300 English freeholders and even some serfs were having their property transactions recorded in writing. The production and preservation of government documents increased spectacularly: surviving papal letters number about thirty-five per year around 1100 but rise to thirty-six hundred per year by the early fourteenth century, and the same hundredfold explosion of paperwork occurred at royal courts.

Financial records, too, were becoming more and more widespread and systematic. Annual written accounts of royal revenues commenced in England around 1110, in France around 1190. Taken altogether, these new records bear witness to increasingly effective and complex royal administrative systems which by 1300 were evolving into modern states. All across Europe, skills such as reading, writing, and mathematical calculation were becoming vital to the functioning of secular and ecclesiastical governments, urban businesses, and even agricultural enterprises. Possessors of these skills, the reasoners and reckoners, sifted into positions of control throughout society, changing its attitudes and its character. Schools sprang up everywhere, and the age of the university dawned. Indeed, high medieval Europe witnessed the first appearance, in large numbers, of professional intellectuals—professors and scholars.

The growing complexity of high medieval society opened much greater possibilities than before for social mobility. Clever social nobodies could rise to power in royal and ecclesiastical administrations. Devout Christians could now choose from a rapidly increasing number of new monastic and religious orders. And to restless serfs and poor freeholders, the city beckoned. Most sons and daughters continued to follow in their parents' footsteps, but the more daring and ambitious found opportunities to break from the family pattern. The result was greater social vitality and, for many, increased anxiety. One's career choice was no longer as predetermined as before, and it could be a traumatic experience to move from a small community of one or two hundred familiar faces into a city of ten or twenty thousand strangers. Some historians have seen as a consequence of this fluidity a growing sense of anxiety—sometimes to the point of xenophobia—and an increase in self-awareness. More people were collecting and preserving their personal letters; autobiographies began to appear for the first time since St. Augustine wrote his *Confessions*.

CHRONOLOGY OF THE HIGH MIDDLE AGES

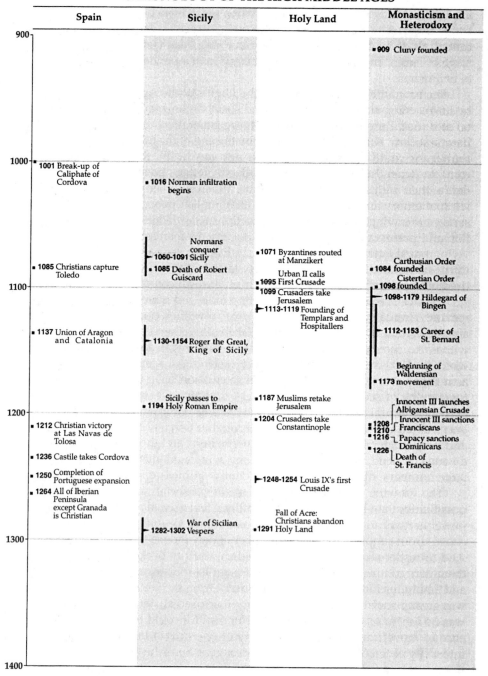

	Spain	Sicily	Holy Land	Monasticism and Heterodoxy
900				▪ **909** Cluny founded
1000	▪ **1001** Break-up of Caliphate of Cordova	▪ **1016** Norman infiltration begins		
	▪ **1085** Christians capture Toledo	▪ **1060-1091** Normans conquer Sicily ▪ **1085** Death of Robert Guiscard	▪ **1071** Byzantines routed at Manzikert ▪ **1095** Urban II calls First Crusade	▪ **1084** Carthusian Order founded ▪ **1098** Cistertian Order founded
1100			▪ **1099** Crusaders take Jerusalem ⊢ **1113-1119** Founding of Templars and Hospitallers	⊢ **1098-1179** Hildegard of Bingen
	▪ **1137** Union of Aragon and Catalonia	⊢ **1130-1154** Roger the Great, King of Sicily		⊢ **1112-1153** Career of St. Bernard
				▪ **1173** Beginning of Waldensian movement
1200		▪ **1194** Sicily passes to Holy Roman Empire	▪ **1187** Muslims retake Jerusalem	Innocent III launches Albigansian Crusade
	▪ **1212** Christian victory at Las Navas de Tolosa		▪ **1204** Crusaders take Constantinople	▪ **1208** Innocent III sanctions ▪ **1210** Franciscans ▪ **1216** Papacy sanctions Dominicans
	▪ **1236** Castile takes Cordova			▪ **1226** Death of St. Francis
	▪ **1250** Completion of Portuguese expansion ▪ **1264** All of Iberian Peninsula except Granada is Christian		⊢ **1248-1254** Louis IX's first Crusade	
1300		⊢ **1282-1302** War of Sicilian Vespers	▪ **1291** Fall of Acre: Christians abandon Holy Land	
1400				

CHRONOLOGY OF THE HIGH MIDDLE AGES

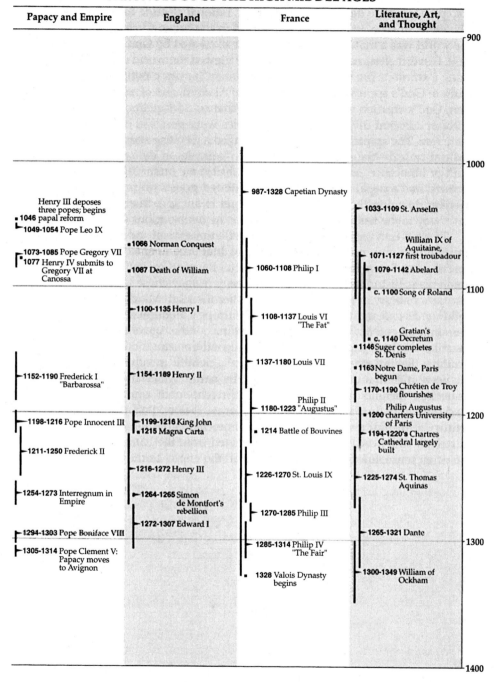

Papacy and Empire	England	France	Literature, Art, and Thought
			— 900
			— 1000
		987-1328 Capetian Dynasty	
Henry III deposes three popes; begins 1046 papal reform 1049-1054 Pope Leo IX			1033-1109 St. Anselm
1073-1085 Pope Gregory VII 1077 Henry IV submits to Gregory VII at Canossa	1066 Norman Conquest 1087 Death of William	1060-1108 Philip I	William IX of Aquitaine, 1071-1127 first troubadour 1079-1142 Abelard
			c. 1100 Song of Roland — 1100
	1100-1135 Henry I	1108-1137 Louis VI "The Fat"	
		1137-1180 Louis VII	Gratian's c. 1140 Decretum 1146 Suger completes St. Denis 1163 Notre Dame, Paris begun
1152-1190 Frederick I "Barbarossa"	1154-1189 Henry II	Philip II 1180-1223 "Augustus"	1170-1190 Chrétien de Troy flourishes
1198-1216 Pope Innocent III	1199-1216 King John 1215 Magna Carta	1214 Battle of Bouvines	Philip Augustus 1200 charters University of Paris — 1200 1194-1220's Chartres Cathedral largely built
1211-1250 Frederick II	1216-1272 Henry III	1226-1270 St. Louis IX	1225-1274 St. Thomas Aquinas
1254-1273 Interregnum in Empire	1264-1265 Simon de Montfort's rebellion 1272-1307 Edward I	1270-1285 Philip III	1265-1321 Dante
1294-1303 Pope Boniface VIII		1285-1314 Philip IV "The Fair"	— 1300
1305-1314 Pope Clement V: Papacy moves to Avignon		1328 Valois Dynasty begins	1300-1349 William of Ockham
			— 1400

One of the twelfth century's best known autobiographers, Peter Abelard, also pioneered the development of a new, rational attitude toward the cosmos. The seeds of such an attitude had existed in the Judeo-Christian doctrine that the world was a material, physical universe, created by God yet separate from God. Nevertheless, early medieval people viewed the world as a theater of miracles: a storm or fire was a divine punishment for sin; a military victory was a mark of God's approval. But in the view of Abelard, and of many who followed him, God's creation was a natural order that could function by its own rules, without constant divine tinkering. Miracles were possible, of course, but they were rare. The spread of this idea encouraged a growing skepticism toward the judicial ordeal—the appeal to God for a "miracle on demand" to determine guilt or innocence (see pp. 33–34). The ordeal came under attack in the twelfth century, and a papal council of 1215 prohibited priests from participating in it, thereby dooming the procedure to gradual extinction. The judgment of God gave way to the testimony of witnesses or the deliberations of juries.

These deeply significant shifts in attitude toward self and toward the world, and the vast economic and social changes that accompanied them, have been described as Europe's coming of age. Such biological metaphors are obviously inadequate; historians might argue endlessly (if they chose to) over the date of Europe's puberty or adulthood. But whether the High Middle Ages are seen as childhood's end, or the opening phase of Europe's modernization, or the time of economic takeoff (or, for that matter, the climax of the Age of Faith), the changes described in these pages were essential preconditions for modern European civilization. Behind the seventeenth-century scientific revolution lay the high medieval idea of a universe functioning by natural rules and open to rational inspection. Behind the fifteenth-century invention of printing lay the high medieval shift from a preliterate to a literate society. Behind the nineteenth-century industrial revolution lay the commercial revolution of the twelfth and thirteenth. Our word "civilization" is derived from the Latin *civitas*—"city." In this strict sense, Europe became civilized in the High Middle Ages.

Town, Countryside, and Economic Takeoff

THE COMMERCIAL REVOLUTION

Towns and Commerce

There had been towns in Western Europe ever since antiquity. The administrative-military towns of the Roman Empire evolved into the cathedral towns of the early Middle Ages, with their episcopal courts and churches and the sacred legends and relics of their saints. As commerce revived in the tenth and eleventh centuries, old towns were invigorated and new ones emerged as centers of trade and production. The high medieval city remained faithful to its saints and religious establishments, while at the same time expanding its commercial districts and developing its political and legal institutions. Church, commerce, and urban government coexisted in a balanced relationship within the city's walls, but where trade was lively, merchants spilled outside the walls into new suburbs. It was commerce that transformed Europe's cities into economic centers that, for the first time, earned their own way from the activities of their traders and artisans.

The commerce of early post-Carolingian Europe owed much to the activities of Jewish merchants, who linked Western Christendom with the wealthier civilizations of Islam and Byzantium. Commercial activity intensified between the ninth century and the eleventh as Jewish merchants in European towns conducted a regional and international trade in such commodities as cloth, grain, salt, slaves, and wine. They enjoyed the great advantage of commercial contacts with Jewish communities in Islamic and Byzantine cities, and they shared with these communities a familiarity with accounting techniques, commercial contracts, and other business methods otherwise little-known in the West. During the eleventh and twelfth centuries Christians moved increasingly into commercial life, first in Italy, then to the north. By then the commercial revolution was well under way.

As it gathered momentum, commercial settlements began springing up all across Western Europe—sometimes as suburbs of older cathedral towns, sometimes outside the walls of monasteries, and often around one or another of the many fortresses that had risen in post-Carolingian Europe. These strongholds were generally known by some form of the Germanic word "burgh," and in time the term came to apply to the town itself rather than the fortress that spawned it. By the twelfth century a burgh, or "borough," was an urban commercial center, inhabited by "burghers" or "burgesses," who constituted a new class known later as the "bourgeoisie."

The earliest and largest commercial towns were those of northern Italy, where the immense opportunities of international commerce were first exploited. As we have seen, Venetian merchants had long been trading with Constantinople and Islam, while other Italian ports—Genoa, Pisa, and Amalfi—soon followed Venice into the profitable markets of the eastern Mediterranean. We have seen, too, how the ramifications of their far-flung trade brought vigorous new life to towns of interior Italy such as Milan and Florence. During the High Middle Ages the Muslims were virtually driven from the seas; Italian merchants dominated the Mediterranean, bringing Eastern goods to the markets of Italy and carrying them overland across the Alps into Germany and France. As a consequence of these commercial activities, Milan's population rose from about twenty thousand to something like one hundred thousand, and Venice, Florence, and Genoa reached almost comparable size.

Far to the north, the towns of Flanders (roughly modern Belgium) were growing wealthy from commerce and manufacturing. Their trade extended throughout northern France and the British Isles, the Rhineland, and the shores of the Baltic Sea. Flanders had long been a great sheep-raising district, and its growing towns—Bruges, Ypres, St-Omer, Ghent, and others—became centers of woolen textile production. In time, international demand for Flemish cloth grew to the point where the Flemish wool supply became insufficient, and Flemish merchants began importing wool from England on an ever-larger scale. By then Flanders was the industrial center of northern Europe, and its textile industry was the supreme manufacturing enterprise of the age. The exporting of textiles to eastern Europe, the Middle East, and beyond—from both Flanders and the Italian cities—was a crucial factor in reversing Europe's age-long trade deficit.

Centers of commerce and manufacturing, formerly isolated from one another, now became linked into a single network of commerce. The Flemish and Italian towns, for example, were becoming joined together in an emerging commercial axis running through the Rhine and Rhône valleys. As other centers of production developed similar commercial ties, much of western and central Europe came to be bound together into a single network of commerce.

As this process continued, agricultural specialization increased significantly. Money and merchants made it possible for local areas to concentrate on whatever goods they could produce most efficiently, using their profits to import other necessities. Thus, the Paris basin exported grain, Scandinavia exported timber, Poland exported salt, northern Germany exported salt and fish, England exported wool and beer, Flanders exported cloth, and Burgundy exported wine. A thirteenth-century visitor to a Burgundian religious house reported that the surrounding lands were devoted exclusively to vineyards: "They send their wine to Paris, because they have a river at hand that flows there (the Seine), and they sell their wine for a good price from which they buy all their food and clothes."

Throughout Western Christendom commerce was lubricating the economy with an ever-increasing flow of money, causing the Angevin writer Marbod of Rennes, writing around AD 1100, to burst into poetry:

Money! He's the whole world's Master.
His the voice that makes men run:
Speak! Be quiet! Slower! Faster!
Money orders—and it's done.

Godric of Finchale

The life of St. Godric of Finchale (c. 1069–1170) provides a unique portrayal of the rags-to-riches business career of a native Englishman in the generations following the Norman Conquest. Godric had many contemporaries of humble birth who, like him, prospered greatly from the burgeoning commerce of the era. But writers of the time were not interested in recording such economic success stories. We know of Godric's rise to fortune only because he later rejected his worldly wealth to become a hermit-saint whose austere life of prayer and self-sacrifice came to be known and admired throughout Western Europe. For that reason, he was the subject of no less than three pious biographies.

From these sources, we learn that Godric was born shortly after the Norman Conquest of England in a small town in Norfolk. His name marks him as one of the conquered English rather than the conquering Normans, and the names of his parents, Ailward and Aedwin, are similarly Anglo-Saxon. Godric was their firstborn, and he remained at home with his parents and younger siblings throughout his boyhood and early adolescence.

At about the age of sixteen Godric left his family and set off to seek his fortune. After four years as a wandering peddler, scavenging for lost or castoff goods and then selling them, he had prospered to the point that he could afford to make a pilgrimage to Rome—which he probably undertook not only for reasons of piety but also out of curiosity and a longing for adventure.

Godric then became a seafaring merchant, plying his wares between England, Flanders, Denmark, and Scotland. Soon he was able to buy a half-share in one merchant ship and a quarter-share in another. He became an accomplished sea captain, steering his own ships from port to port and sometimes saving them from shipwreck (or so it was later said) by his uncanny skill at weather forecasting.

At this stage Godric was far from being the saint he would later become. In future years he bitterly repented the sins of lust and dishonesty that he had so often committed during his youthful years as a merchant and sailor. In 1101 he sailed to the Holy Land on what was said to have been a "pilgrimage to Jerusalem," and he doubtless set out on the voyage with a pious intent. Nevertheless, he probably did some trading and perhaps even plundering along the way. It was probably he whom Crusade chronicles describe as "Godric the pirate from the kingdom of England," who rescued King Baldwin I of Jerusalem in 1102 after the king had suffered a major defeat at the hands of a Muslim army. Godric in his early thirties is described by a friend as short, agile, and strong, with a broad forehead, sparkling gray eyes, and bushy eyebrows that almost met. He had an oval face, a long nose, a thick beard, and black hair that in later years would turn pure white.

On his return to England from Jerusalem, Godric seems to have been torn between resuming his worldly life and devoting himself to God. He served for a time as business manager for a rich nobleman but soon gave it up to go on more pilgrimages—to Rome, to the shrine of St. Gilles in southern France, and to Rome again. Finally, in his mid-thirties, Godric abandoned his business career for good. He disposed of all his wealth and became a hermit, moving from place to place in the forests of northern England. Eventually, after returning from one last penitential pilgrimage to Jerusalem, he settled down at a lonely, beautiful site on the River Wear, just north of Durham, called Finchale (pronounced—regrettably—"Finkle").

There Godric lived as a pious hermit for well over sixty years. Gradually his reputation for sanctity spread across England and Europe. He was visited by the great abbots and bishops of northern England. He was venerated as a prophet of such potent gifts that some of the most celebrated leaders in Christendom—prelates such as Archbishop Thomas Becket and Pope Alexander III—sought his prayers and his counsel. He was also admired as a religious poet who set his verse to music, some of which still survives. His poetry is not for every taste, yet it represents something of a milestone in the history of English literature, constituting as it does the earliest surviving Middle English verse. Godric was revered also for his love of animals. Throughout the icy northern winters he would bring rabbits and field mice to his cottage to enjoy the warmth of his fire.

The evidence suggests that Godric lived to be at least one hundred years old. During his final illness he was nursed by the monks of Durham Cathedral. After his death, in April 1170, the monks built a priory on the site of his hermitage at Finchale, the ruins of which remain to this day in an unspoiled vale alongside the River Wear.

Godric was only one of many holy men whose careers were subsequently recorded by admiring biographers. In his case, however, the record of his youthful years as a merchant and seafarer provides us with an unparalleled portrait of a self-made entrepreneur in an early phase of the medieval commercial revolution.

With the increasing abundance of money, princes could now collect their taxes in silver coins rather than in goods, govern through salaried officials, and wage war with hired troops. Enterprising peasants could accumulate liquid wealth. Aristocrats could pamper themselves with imported luxury goods. And burghers, the chief beneficiaries of the new economy, could honor their civic saints (and express their civic pride) by building vast, richly decorated churches. Often, too, they honored themselves by building elaborate town halls, and even more so by building impressive stone houses where they dwelt in conspicuous elegance.

Urban Liberties

The new urban class emerged from a society that had heretofore been almost exclusively agrarian. The town dwellers were drawn primarily from the wealthier peasantry but also included vagabonds, runaway serfs, ambitious younger offspring of the lesser nobility, and, in general, the surplus of a mushrooming population.

At an early date traders began to form themselves into merchant guilds to protect themselves against exorbitant tolls and other exactions levied by the landed aristocracy. A town was almost always situated in the territory of some lord—baron, bishop, count, duke, or king. And merchants found that only by collective action could they win the privileges essential to their calling: freedom from servile dues, freedom of movement, freedom from inordinate tolls at every bridge or castle, and the rights to own town property, to be judged by the town court rather than the lord's court, to execute commercial contracts, and to buy and sell freely.

By the twelfth century, lords were issuing charters to their towns that guaranteed many or all of these privileges. Some lords were forced to do so in response to urban riots and revolts; others did so voluntarily, recognizing the economic advantages of having flourishing commercial centers in their territories. Indeed, some farsighted lords began chartering new towns on their own initiative, laying out streets on a gridiron plan within the new walls, and attracting commercial settlers by offering generous privileges.

The first urban charters varied greatly from one another, but in time it became common to pattern them after certain well-known models that were copied repeatedly throughout England, France, Germany, Spain, and Flanders. The privileges enjoyed by the burghers of Newcastle-on-Tyne under King Henry I of England, and the charter granted by the French king Louis VI to the community of Lorris, became prototypes for the charters of many other communities. In effect, such privileges created semi-autonomous political and legal entities, each with its own local government, its own court, its own tax-collecting agencies, and its own customs. The merchants and artisans who inhabited these communities paid well for their charters and continued to render regular taxes to their lord. But—and this is all-important—they did so collectively, through their urban governments. Individual merchants were freed from the harassments of their lords' agents. Townspeople enforced their own law in their own courts, collected their own taxes, and paid their dues to their lord in a lump sum. In short, they had won the invaluable privilege of handling their own affairs. And wise lords had no objection to simply gathering the golden eggs without administrative effort.

One should not conclude that the medieval towns were even remotely democratic. It was the prosperous merchants and master craftsmen who profited chiefly from the charters, and it was they who came to control the town governments, ruling over the towns' less exalted inhabitants. Some towns witnessed the beginnings of a significant split between large-scale producers and wage-earning workers. Indeed, the medieval town is regarded by many economic historians as the birthplace of European capitalism. For as time progressed towns tended to become centers of industry as well as commerce. Manufacturing followed in the footsteps of trade. And although most industrial production took place in small shops rather than large factories, some enterprising manufacturers employed considerable numbers of workers to produce goods, usually textiles, on a large scale. Normally, these workers did not labor in a factory but instead worked in their own shops or homes. Since the entrepreneur sent raw materials out to the workers, rather than bringing the workers to the materials, this mode of production has been called the "putting-out system." As a direct antecedent of the factory system, it was a crucial phase in the early history of capitalism.

Craft Guilds and Artisans

The more typical medieval manufacturers worked for themselves in their own shops, producing their own goods and selling them directly to the public. As early as the eleventh century, these artisans were organizing themselves into craft guilds, as distinct from merchant guilds. These guilds had many functions: social interaction, group drinking, charitable activities, and religious observances. They also had significant economic functions. To limit competition and ensure the quality of their goods, the craft guilds established strict admission requirements and stringent rules on prices, wages, standards of quality, and operating procedures. Young artisans learned their trade as apprentices in the shops of master craftsmen. After a specified period, sometimes as long as seven years, the apprenticeship ended. With good luck and rich parents, the apprentice might then become a master. But young artisans normally had to work for some years beyond their apprenticeships as day laborers—"journeymen" (after *journée*, the French word for "day")—improving their skills and saving money in the hope of someday establishing their own shop and becoming guild masters. Many never made it; as time progressed and urban society crystallized, it became increasingly common for artisans to spend their whole lives as wage earners, never becoming masters.

Throughout the High Middle Ages and beyond, women took an active part in town life. Since the master craftsman's shop was also his home, the modern distinction between home and workplace, between public and private spheres of activity, did not exist (nor did it in aristocrats' castles or peasants' cottages). This blurring of domestic and business life worked to women's advantage: a master's wife and daughters could learn his skills just as his apprentices could, by observing and practicing. Indeed, master craftsmen and their wives normally shared authority over apprentices, on the assumption that the wife was well acquainted with her husband's craft. Widows commonly carried on the businesses of their deceased husbands—and the tendency for urban women in their teens to marry established businessmen in their late twenties or thirties resulted in an abundance of lively, prosperous widows. Even while still married, women sometimes owned and operated their own businesses, distinct from their husbands. And women dominated such economic activities as the spinning of silk, the manufacture of female headgear and purses, and, in Paris, the managing of hotels and taverns. Women could also be members of some guilds, though by no means all. And town records show women collecting taxes, lending and exchanging money, illuminating and copying books, working as druggists and barbers, and engaging on their own in a wide variety of craft and merchant enterprises.

Economic and Cultural Vitalization

There were many who made their fortunes in commerce and manufacturing. Europe was astir with new life, and for one who was clever and enterprising, the possibilities were vast. In the twelfth and thirteenth centuries, merchants were moving continuously along the roads and rivers of Europe. A series of annual fairs on the overland trade routes provided them with excellent opportunities to sell their goods. As commerce grew, credit and banking grew with it, and by the thirteenth century several Italian banking families had amassed huge fortunes.

Money and religious piety blended in the new towns to vitalize the Christian culture of the High Middle Ages. It was money that built the great cathedrals, supported the Crusades, financed the charities of Christian princes, and gave life and substance to the magnificent religious culture of the thirteenth century— money and of course an ardent faith. For townspeople, by and large, exhibited a piety that was more vibrant and intense than that of the peasantry and aristocracy. The surge of urban piety became a crucial factor in the development of high medieval Christianity—spawning cathedrals, abbeys, priories, and hospitals, universities and colleges, saints and heretics. The most celebrated saint of the era, Francis of Assisi, and the best known heretic, Peter Waldo, were both townsmen. In the electric atmosphere of the new cities, Christianity acquired an emotional intensity unknown to the villages and manor houses.

At some point in the course of the medieval commercial revolution, perhaps toward the end of the twelfth century, commerce outdistanced agriculture to become the dominating force in the European economy that it has remained ever since. What occurred was more than a great economic boom. It was a permanent change, and of such historic magnitude that several distinguished scholars have described it as Europe's "economic takeoff." In centuries thereafter, Europe would endure depressions, plagues, and devastating wars, but it would never revert to the primarily agrarian economy of the early Middle Ages.

Life in Twelfth-Century London

We can gain some impression of life in a medieval city by looking at London as it existed toward the end of the twelfth century. With a population of about thirty thousand, London was by far the largest city of its time in the British Isles and one of the leading commercial centers of northwestern Europe. Many of England's bishops, abbots, and barons maintained townhouses there, and the king himself conducted much of his business at a palace (completed in 1099 and standing to this day) in London's western suburb of Westminster. Londoners of the later twelfth century were served by 139 churches, whose bells pealed across the city and its suburbs to mark the hours of the day.

London's narrow streets were lined with houses and shops, most of them built of wood. Fire was an ever-present danger. During the day the streets, mostly unpaved, were crowded with people, dogs, horses, and pigs. (Half a century earlier a crown prince of France was killed when his horse tripped over a pig in the streets of Paris.) But from the perspective of its twelfth-century inhabitants, London was a great, progressive metropolis. The old wooden bridge across the River Thames was being replaced by a new London Bridge made entirely of stone. City sanitation workers cleared the streets of garbage. There was a sewer system—the only one in England—consisting of open drains down the centers of streets. There was even a public lavatory, established by Queen Matilda II in the early twelfth century, the first of England's impressive network of "Public Conveniences."

By today's standards, the city was a small, filthy, odoriferous firetrap. But twelfth-century Londoners were proud of it. One of them, William fitz Stephen, writing around 1175, described it in these glowing words:

> Among the noble and celebrated cities of the world, London, the capital of the kingdom of the English, extends its glory farther than all others and sends its wealth and merchandise more widely into far distant lands. It holds its head higher than all the rest. It is fortunate in the healthiness of its air, in its observance of Christian practice, in the strength of its fortifications, in its natural setting, in the honor of its citizens, and in the modest behavior of its wives. It is cheerful in its sports and the fruitful mother of noble men.[1]

All medieval cities were fortified, and London more strongly than most:

> It has on the east the Tower of London, very great and strong. . . . On the west there are two powerful castles, and from there runs a high and massive wall with seven double gates and with towers along the north at regular intervals.

Within these walls, London was a hive of commercial activity:

> Those engaged in businesses of various kinds—sellers of merchandise, hirers of labor—go off every morning into their various districts according to their trade. Besides, there is a public cook shop in London, located on the riverbank in the district where wines are offered for sale in ships and in the cellars of the wine merchants. Each day, at this cook shop, you will find food according to the season—dishes of meat, roasted, fried, and boiled; large and small fish; coarser meats for the poor and more delicate for the rich, such as venison and large and small birds.

The delicacies offered by this medieval KFC could be enjoyed not only by Londoners but also by visitors from afar:

---

[1] Among the noble "men" born in twelfth-century London, William fitz Stephen proudly included Empress Matilda.

To this city merchants delight to bring their trade by sea from every nation under heaven. The Arabian sends gold; the Sabaean spice and incense. The Scythian brings arms, and from the rich, fat lands of Babylon comes palm oil. The Nile sends precious stones; the Norwegians and Russians send furs and sables; nor is China absent with its purple silk. The French come with their wines.

William fitz Stephen went on to describe London's entertainments and sports: the miracle plays, the annual Carnival Day with its cockfights and athletic contests, when ball teams from various London guilds and schools competed in the fields outside the city's walls. "On feast days throughout the summer, the young men engage in the sports of archery, running, jumping, wrestling, slinging stones, hurling javelins beyond a certain mark, and fighting with sword and buckler." And in winter,

> Swarms of young men come out to play games on the ice. Some, gaining speed in their run, slide sideways over a vast expanse of ice, their feet set well apart. Others make seats out of a large lump of ice, and while one person sits on it, the others, with linked hands, run in front and drag him along behind them. So swift is their sliding motion that sometimes their feet slip, and they all fall on their faces. Others, more skilled at winter sports, put on their feet the shin bones of animals, binding them firmly around their ankles, and then, gripping iron-shod poles, which they strike from time to time against the ice, they are propelled as swiftly as a bird in flight.

William fitz Stephen was prone to exaggeration. He wrote of the healthiness of London's air, and yet we know that London had a smog problem even in the twelfth century. The author's chamber-of-commerce viewpoint contrasts sharply with the testimony of a twelfth-century Jewish merchant from France, who gave this warning to a friend about to leave for England:

> If you go to London pass through it quickly. . . . Every evil or malicious thing that can be found anywhere on earth you will find in that one city. Steer clear of the crowds of pimps; don't mingle with the throngs in eating houses; avoid dice and gambling, the theater and the tavern. You will meet with more braggarts there than in all of France. The number of parasites is infinite. Actors, jesters, smooth-skinned lads, Moors, flatterers, pretty boys, effeminates, degenerates, singing girls and dancing girls, quacks, belly dancers, sorceresses, extortioners, night wanderers, magicians, mimes, beggars, buffoons: all this tribe fill all the houses. So if you don't want to deal with evildoers, don't go to London.

The same Jewish merchant provided equally bad reports about other English towns: In Exeter both men and beasts are provided the same food. Bath, lying amidst "exceedingly heavy air and sulphurous fumes, is at the gates of hell." At Bristol, "there is nobody who is not or has not been a soap maker." Ely stinks perpetually from the surrounding marshes. And York is "full of Scotsmen—filthy and treacherous creatures, scarcely men."[2]

---

[2]These views are ascribed to the merchant by the English chronicler Richard of Devizes, who may himself have invented the whole business.

The warnings of the French merchant are reinforced by a recent calculation of the murder rate in thirteenth-century London: twelve homicides per one hundred thousand people, thirty times the per-capita murder rate of modern Britain (though far less than the rate of Los Angeles or New York in the 1990s). The violence of medieval London may be attributable in part to the existence (in 1309) of 354 taverns and more than thirteen hundred ale shops, a fact that provides added significance to the term "High Middle Ages." Ale consumption seems to have been still more heroic in the medieval English countryside, where the murder rate was even higher than in the towns.

The Jews of Medieval Europe

Well might a twelfth-century Jewish merchant be unenthusiastic about urban life in England—or, for that matter, throughout much of Western Christendom. For in a civilization that was almost unanimously Christian, members of a minority faith were apt to suffer. In most regions of Christian Europe, Jews had long been subjected to legal disabilities and popular bias. And their condition worsened in the High Middle Ages with the growth of Christian self-awareness, militancy, and popular devotion to the suffering Christ. Good Christian theology insists that Christ died for the sins of all humanity, but popular sentiment often held that he was murdered by the Jews. And there were those who arrived at the grotesque conclusion that the "murder" should be avenged. The persecution of Jews—and of other dissenting groups such as heretics and magicians—represents the dark underside of high medieval Christian piety.

Jews had played a vital part in the earlier phases of medieval urban growth, as we have seen. They were active in the commercial life of Italian cities throughout the early Middle Ages, and in 875 King Charles the Bald brought a community of Jews home with him from a visit to Italy and settled them in his kingdom. They spread into numerous cities of France and Germany and finally into England in the wake of the Norman Conquest of 1066. Wherever they settled, they stimulated commerce through their mercantile expertise.

Ever since the Christian conversion of the Roman Empire, however, Jews had been at best second-class citizens. A Church council of 451 had prohibited Christians from marrying Jews, having dinner with them, or even going to Jewish physicians. Jews were not to hold Christian slaves, to take Christian oaths of fealty, or to be lords over Christians. Such rules were not strictly enforced in the Early Middle Ages, but by the later twelfth century, Jews were required to wear special badges or hats so that Christians might be warned to keep their appropriate social distance.[3] The papacy was never a friend of Jews, but it did endeavor to protect them from the violence of popular prejudice, and Jewish intellectuals responded by supporting the growth of papal authority. An eleventh-century pope wrote to the bishops of Spain,

---

[3]Similar stigmas were imposed on non-Muslims under Islamic rule.

> We are pleased with the account we have recently heard concerning the way you have protected the Jews who live among you from destruction by those who are setting out to fight the Saracens. For these warriors, moved by stupidity or perhaps blinded by avarice, wished to behave like savages, destroying those whom divine, fatherly love may well have intended for salvation. . . . Indeed, the cases of the Jews and Saracens are altogether distinct: warfare is rightful against the Saracens, who persecute Christians and drive them from their own towns and lands; but the Jews are everywhere ready to do service.

As this passage suggests, Crusades against Islam could escalate Christian anti-Semitism to the point of bloodthirsty violence. Such was the effect of the First Crusade to the Holy Land in 1096. It dawned on some crusaders that their mission to extend Christian power over infidels abroad might be prefaced by slaughtering the "infidel" minority in Christendom itself. The Jews of France and England survived the crusading fervor largely unscathed, but those of central Europe did not. According to one Christian writer, the crusaders

> should have traveled their road for Christ, recalling the divine commands and holding to the discipline of the Gospel, while instead they turned to madness and shamefully, wantonly, cruelly cut down the Jewish people in the cities and towns through which they passed.

Massacres of Jews did not begin with the Crusades, but they became more frequent thereafter. Most were products of prejudice among common Christian town dwellers, whipped to a frenzy by popular rumors that Jews desecrated the transfigured bread of the Holy Eucharist or that they murdered Christian infants (as they had allegedly murdered Christ). A pope decreed in 1272 "that Jews arrested on such an absurd pretext be freed from captivity."

Here again the papacy was assuming responsibility for protecting Jews from mindless grass-roots savagery, and the responsibility was shared by kings and emperors. But these enthroned guardians demanded much of the Jews in return for protection. They borrowed heavily from Jewish burghers, milked them through arbitrary taxes, seized the property and loan accounts of Jews who had died without heirs, and charged enormous sums for the rights to travel freely, enjoy a fair trial, and pass their property on to their heirs. As the High Middle Ages closed, Jews were being subjected to ever more intense persecution. Whereas the Fathers of the early Church had advocated the toleration of Jews as witnesses to the faith of the Old Testament, many churchmen and theologians had become convinced by the mid-thirteenth century that the Judaism of their own times, with its emphasis on the Talmud, constituted a heretical lapse from the original Mosaic faith. Jews should therefore be punished for blasphemy if they refused to convert to Christianity.

In the years around 1300, Jews were being expelled en masse from one kingdom after another by monarchs who coveted their wealth. By then their services as moneylenders were no longer essential; Italian bankers were providing an alternative source of credit. Many Jews subsequently filtered back or were invited to return when royal policy shifted. But by the fifteenth century, with the coming of the Renaissance, they were being segregated into ghettos.

And persecution continued unabated throughout most of Europe for centuries thereafter, reaching its crescendo in the twentieth century with the horrors of the Nazi Holocaust.

The Jews of the High Middle Ages have usually been associated almost exclusively with such activities as moneylending and commerce. But although it is true that Jews were excluded from Christian guilds and forbidden to be lords of Christian peasants, more recent scholarship suggests that many Jews, particularly in southern Europe, blended almost invisibly into the general urban society. Their activities were less strictly limited in the south than in the north, and it is certain that, throughout Christendom, moneylending and commerce occupied only a small, highly visible minority of medieval Jews. Still, they differed from Christians in ways other than faith alone: they achieved a much higher literacy rate than their Christian contemporaries (every substantial Jewish community had its own school), and their contributions to medieval medicine, Biblical scholarship, and philosophy were all out of proportion to their numbers. The Jewish communities of medieval Europe produced such eminent thinkers as the Frenchman Rabbi Solomon ben Isaac (better known as Rashi), and the great Jewish philosopher from Spain, Moses Maimonides (1135—1204), whose highly creative use of Aristotle did much to shape both Jewish and Christian thought in the thirteenth century and long thereafter. Indeed, Miamonides was a major influence on such celebrated Christian philosophers as St. Thomas Aquinas (see pp. 309–311). In the areas of medicine and philosophy, as in commerce, the contacts of European Jews with their Jewish counterparts in Islam and Byzantium contributed much to the ending of Europe's isolation.

THE LANDHOLDING ARISTOCRACY

The commercial revival had a substantial impact on medieval aristocratic life in the north European countryside. For one thing, the much-increased circulation of money gradually eroded the tenure-service relationships of the early Middle Ages. Rulers came to depend less on the military and administrative services that vassals performed in return for their lands and resorted increasingly to the use of mercenary troops and paid officials, first in England and later on the Continent. Beginning in the twelfth century, English kings often required their aristocratic landholders to pay a tax called *scutage* ("shield money") in lieu of personal service in a royal campaign, and in time this practice spread to France and elsewhere.

Moreover, money and commerce made new luxuries available to the landed aristocracy: pepper, ginger, and cinnamon for baronial kitchens; finer and more colorful clothing, jewelry, fur coats for the cold winters (and to impress the less fortunate); and—for the castle—carpets, wall hangings, and more elaborate furniture. These amenities, in turn, drove many nobles into debt, thus increasing the business (and unpopularity) of Jewish lenders. Many aristocrats, women and men alike, regarded overspending as a virtue—the mark of a generous spirit.

Hugh, Earl of Chester

Although not the greatest nobleman of his era, Hugh, earl of Chester, nevertheless inherited considerable landed wealth and acquired far more in the course of his eventful career. His life was in some important respects typical of his age and class; in other respects, however, he emerges as a unique individual with a style all his own.

Hugh was born in Normandy about eighteen years before the Norman Conquest of England (c. 1048). Like other Norman nobles, he was of Viking descent: his great-grandfather was known as Ansfrid the Dane. But several generations in Normandy had transformed Ansfrid's descendants and those of his fellow Viking settlers into a French-speaking aristocracy hardly distinguishable from the aristocracies of neighboring French provinces.

Hugh's father, Richard of Avranches, was a wealthy Norman landholder and was an important regional official—a vicomte—of William, duke of Normandy, the future conqueror of England. Hugh inherited his father's estates and office of vicomte. And as a result of the Norman Conquest of 1066, in which Hugh probably participated as a teenaged commander of a large contingent of knights, he acquired lands and power in England far exceeding his inheritance in Normandy. King William the Conqueror showered wealth on his young vassal, granting him estates scattered across some twenty shires and raising him to the prestigious office of earl. It was Hugh's responsibility as earl to consolidate Norman power in the county of Cheshire on the frontier of Wales, and to expand Norman authority into the northern regions of that as yet unconquered land. To assist Hugh in meeting these responsibilities, King William gave him all the lands in Cheshire, except those belonging to the Church, and granted him virtually kingly authority there: Hugh was empowered to summon all the Cheshire knights on his own authority, to collect his own taxes, and to appoint his own sheriff and lesser shire officials.

Hugh never abused these privileges. Unlike many other great magnates of post-Conquest England, he remained steadfastly loyal to William the Conqueror and his royal successors. In the course of several baronial rebellions, Hugh gave the monarchy his total support—and he and his family consequently basked in the royal favor.

Hugh was distinctly less popular among the Welsh. They called him "Hugh the Wolf" because of his ruthless and savage military campaigns against northern Wales. The Normans were known at the time as a conquering people, and Hugh was in this respect a typical Norman. He did not succeed in subduing all of northern Wales, but he and his men occupied large portions of it, slaughtering the Welsh in great numbers.

He was also known as "Hugh the Fat," and a contemporary writer went on at some length deploring his flamboyant lack of self-restraint:

He was a great lover of the world and its pomp, which he regarded as the greatest blessing of the human lot. He was always in the forefront of battle, lavish to the point of prodigality, a lover of games and luxuries, actors, horses, dogs, and similar vanities. He was always surrounded by a huge following, noisy with swarms of boys of both high and low birth. Many honorable men, clerics and knights, were also in his entourage, and he cheerfully shared his riches with them. . . . He kept no check on what he gave or received [an interesting observation suggesting that contemporary magnates normally kept accounts of receipts and expenditures].

His hunting was a daily devastation of his lands, for he thought more highly of hawkers and hunters than of peasants or monks. A slave to gluttony, he staggered under a mountain of fat, scarcely able to move. He was given over to carnal lusts and sired a multitude of bastards by his concubines.

The author of these lines, an Anglo-Norman monk named Orderic Vitalis, probably got carried away in singling Hugh out from his fellow aristocrats. In the absence of our modern obsession with dieting and fitness, most medieval nobles, because they could afford to eat well, tended to put on weight as they grew older. All the French and English kings of Hugh's era were corpulent. Similarly, Hugh's enthusiasm for hunting and hawking was widely shared among his royal and aristocratic contemporaries, even if most of them engaged in these sports with less care-free abandon. And as against Hugh's bacchanalian antics, one must bear in mind that he was also a faithful and trusted vassal of the kings of England and an extremely generous benefactor of the Church. In Normandy, Hugh founded a great (and vastly expensive) Benedictine abbey—St-Sever, close to Avranches—granting it extensive lands from his family estates scattered across the central and western districts of the Norman duchy. With his wife, Ermentrude, the daughter of a French count and countess, he founded a second, equally expensive Benedictine abbey in his English earldom: St. Werburg's, Chester. He established St. Werburg's in consultation with his close friend St. Anselm, abbot of Bec, then archbishop of Canterbury, and one of the wisest and holiest saints of the Middle Ages (see p. 304). Anselm and Hugh were an odd couple, yet they accomplished much together. Under Anselm's guidance, Hugh filled his new abbey with pious and dedicated monks from Bec, and St. Werburg's became a center of church reform. It stands to this day as Chester Cathedral.

In 1101, while in his early fifties, Hugh fell gravely ill. By July he knew that he was nearing death, and like other noble abbey patrons in similar situations, he took his vows as a Benedictine monk and was welcomed into the austere monastic community of St. Werburg's. His timing could hardly have been better; having lived a shamelessly worldly life for half a century, and having submitted to the monastic discipline for only four days, he died.

From Orderic Vitalis's vivid description, Earl Hugh emerges as a festive, cheerfully disorganized individual. From the broader viewpoint of Anglo-Norman warfare and diplomacy, his career was a dazzling success. He always managed to make the right moves; he thereby added an extraordinarily wealthy English earldom to his Norman vicecomital estates and succeeded in holding both simultaneously throughout the later decades of his life. Perhaps most striking of all is the contrast between his ostentatious flouting of contemporary Christian moral principles—his savage campaigns against the Welsh, his unbridled gluttony and sexual license—and, on the other hand, his lavish generosity toward the Church. But here again the contradiction was not peculiar to Hugh himself; it was characteristic of the medieval aristocracy as a whole during the earlier generations of the High Middle Ages.

The Flowering of Knighthood

The medieval aristocracy was, above all, a military class, trained from early youth in the practice of mounted combat. As we saw in the last chapter, the aristocracy was two-tiered, divided between nobles (the great landholders) and knights (their followers). With the passing of generations, however, the social boundary between nobles and knights grew indistinct. The term "knight" gradually acquired high prestige: the Church emphasized more and more the idea of Christian knighthood, the crusading movement glamorized the "knights of Christ," and fictional knights such as Roland, Tristan, Lancelot, and Perceval became heroes of high medieval literature. The dubbing ceremony was shared by nobles and ordinary knights alike, and under the influence of the Church it became a kind of "sacrament of knighthood." In the end even the grandest nobles were proud to be called "knights" and to share with less wealthy warriors a common code of knightly behavior known as "chivalry" (from *cheval*, the French word for "horse"). Common knights, in the meantime, were acquiring more extensive lands, along with privileges and jurisdictional rights formerly limited to the old nobility. They were building fortified dwellings on their estates and marrying into noble families. By the thirteenth century, knights and nobles were blending into a single aristocratic order. The two groups continued to vary greatly in wealth and power, but they shared a common chivalric ideology and knightly status.

For all the romantic images that today surround the medieval knight, he was, essentially, a warrior. Mounted on a charger and clad in helmet and chain mail, he was a kind of "military machine"—the medieval equivalent of the modern tank. The analogy becomes still closer when, after 1300, chain mail gave way to plate armor in response to the coming of the longbow.

Warfare was all too common in the High Middle Ages, not only among kings and great princes, but also between neighboring barons. In time the growing authority of monarchs and princes curtailed private wars, particularly in England. But it was a slow process and did not seriously affect the French countryside until well into the thirteenth century. Fighting was what aristocrats had been trained for; it was the chief justification for their existence. They were viewed (ideally) as the protectors of Church and society, but most of them were interested primarily in defending and extending their own estates. And to some, nothing was more fulfilling than to do battle with the enemy—any enemy. As a twelfth-century French writer put it,

> I tell you that I never eat or sleep or drink so well as when I hear the cry, "Up and at 'em!" from both sides, and when I hear the neighing of riderless horses in the brush and hear shouts of "Help! Help!" and see men fall . . . and the dead pierced in the side by gaily-pennoned spears.

War could ravage the land, destroying farms and churches, but it was less dangerous to the aristocracy than might be imagined. Great battles were rare, and even when they occurred, the knight was well protected by his armor. Most medieval warfare consisted of castle sieges and the harrying of an enemy's possessions, including his peasants. For a knight, the great risk was to be taken captive in battle, which obliged the victim to raise a large ransom in return for his release. On the other hand, a skillful and lucky knight might take many captives in the course of his campaigning and enrich himself from their ransoms.

In peacetime, tournaments took the place of battles. The Church legislated against tournaments, fruitlessly but with good reason, for they often involved daylong mock battles among groups of as many as a hundred knights, in the course of which a participant might be killed, maimed, or, most likely, taken for ransom. The aristocracy relished these melees as opportunities to train for war or to collect ransoms—or simply for the fun of fighting.

Magnates had more sober tasks to perform as well: presiding at the castle court, giving counsel to their lords, and managing their revenues and estates—a responsibility that they took more and more seriously as the commercial revolution increased the circulation of money and encouraged a profit mentality. For recreation, aristocrats went hunting or hawking in their private forests or parks. Besides the sheer enjoyment of it, hunting rid the forests of dangerous beasts—wolves and wild boars—and provided tasty venison for the baronial table. Lords and ladies alike engaged in falconry, a sport that consisted of releasing a trained falcon to soar upward, kill a wild bird in flight, and return it to earth uneaten. Both hunting and falconry were refined during the High Middle Ages into complex arts.

Indeed, the process of gradual refinement characterized high medieval aristocratic life as a whole, and it was much needed. Most baronial castles of the eleventh and early twelfth centuries were nothing more than square wooden towers of two or three stories. They were usually set atop hills or artificial mounds and surrounded by barracks, storehouses, stables, workshops, kitchen gardens, manure heaps, and perhaps a chapel—all enclosed, along with assorted livestock, within a moat or stockade, or both. The tower, or "keep," was apt to be stuffy, leaky, gloomy, and badly heated. Since it was built for defense, not comfort, its windows were narrow slits for outgoing arrows, and its few rooms had to accommodate not only the lord and lady and their family but servants, retainers, and guests as well. It was a world of enforced togetherness in which only the wealthiest of aristocratic couples could enjoy the luxury of a private bedchamber.

By the thirteenth century, however, rich aristocrats were living in much more commodious dwellings, usually built of stone and mortar. The advent of chimneys in the twelfth century, replacing the central fire, made it possible to heat individual rooms and thus contributed to the spread of the modern notion of privacy—private bedrooms and separate servants' quarters. Privacy remained relatively rare, for great lords now commanded larger retinues than before. But the sweaty, swashbuckling life of the eleventh-century baron had evolved by 1300 into a new, courtly lifestyle of good manners, troubadour songs, and gentlemanly and ladylike behavior. In much of Christendom war had become less incessant, and the barracks atmosphere was softening. The old military elite was becoming a "high society," increasingly conscious of itself as a separate class. Distinguished from lesser folk by its good breeding and good taste, the aristocracy became more exclusive and more rigidly defined than in its earlier, less stylish days.

"September," from the *Tres Riches Heures* of the
Duke de Berry, Limbourg brothers, 1413–1416,
showing the castle of Saumur in Anjou. The castle
still stands but is a bit the worse for wear.

Aristocratic Women

It stands to reason that a society of landholding warriors would relegate
women to supporting roles. Women were indeed subordinated to men in many
respects, but not in all. Shortly after the Norman Conquest of England in 1066,
so we are told by a contemporary monk,

> certain Norman women, consumed by raging lust, sent message after message
> to their husbands urging them to return at once, and adding that, unless they
> did so with all possible speed they would find other husbands for them-
> selves. . . . Many men left England heavy-hearted and reluctant, because they
> were abandoning their king while he struggled in a foreign land. They
> returned to Normandy to oblige their wanton wives.

The monk who related this story objected to the women's initiative, but their all-conquering husbands rushed home nonetheless.

Women were subordinated to men in virtually all premodern societies—less so in Western Christendom than, for example, in Islamic civilization, where the veil and harem flourished. We have traced in earlier chapters the gradual improvement of women's status in the later Roman Empire and the ways in which late Roman and Christian influences softened the antifeminine attitudes embodied in early Germanic law codes. According to an early Anglo-Saxon law, "If a free man lies with another free man's wife, he shall pay the husband [a sum of money] and shall buy the husband another wife." By the tenth century, however, Anglo-Saxon women were holding property on a sizable scale and were willing it to their sons and daughters, sometimes in equal portions.

Christianity itself could be highly inconsistent in its attitude toward women. St. Paul—at once a Christian evangelist and a Roman citizen—injected a typically Roman antifeminine bias into the Christian mainstream. He conceded that in God's eyes there was no distinction between men and women or between slave and nonslave: "All are one in Christ." But this heavenly equality did not, in St. Paul's opinion, extend to earthly affairs: "Let your women keep silent in churches," he wrote, "for it is not permitted to them to speak. . . . And if they want to learn anything, let them ask their husbands at home."

Medieval Christianity echoed some of St. Paul's antifeminism. Women could not be priests; they could hold no Church office except as an abbess or lesser official in a nunnery (though "double monasteries" admitting both men and women were occasionally presided over by abbesses). Holy men were apt to regard women as threats to male purity, and thus as less than human—as objects. The canons of a thirteenth-century priory expelled the nuns from their community on these grounds:

> Recognizing that the wickedness of women is greater than all the other wickedness in the world, and that there is no anger like that of a woman, and that the poison of snakes and dragons is easier to cure and less dangerous to men than associating with women, we and our whole community have unanimously decreed—for the preservation of our souls no less than of our bodies and property—that we will on no account receive any more nuns, to the increase of our damnation, but will avoid them as we would avoid poisonous beasts.

Many churchmen would have taken strong exception to this tirade. Meister Eckhart, writing in the fourteenth century, observed that God had made woman "from man's side, so that she should be equal with man—neither below nor above." And a thirteenth-century Dominican argued that God had favored women over men from the beginning:

> For God made man from the vile earth, but he made woman in Paradise. Man he formed of slime, but woman of man's rib. She wasn't formed of a lower limb of man—for example, of his foot—lest man should regard her as his servant, but of his midmost part, so that he should regard her as his fellow.

Geoffrey Chaucer, writing in the fourteenth century, told the story of an oft-married Wife of Bath whose fifth husband persisted in reading aloud to her from a "book of wicked wives," which recounted the evil deeds of innumerable wives from Biblical, classical, and later times. As the Wife of Bath explained it,

> When I saw that he would never stop
> Reading this cursed book, all night no doubt,
> I suddenly grabbed and tore three pages out
> Where he was reading, at the very place,
> And fisted such a buffet in his face
> That backwards down into our fire he fell.

Alongside notions of wanton women and wicked wives, high medieval Christianity developed a concept of idealized womanhood from its emphasis on Mary, the virgin mother of Jesus. As the great symbol of maternal compassion, Mary became the subject of countless miracle stories. Sinners who trembled at the prospect of God's judgment would turn their prayers to Mary, confident that she could persuade Christ to forgive them—for what son could refuse his mother? Many of Europe's greatest cathedrals were dedicated to Mary under the name of *Notre Dame*, "our Lady."

The high medieval troubadour songs and the rise of stylized courtesy in noble households resulted in still another kind of idealization. As romanticized ladies-fair, women were placed on pedestals, from which they are only now descending. This idealization of women was itself a kind of dehumanizing process; for high atop their pedestals, women remained objects still. But the pedestals tended to raise women from their former inferior status as threats to male purity, or objects of casual knightly seduction and rape, or victims of boorish, wife-beating husbands. The courtly lady remained an object, but a more revered and idealized object than before.

But medieval lords and ladies did not ordinarily behave like characters in some courtly romance. Wife-beating persisted, and, on a far lesser scale, husband-beating as well (recall the Wife of Bath). Wives of all classes were immobilized for long periods by the bearing and nursing of numerous offspring, necessary for the preservation of family lines in an era of high infant mortality. Eleanor of Aquitaine (see cover photo), one of the great women of twelfth-century Europe and a patroness of troubadours, had no less than eleven children but was survived by only two. She was imprisoned by her husband, King Henry II of England, for urging their sons to rebel, and spent many years in (relatively luxurious) confinement. Only at her husband's death was she released to live out her final years as a valued adviser to her royal sons and as a wealthy and independent *grande dame* of the realm.

Other medieval queens and noblewomen often served as regents, ruling the dominions in their husbands' absences. In the thirteenth century Blanche of Castile, mother of King Louis IX (St. Louis), ruled France for eight years in her son's name until he came of age and again when he was off crusading. A person of uncommon intelligence and resolution, Blanche of Castile put down a major baronial rebellion at the beginning of St. Louis' reign through an adroit blend of warfare and diplomacy. "To all intents and purposes," wrote a modern French historian, "she may be counted among the kings of France."

Blanche and Eleanor were exceptional. In general, medieval society was a warrior's world, and women were not expected to fight in battle. Still, the convention could occasionally be defied: Isabel of Conches, the wife of a Norman baron of about the year 1100, was described by a contemporary writer as generous, daring, and high-spirited: "In war she rode among the knights, dressed as a knight herself."

Isabel was a newsworthy exception to the male domination in warfare, but women could be influential in other ways as well. For if the aristocracy was a warrior class, it was also a class of hereditary landholders, and women could play a key role in the inheritance of land. In the absence of sons, a daughter might become a wealthy and coveted heiress; even if she had brothers, a well-born daughter might bring a large estate to her husband as a dowry and retain some control over it. Women, whether married or single, could sometimes hold and grant fiefs. They could own goods, make contracts and wills, and, under certain conditions, engage in litigation. A widow normally received a third of her husband's lands (their eldest son received the rest), and since aristocratic wives, like urban wives, were frequently much younger than their husbands, landholding widows were commonplace.

A strong king might compel a wealthy maiden or widow to marry some royal favorite. Indeed, the granting of an heiress in marriage to a loyal courtier was an important element of royal patronage—and a source of royal revenue as well. In the financial accounts of King Henry I of England (1100–1135) one finds such items as these: "Robert de Venuiz renders account to the king for sixteen shillings eightpence for the daughter of Herbert the Chamberlain with her dowry"; "The sheriff of Hampshire renders account to the king for a thousand silver marks for the office, lands, and daughter of the late Robert Mauduit." And one great English heiress, the thrice-widowed Lucy, countess of Chester, was charged a handsome sum for the privilege of not having to marry again for five years.

Favorable marriages could bring wealth and greatness to a family. Many a family fortune was built on strategic marriages of heirs to heiresses. In a landed society such as medieval Europe's, marriages were crucial to a family's well-being, and marriages for love alone were luxuries that no noble family could afford. Medieval Church law insisted that both partners must consent to their marriage, but family interests usually superseded the wishes of the bride and groom. Marriages based on family interests sometimes did, in time, become loving relationships, but they also encouraged the emphasis on extramarital romance in courtly literature—and sometimes in the real world as well. We have already encountered the numerous bastards of Earl Hugh of Chester. Eleanor of Aquitaine was suspected of an extramarital affair with her uncle, and Henry I of England had at least twenty-two bastard children. The Church condemned adultery as a mortal sin, but aristocratic society looked tolerantly on the escapades of well-born husbands. Their wives, however, were judged by a double standard that demanded wifely fidelity to ensure the legitimacy of family lines. Earl Hugh could sire bastards across the Cheshire countryside but expected his wife's children to be his own. This double standard of male "wild-oat sowing" and female virtue has persisted into the present century.

Notwithstanding their dowry rights, wives were very much under their husbands' control according to baronial law. But in the actual day-to-day functioning of aristocratic life, the wife might exercise a great deal of power. In the castle, as in the urban shop-dwelling, home and workplace were one. The wife usually governed the castle and barony when her husband was absent (as husbands often were—on wars or Crusades). If the castle was attacked while the lord was away, his wife frequently commanded its defense.

Even when the lord was home, the wife might enjoy considerable authority. In medieval marriages as in modern ones, husband and wife might relate in a wide variety of ways. Some husbands were cruel and domineering. Others were ineffectual or senile, in which case—despite social and legal conventions—the wife ruled the castle. One such person was Avicia, countess of Évreux:

> The count of Évreux's intellect was by nature somewhat feeble as well as being blunted with age. And putting perhaps undue trust in his wife's ability, he left the government of his county entirely in her hands. The countess was distinguished for her wit and beauty. She was one of the tallest women in all Évreux and of very high birth. . . . Disregarding the counsels of her husband's barons, she chose instead to follow her own opinion and ambition. Often inspiring bold measures in political affairs, she readily engaged in rash enterprises.

The Norman monk who wrote these words clearly disapproved, but his description of Countess Avicia shows us an aspect of aristocratic womanhood absent from the arid accounts of legal custom and the romances of the troubadours.

Medieval Children

Until recently, historians of the new and expanding field of childhood have viewed the Middle Ages as pitch dark. Medieval people, they argued, had no conception of childhood as a distinct phase of human life but regarded children simply as "little adults." Childhood thus had to be "invented" at some point in modern history (it was never clear exactly when). This is nonsense.

Even in the early Middle Ages, Gregory of Tours had written of a plague that was particularly fatal to young children: "And so we lost our little ones, who were so dear to us and sweet, whom we had cherished in our bosoms and dandled in our arms, whom we had fed and nurtured with such loving care. As I write I wipe away my tears."

With the advent of the High Middle Ages, children were cherished even more. The revolutionary high medieval changes in commerce and social organization required increasing numbers of well-trained specialists in a wide variety of vocations—trading, manufacturing, estate management, ecclesiastical and secular governance—and, hence, much greater emphasis than before on the rearing and training of children. Schools sprang up on all sides; to the old monastic schools were now added an abundance of urban schools and village schools. It has been estimated that about half the boys and girls of early-fourteenth-century Florence received at least a grammar school education. Other medieval cities probably did not do so well (we lack the figures), and widespread illiteracy continued in the countryside until fairly recent times. But there can be no question that high medieval society invested heavily in the education of its children.

Aristocratic and urban children, particularly boys, were usually sent away from home at an early age for training in another noble household or urban business. Nevertheless, there is unmistakable evidence that many medieval parents were devoted to their children, whether at home or away. Despite the vexations of large families, and the danger of lavishing affection on a child who might not survive infancy, parents could love their children dearly and care for them tenderly. Voices began to be raised against the age-long custom of child-beating: the thirteenth-century writer, Vincent of Beauvais, cautioned that "children's minds break down under excessive severity of correction: they despair, they worry, and finally they hate. And this is most injurious, for where everything is feared, nothing is attempted."

Beginning in the twelfth century, books on the rearing and training of children began appearing in considerable number. One of the most popular of them, by the Spanish writer Raymond Lull, included sections on breast-feeding, weaning, early education, and the care and nourishment of children. "Every person," Raymond Lull observed, "must hold his child dear."

Even the traditional Christian doctrine that baptism was necessary for salvation was modified in the twelfth century with respect to unbaptized babies. Previously they had been condemned to hell; now they were assigned to "limbo," where they could exist for eternity in innocent happiness even though denied the direct presence of God. There also emerged in high medieval piety a special devotion to the Child Jesus, whose beauty and innocence were reflected, to a lesser degree, in all children. "O sweet and sacred childhood," wrote a Cistercian monk, "which brought back humanity's true innocence."

Actual child-rearing practices varied widely from family to family and class to class, and as in most ages they usually fell short of the social ideal. Warnings against excessive child-beating show not only that it was frowned on but that it continued. And infanticide, though severely forbidden, was never eliminated. Nevertheless, whether judging by the proliferation of schools, the popularity of books on child rearing, or the sympathetic literary portrayals of childhood, the people of the High Middle Ages placed a large emotional and material investment in their children. They were by no means blind to the existence of childhood; instead, they idealized it.

THE EVOLUTION OF AGRARIAN LIFE

Good Times and Bad

The new social and economic conditions of the late eleventh and twelfth centuries transformed the landscape of northern Europe. In response to the stimulus of a growing population and the need for higher food production, people drained swamps and marshes and cleared forests, and inhabitants of the Low Countries built dikes to reclaim land from the sea. These clearing and draining operations vastly increased the extent of lands open to cultivation. Food production was further augmented by gradual improvements in agrarian technology: a much more efficient horse collar than in antiquity, the development of the tandem harness, axled wheels on wagons, and the wider use of metal farm tools. And with the growth of towns and a rising money economy, agricultural surpluses could now be sold to townspeople and thereby converted into cash. Consequently, peasants were motivated to produce as far in excess of the consumption level as they possibly could.

The initial result was to increase peasants' incomes and elevate their legal status. Slavery, common in Carolingian times, was diminishing by the eleventh century and virtually disappeared in the course of the twelfth. The tillers of the land were now chiefly freeman and serfs. Often the freeman owned his own small farm, but the serf was generally to be found on a manor. Normally, as we have seen, the manor included the peasants' fields intermixed with the lord's fields (demesne), the produce of which went directly to the lord. Among the obligations that the serf usually owed his lord was labor service for a stipulated number of days per week on the lord's demesne. In Carolingian times, manorial lords had augmented the part-time serf labor by using slaves. But in the twelfth century, with slavery dying out, lords were faced with a labor shortage on their demesnes.

As a result of this problem, and in keeping with the trend toward transforming service obligations into money payments, some lords abandoned demesne farming altogether. They leased out their demesne fields to peasants and, in return for a fixed-money payment, released their serfs from the traditional obligation to work part-tie on the demesne. At about the same time, many lords were translating the serf's food rent into a money rent. In shedding their burden of laboring on their lord's fields, serfs were elevating themselves to the status of tenant farmers. Their obligations, like those of their baronial lords, were gradually being placed on a cash basis.

Throughout much of the eleventh and twelfth centuries, lords were under pressure to improve the condition of their peasants in order to keep them from migrating to the towns or to newly cleared lands. Peasants were in demand, and enterprising land developers who were turning woods and marshes into field competed for their services. As a consequence, the twelfth century witnessed the elevation of many peasants from servile status to freedom. One of the clearest expressions of this trend was the emergence of rural communes—communities of peasants whose lord had granted them a charter freeing them from servile obligations and permitting them to pay their dues collectively, on the pattern of the chartered town.

But even in the booming twelfth century, the reduction of demesne farming and the freeing of serfs occurred slowly and unevenly. And by the thirteenth century, these trends were beginning to reverse themselves. For population growth was gradually outstripping the increase in arable lands, creating a rise in land values and a surplus of peasant labor. As land became more valuable than laborers, lords throughout much of northern Europe began farming their demesnes more intensively than before, often employing landless peasants at low wages or strictly enforcing the labor services of their remaining serfs.

Moreover, the thirteenth century witnessed a growth of legal consciousness and a hardening of custom that gave rise to stricter class divisions and made it much more difficult for serfs to gain their freedom. On the other hand, a freeman might easily sink back into serfdom. It was the custom of some districts, for example, that a free peasant forfeited his freedom by marrying a servile woman, and a free woman suffered the same descent if she married a serf. In thirteenth-century England there were instances of landless free peasants submitting to serfdom in return for a plot of land. And quite apart from the matter of legal status, peasants of the thirteenth century, lacking the leverage they had enjoyed in the earlier generations of land clearance and labor shortage, were subjected to heavy economic exploitation by their lords. They were burdened with higher rents and taxes, higher fines at the manorial court, higher charges for the use of the lord's mill, winepress, and ovens. And a peasant who refused to pay could be replaced by someone else from among the growing body of landless laborers that the high medieval population explosion produced.

Again, these processes varied a great deal from place to place and from region to region. But generally speaking, the combined effects of population growth and land clearance profited lords and peasants alike throughout the later eleventh century and much of the twelfth, but worked to the peasants' disadvantage during the thirteenth, when land clearance and advances in farming techniques failed to keep pace with the continually rising population. Western Europe remained prosperous throughout most of the thirteenth century, but the easy years of limitless land were passing, and there was trouble ahead.

Peasant Life in a North-European Village

The life of a high medieval peasant is almost beyond our imagining. Village life was tied to the cycle of the seasons and vulnerable to the whims of nature—drought, flooding, epidemics among humans and animals, crop diseases, the summer's heat and the winter's chill. Today we are insulated from nature by a screen of modern technological wonders: central heating, refrigeration, air conditioning, a secure food supply, plumbing, deodorants, modern medicine, and many more—some of which may well be threatening our environment. We enjoy the protection of police and fire departments; we defy distance and terrain with our freeways and jets. All these things and others we take for granted, but they are all products of the recent past. They were undreamed of in the Middle Ages and remained unknown for many centuries thereafter.

From the viewpoint of modern middle-class America, the medieval peasant lived in unspeakable filth and poverty. A typical peasant's house, although more substantial than in earlier times, consisted of a thatched roof resting on a timber framework, with the spaces between the framing filled with webbed branches covered with mud and straw. The houses of wealthier peasants sometimes had two rooms, furnished with benches, a table, and perhaps a chest. But poorer peasants often lived in one-room cottages virtually bare of furniture.

The straw on which the family slept was apt to be crawling with vermin. The smells of sweat and manure were always present, and therefore largely unnoticed. Flies buzzed everywhere. The cottage might shelter not only a large family but its domestic livestock as well: chickens, dogs, geese, occasionally even cattle. In winter animals provided added heat, and for the same reason, all family members usually slept in the same bed. Windows, if any, were small and few (and of course had no glass). The floor was usually of earth; it froze in the wintertime and turned damp and oozy with the coming of a thaw. Arthritis and rheumatism were common, along with countless other diseases whose cure lay far in the future. A simple fire served for cooking and heating, but in the absence of chimneys the smoke filled the room before escaping through holes or cracks in the ceiling. Candles were luxury items, and peasants had to make do with smoky, evil-smelling torches made of rushes soaked in fat. And there was always the danger that a stray spark might set the thatched roof afire.

The daily routine of a family of village-dwelling serfs might run more or less as follows: there would be a predawn breakfast—perhaps of coarse black bread and diluted ale—after which the husband, wife, and post-toddling off-spring would work from daybreak to nightfall. Peasants' work involved a close partnership between husband and wife; indeed, young peasant men were expected to marry before inheriting land, because women and children played essential roles in the peasant work force. The father and his sons did most of the heavy plowing. The wife and daughters took primary responsibility for the "inside" work—not only doing such domestic chores as cooking and cleaning, but also manufacturing the family's food and clothing: making cheese and butter, spinning and weaving cloth. They milked the cows, fed the livestock, tended the vegetable garden outside the cottage, and joined with the men in such activities as haymaking, thatching, shearing the sheep, sowing and reaping the grain, weeding the open fields, and sometimes even plowing. Or in the winter, when the fields were often frozen, the whole family might stay indoors constructing or repairing their tools. The evening meal might consist of a pot of vegetable broth, more coarse black bread, more ale, and possibly an egg. Then it was early to bed, to rest for the toils of the following day.

Even this somber picture is a bit idealized. Often one or more members of the peasant family would be immobilized by illness (for which there were very few available doctors or effective medicines) or tormented by injuries, wounds, aches, and pains (no aspirin, just ale). Wives had to endure one pregnancy after another; childbirth was a mortal danger to mother and baby alike, and infant mortality was very high. (In medieval and early modern Europe, approximately two-thirds of all children died before the age of ten, and well over a third died during their first year.)

Occasionally famine would strike a large region, as in 1125 when a great August flood inundated numerous villages of eastern England: "Many people drowned and bridges collapsed and grain and meadows were utterly ruined, and famine and disease afflicted people and cattle." Worse still, the frequency of warfare meant that a peasant village might be pillaged or burned by its lord's enemy or might even become a battleground. From a French poem of c. 1200 comes this chilling tale:

> They start to march. The scouts and the incendiaries lead. After them come the foragers who are to gather the spoils and load them into the great baggage train. The tumult begins. The peasants, having just come out to the fields, turn back uttering loud cries. The shepherds gather their flocks and drive them toward the neighboring woods in the hope of saving them. The incendiaries set the villages afire and foragers visit and plunder them. The distracted inhabitants are burned to death or led away with tied hands to be held for ransom. Everywhere alarm bells ring. Fear spreads from one side to another and becomes general. Everywhere one sees helmets shining, pennons floating, and horsemen covering the plain. Here money is seized; there cattle, donkeys, and flocks are taken. The smoke spreads; the flames rise; the terrified peasants and shepherds flee in all directions.

Such disasters were rare in the life of a single village, but when they occurred, the helpless inhabitants had no choice but to rebuild, replant, and pray for survival through a cold, hungry winter.

In a typical peasant village the most substantial buildings, as we have seen, were the lord's or bailiff's residence and the parish church. The lord's residence, the headquarters of the manor, was commonly surrounded by a walled enclosure that also contained a bakehouse, kitchen, barns, and other structures. To the manor house the peasants would bring portions of their crops, which they owed as customary dues. Here, too, they would bring their disputes to be settled in their lord's court. The parish church often stood at the center of the village. Its priest (assuming it had one) was seldom well educated, though he might have learned the rudiments of reading and writing. He played a central role in the villagers' lives—baptizing infants, presiding at marriages and burials, and regularly celebrating the Mass. The church was likely to be painted inside with scenes from the Bible or the life of the local patron saint; such paintings provided an elementary form of religious instruction to an illiterate congregation.

The church usually doubled as a village meeting hall, and on festival days it might be used for dancing, drinking, and revelry. The feast days of the Christian calendar—Christmas, Easter, and many lesser holy days (holidays)—provided joyous relief from an otherwise grinding routine. In some districts the feast of Candlemas (February 2) was celebrated by a candlelight procession followed by a pancake dinner. On the eve of May Day the young men of some villages would cut branches in the forest and lay them at the doors of houses inhabited by young unmarried women. St. John's Day (midsummer) brought bonfires and dancing. And throughout the year, time could be found for informal sports—wrestling, archery, cockfights, drinking contests, and a rough form of soccer.

But for most of their days medieval peasants labored to raise the food on which their families and communities depended for survival. An English writer of the late tenth century attributed these words to an imaginary but typical serf of his times:

I work hard. I go out at daybreak, driving the oxen to the field, and then I yoke them to the plow. Be the winter ever so stark, I dare not linger at home for awe of my lord; but having yoked my oxen, and fastened plowshare and coulter, every day I must plow a full acre or more. . . . I have a boy, driving the oxen with an iron goad, who is hoarse with cold and shouting. Mighty hard work it is, for I am not free.

Changes in Diet and Female Mortality

The last several paragraphs should banish any illusions about the happy pre-industrial farmer (close to nature, living in rhythm with the seasons, free of urban anxieties, etc.). But they must not blind us to the fact that conditions were improving. The spread of iron or iron-tipped tools, better plows, better systems of crop rotation, water mills, and (beginning in the twelfth century) wind-mills—these and other new devices contributed to the increase in food production and to gradual but significant improvements in diet. The High Middle Ages saw a marked increase in the consumption of protein-rich and iron-rich foods: peas and beans (products of the new three-field rotation), cheese and eggs, fish and meat. Pork was beginning to appear more often on peasant tables, and the rabbit, introduced from Spain, had hopped to France by late Carolingian times and to England by the twelfth century. By the late Middle Ages, Europe had become, in the words of one historian, "the most meat-eating culture in the world."

These dietary changes appear to have produced a shift of the most fundamental importance in the relative life expectancies of women and men. There is scattered but fairly consistent evidence that throughout classical antiquity and the early Middle Ages men outnumbered and outlived women. Back in the fourth century BC, Aristotle had explained that men live longer than women because the male is a "warmer creature than the female," and while other classical writers differed on the explanation, they were agreed on the fact. Early medieval estate surveys likewise disclose a preponderance of males to females, particularly in the older age groups. By the thirteenth and fourteenth centuries, however, writers were alluding to a surplus of women over men. The thirteenth-century scholar Albertus Magnus attributed women's greater longevity to the cleansing effect of menstruation and the fact that sexual intercourse drains the female less than the male. Whatever the merits of these intriguing hypotheses, they fail to explain the basic shift: more males than females until the High Middle Ages; more females than males from then until now.

The explanation may well be found in the increased consumption of iron-rich foods such as meat, beans, and other green vegetables. Women require iron in much greater amounts than men. Menstruation, pregnancy, and breast-feeding drain iron from the body to such a degree that a woman of menstrual age requires twice as much iron as a man, and a pregnant woman requires three times as much. The scarcity of iron in the diet of common people of ancient and early medieval times probably resulted in many women becoming severely anemic by their early twenties and therefore highly vulnerable to death from a variety of diseases. The improved diet of the High Middle Ages would have seriously reduced the high rate of female mortality resulting from iron-deficiency anemia. The whole population would live longer and more energetic lives than ever before, but the effect of the new foods on women would be particularly striking—altering the sex ratio in women's favor throughout European society down to the present day.

Conclusion

This chapter has attempted to catch the flavor of life among the townspeople, aristocrats, and peasant villagers of the High Middle Ages. For all these groups I have tried to show not only what their lives were like but also how their lives were changing. Across the generations between about 1050 and 1300, the changes were most evident among the townspeople and aristocrats: the former were participants in a commercial and urban revolution of decisive significance to European history; the latter experienced a drastic transformation in taste and style as they moved from grim, square towers into elaborate, well-furnished castles echoing with the songs of troubadours.

Changes in the life of the peasant village were no less important. Villagers, too, were drawn increasingly into the web of a burgeoning money economy that provided markets and profits for surplus food. With the vast increase of cultivated fields, the European landscape was permanently transformed. And the gradual improvement of the peasant diet, too gradual to have been perceived at the time, may well have contributed a great deal to the vitality and longevity of Western man—and, more particularly, Western woman.

CHAPTER 10

Conquests and Crusades

TERRITORIAL EXPANSION

Europe's transformation during the High Middle Ages was marked by a significant advance of its external and internal frontiers—an advance that continued until the late thirteenth and early fourteenth centuries when it slowed to a halt. The clearing of forests and the draining of swamps to create new farmlands represent the conquest of a great *internal* frontier. It is paralleled by external expansion all along the periphery of Western Christendom that brought areas of the Arab, Byzantine, and Slavic worlds within the ballooning boundaries of European civilization and vastly enriched it.

Western Christian Expansion in the Early Middle Ages

Western Europe had been expanding ever since Charles Martel repelled the Arabs in 732. Charlemagne had introduced Frankish government and Christianity into much of Germany and had established a Spanish bridgehead around Barcelona. The stabilization and conversion of Hungary, Scandinavia, Bohemia, and Poland around the turn of the millennium pushed the limits of Catholic Christianity and Western civilization far northward and eastward from the original Carolingian core. Now, in the eleventh, twelfth, and thirteenth centuries, the population boom, along with the growing custom of primogeniture, prompted multitudes of landless aristocratic younger sons to seek wealth and military glory on Christendom's frontiers. And the expanding peasant population provided a potential labor force for the newly conquered lands. While the warrior of the frontier was carving out new estates for himself, he was also storing up treasures in heaven by pushing Western Christianity into Muslim Spain, Sicily, Syria, and great tracts of Slavic Eastern Europe. Land, gold, and eternal salvation—these were the alluring rewards of the medieval frontier.

Chronology of the European Frontier Movement

Spain		Sicily		Holy Land	
1002	Breakup of caliphate of Cordova	c. 1016	Norman infiltration begins		
1085	Capture of Toledo	1060–1091	Normans conquer Sicily		
		1085	Death of Robert Guiscard	1095	Calling of First Crusade
		1130	Coronation of Roger the Great	1099	Crusaders take Jerusalem
1137	Aragon unites with Catalonia	1154	Death of Roger the Great	1187	Muslims retake Jerusalem
1212	Christian victory at Las Navas de Tolosa			1204	Crusaders take Constantinople
1236	Castile takes Cordova			1291	Crusaders driven from Holy Land

SPAIN

So it was that knightly adventurers from all over Christendom—and particularly from France—flocked southwestward into Spain during the eleventh century to aid in the reconquest of the Iberian Peninsula from Islam. The Muslim Caliphate of Cordova had broken up after 1002 into warring fragments, providing the Christians a superb opportunity to conquer them or, as was often the case, to extort tribute from them. The Christians, however, were themselves divided into several kingdoms and seldom capable of united action. More often, they fought among themselves.

Taking the lead in the reconquest, the Christian kingdom of Castile captured the great Muslim city of Toledo in 1085. In later years Toledo became a crucial contact point between Islamic and Christian culture, with a considerable Jewish population serving as intermediaries. Here Arab scientific and philosophical works were translated into Latin and then disseminated throughout Europe to challenge and invigorate Western thought.

Early in the twelfth century the Spanish Christian kingdom of Aragon contested the supremacy of Castile and undertook an offensive of its own against the Moors (Muslims originally from North Africa). In 1137 Aragon was strengthened by its unification with the prosperous county of Barcelona—the Spanish March of Charlemagne's time—centered on one of the major seaports of the western Mediterranean. And meanwhile still another Christian state, Portugal, was establishing itself as an independent kingdom in the far west, facing the Atlantic.

Yet for more than a century following the capture of Toledo in 1085, the reconquest made little progress. Muslim resistance stiffened as reinforcements poured into Spain from North Africa, while the Christian kingdoms exhausted themselves fighting one another or intervening in the affairs of southern France. It was not uncommon for a Christian prince to ally with Muslims against another Christian prince.

Under Roger and his successors the kingdom enjoyed a diverse intellectual life. Its history was well chronicled by talented historians; the Muslim scholar Idrisi, the greatest geographer of his age, contributed a comprehensive geographical work that drew from classical and Islamic sources. Idrisi dedicated his masterpiece to Roger the Great, and the treatise has been known ever since as "The Book of Roger." Sicily, like Spain, became a significant source of translations from Arabic and Greek into Latin. The Sicilian translators provided Western European scholars with a steady stream of texts drawn from both classical Greek and Islamic sources, and these texts, together with others passing into Europe from Spain, served as the essential foundations for the intellectual achievement of thirteenth-century Christendom.

Conclusion

In many ways Norman Sicily was Western Europe's most interesting and fruitful frontier state. A center of intense interaction between Christian, Muslim, and Byzantine cultures, it demonstrated that the outer limits of Europe were not only advancing but also open. Europe besieged had given way to a new, expanding Europe, exposed to the invigorating influences of surrounding civilizations. And nowhere was this cultural contact more intense than in Norman Sicily. East and West met in Roger the Great's glittering, sun-drenched realm, and worked creatively side by side to make his kingdom the most sophisticated European state of its day.

THE CRUSADES

The crusading movement, which proved so costly to Europe's Jews, was prompted by a major political crisis in the Near East. During the eleventh century a new warlike tribe from central Asia, the Seljuk Turks, had swept into Persia, taken up the Islamic faith, and turned the Abbasid caliphs of Baghdad into their pawns. In 1071 the Seljuk Turks inflicted a nearly fatal wound on the Byzantine Empire by smashing a Byzantine army at the battle of Manzikert and occupying Asia Minor.[1] Stories began filtering into the West of Turkish atrocities against Christian pilgrims to Jerusalem, and when the desperate Byzantine emperor, Alexius Comnenus, swallowed his pride and appealed to the West for help, Europe, under the leadership of a reinvigorated papacy, was ready to respond.

The Crusades represented a fusion of three characteristic medieval impulses: piety, pugnacity, and greed. All three were essential. Without Christian idealism, the Crusades would be inconceivable, yet the dream of liberating Jerusalem and the Holy Land from the infidel and reopening them to Christian pilgrims was reinforced mightily by the lure of new lands and vast wealth. The

---

[1]For a discussion of the Seljuk Turks and the battle of Manzikert, see p. 53–54. The fall of Bari to Robert Guiscard in the same year was an added blow to Byzantium, although a less crippling one.

crusaders were provided a superb opportunity to employ their knightly skills in God's service—and to make their fortunes in the bargain.

It was to Pope Urban II that Emperor Alexius Comnenus sent his envoys asking for military aid against the Turks, and Urban II, a masterful reform pope, was quick to grasp the opportunity. The Crusade presented many advantages to the Church. It enabled the papacy to put itself at the forefront of an immense popular movement and grasp the moral leadership of Europe. Moreover, the pope saw in the Crusade a partial solution to the problem of private warfare. For more than a century churchmen, with the backing of the peasantry and some nobles, had been attempting to pacify Europe through a movement known as the "Peace of God," which prohibited military operations on noncombatants and their property. The partial success of this effort inspired a similar movement called the "Truce of God," which sought to outlaw warfare on holy days and during holy seasons (including Fridays through Sundays every week). The Crusade, strangely enough, was the climax of these earlier peace movements. For when Urban II proclaimed the Crusade, he also proclaimed a peace throughout the Latin West, forbidding all warfare between Christian and Christian. Although Urban's peace was not everywhere honored, it did have the effect of protecting the lordships of crusaders—to a degree—against the designs of their stay-at-home enemies.

The Crusade also contributed to peace within Christendom by drawing off warlike members of the aristocracy and directing their ferocity outward toward the Muslims. Knights who had previously been condemned by the Church for violating the peace of Christendom were now lauded as soldiers of Christ fighting against the heathen. Thus Christian knighthood became a holy vocation; instead of begging the Church's forgiveness and doing acts of penance for their military violence, knights were invited to achieve salvation *through* the exercise of their warlike prowess. Indeed, the Church pictured crusading as an act of Christian love—toward persecuted fellow Christians in the East and toward Christ himself, whose rightful lordship over the Holy Land had been usurped and polluted by nonbelievers. Just as a good vassal must help his lord recover a stolen lordship, so also must the Christian knight endeavor to restore Jerusalem to the Lord Christ.

The First Crusade

Accordingly, in 1095 Pope Urban II summoned Christian warriors to take up the cross and reconquer the Holy Land. He delivered a spellbinding address to the Frankish aristocracy at Clermont-Ferrand in central France, calling on them to emulate the brave deeds of their ancestors, to avenge the Turkish atrocities (which he described in bloodcurdling detail), to win the Biblical "land of milk and honey" for Christendom and drive the infidel from Jerusalem. Finally, he promised those who undertook the enterprise the highest of spiritual rewards: "Undertake this journey for the remission of your sins, with the assurance of the imperishable glory of the kingdom of Heaven."

With shouts of "God wills it!" French warriors poured into the crusading army. By 1096 the First Crusade was under way. An international military force—with a large nucleus of knights from central and southern France, Normandy, and Norman Sicily—made its way across the Balkans and assembled at Constantinople. Altogether the warriors of the First Crusade numbered around twenty-five or thirty thousand, a relatively modest figure by modern standards but immense in the eyes of contemporaries. Emperor Alexius was gravely disturbed by the magnitude of the Western European response. Having asked for military support, he had, as he put it, a new barbarian invasion on his hands. Cautious and apprehensive, he demanded and obtained from the crusaders a promise of homage for all the lands they might conquer.

From the beginning there was friction between the crusaders and the Byzantines, for they differed both in temperament and in aim. The Byzantines wished only to recapture the lost provinces of Asia Minor, whereas the crusaders were determined on nothing less than the conquest of the Holy Land. Alexius promised military aid, but it was never forthcoming, and not long after the crusaders left Constantinople, they broke with the Byzantines altogether. Hurling themselves southeastward across Asia Minor into Syria, they encountered and defeated Muslim forces, captured ancient Antioch after a long and complex siege, and in the summer of 1099 took Jerusalem itself.

The crusaders celebrated their capture of Jerusalem by plundering the city and pitilessly slaughtering its Muslim inhabitants (as they had slaughtered Jews on their journey eastward). A Christian eyewitness described the sack of Jerusalem in these words:

> If you had been there you would have seen our feet colored to our ankles with the blood of the slain. But what more shall I relate? None of them were left alive; neither women nor children were spared. . . . Afterward, all, clergy and laymen, went to the Sepulcher of the Lord and his glorious temple, singing the ninth chant. With fitting humility they repeated prayers and made their offering at the holy places that they had long desired to visit.

With the capture of Jerusalem after only three years of vigorous campaigning, the goal of the First Crusade had been achieved. No future Crusade was to enjoy such success as the first, and during the two centuries that followed, the original conquests were gradually lost. For the moment, however, Europe rejoiced at the triumph of its crusaders. Most of them returned to their homes and received heroes' welcomes. Others remained in Latin Syria to enjoy the fruits of their conquests. A long strip of territory along the eastern Mediterranean shore had been wrested from Islam and was now divided among the crusader knights. These warriors consolidated their conquests by erecting elaborate castles, whose ruins survive to this day as tourist attractions and guerrilla hideouts.

The conquered lands were organized into four Crusader States: the county of Edessa, the principality of Antioch (ruled by a son of Robert Guiscard), the county of Tripolis, and the kingdom of Jerusalem. This last was the most important of the four states, and the king of Jerusalem was theoretically the overlord of all the crusader territories. In fact, however, he had difficulty enforcing his authority outside his own kingdom, and sometimes even within it. Thus, the Crusader States were tormented from the beginning by rivalries and dissensions.

The Second and Third Crusades

Gradually over the years, the Muslims began to recover their lands. One churchman attributed the crusaders' reverses to their wickedness: "They devoted themselves to all kinds of debauchery and allowed their womenfolk to spend whole nights at wild parties; they mixed with trashy people and drank the most delicious wines." Another cleric offered this explanation: "It's no wonder that the Christians suffer losses from Saracens, rats, and locusts, when they neglect to pay their church dues properly." Whatever the reasons, the crusader county of Edessa fell before Islamic pressure in 1144, and the disaster gave rise to a renewal of crusading fervor in Europe.

A Second Crusade (1147–1148) was inspired by the preaching of the renowned abbot, St. Bernard of Clairvaux (see pp. 212–213), who used his powerful influence to protect Jews from the violence they had suffered during the First Crusade. Led by the kings of France and Germany, the Second Crusade began with high hopes but ended in defeat. The crusaders returned home shame-faced and empty-handed, prompting St. Bernard to describe the campaign as "an abyss so deep that I must call him blessed who is not scandalized by it."

The 1170s and 1180s witnessed the rise of a new, unified Islamic state centered in Egypt and galvanized by the skilled leadership of a warrior-prince named Saladin. Chivalrous as well as able, Saladin negotiated a truce with the Crusader States, but the rise of his new principality was nevertheless an ominous threat to Latin Syria. The breaking of the truce in 1187 by a hotheaded Christian baron resulted in a great showdown battle at Hattin, some distance north of Jerusalem, between Saladin's army and the combined forces of the crusaders. The battle of Hattin, fought on July 4, 1187, ended with an overwhelming Muslim victory. Saladin surrounded the crusader army and virtually annihilated it, and he afterward conquered large portions of the Crusader States without serious opposition. Three months after Hattin, Saladin occupied Jerusalem after a two-week siege. It was not to be retaken by a Christian army for the remainder of the Middle Ages.

The catastrophe at Hattin and the fall of Jerusalem resulted in still another major crusading effort. The Third Crusade (1189–1193) was led by three of medieval Europe's most illustrious monarchs: Emperor Frederick Barbarossa of Germany, King Philip Augustus of France, and King Richard the Lion-Hearted of England.[2] But Frederick Barbarossa drowned on the way, and most of his army trudged back to Germany; Philip Augustus quarreled with King Richard and went home; and Richard, although he enjoyed much military success and won back considerable portions of the Holy Land, failed to take Jerusalem. Worse yet, Richard fell into hostile hands on his return journey and became the

---

[2]All three will be encountered in subsequent chapters.

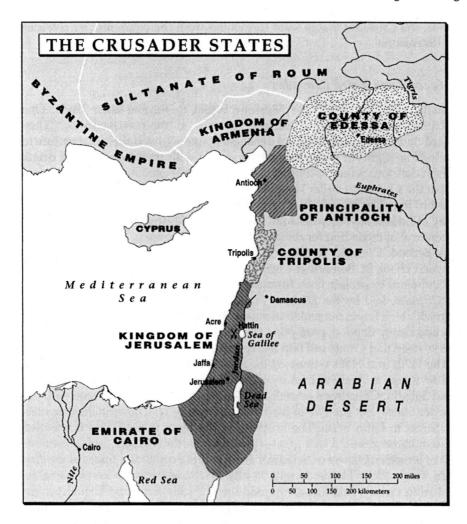

prisoner of Frederick Barbarossa's son, Emperor Henry VI, who released his royal captive only after England had paid the staggering sum of 100,000 pounds—quite literally a king's ransom.

The Fourth Crusade

Within a decade Europe was ready for still another attempt on Jerusalem. The Fourth Crusade (1201–1204) had as its instigator the most powerful of the medieval popes, Innocent III. Like the First Crusade, it was led not by kings but by great territorial princes—most notably, Baldwin IX, count of Flanders. It was, withal, the oddest of the crusades. It never reached the Holy Land at all, yet in its own way it was spectacularly successful.

The crusaders resolved to avoid the perils of overland travel by crossing to the Holy Land in Venetian ships. Unfortunately, the Crusade leaders enormously overestimated the number of their followers and, as a result, contracted with the Venetians for many more ships than were necessary, and at a far greater cost than the crusaders could afford. The doge of Venice nevertheless agreed to take what money the crusaders had and to transport them to the Holy Land if in return they would do him an errand on the way. They were to recapture for Venice the Adriatic port of Zara, which the king of Hungary had seized from Venice some years before. Pope Innocent III was infuriated by this bargain; its effect was to divert the crusading army against a Christian monarchy whose king was not only a good Catholic but a papal vassal as well. When he heard that the crusaders had attacked Zara, Innocent excommunicated them and washed his hands of the whole enterprise.

Nevertheless, the crusaders went doggedly on. Capturing Zara in 1202, they were again diverted, this time by a political dispute in Constantinople involving the succession to the Byzantine throne. One of the two claimants, having recently fled to the West, contacted the crusaders and begged their support, promising them immense wealth, aid against the Muslims, and reunion of the Eastern and Western Churches under Rome.[3] Rising to the challenge, the crusading army moved on Constantinople. The emperor-in-residence panicked and fled the city, and a delegation of citizens, realizing that further resistance was useless, opened Constantinople's gates to the crusaders. Their imperial claimant was installed in power but was murdered shortly afterward by one of his anti-Latin countrymen. Meanwhile, the crusaders had withdrawn from the city as a result of growing hostility and violence between Greeks and Latins. But now, having expended considerable effort in what was apparently a fruitless cause, they resolved to take the city for themselves. Their plan was to elect a new Byzantine emperor from their own ranks and to divide the Eastern Empire among them.

Accordingly, in 1204 the crusaders besieged Constantinople, took it by storm, and subjected it to three long-remembered days of pillage and massacre. The impregnable Byzantine capital had fallen at last to enemy conquerors; the crusaders had succeeded where hordes of Muslims, Persians, Bulgars, Avars, and Germanic tribesmen had failed. Count Baldwin IX of Flanders became emperor, and he and his successors ruled in Constantinople for over half a century. A nucleus of the old Byzantine state held out in Asia Minor, nursing its grievances and gathering its strength, until in 1261 the Latin Empire was overthrown and, after fifty-seven years, Greek emperors reigned once again in Constantinople. But the Fourth Crusade had delivered a blow from which Byzantium never entirely recovered.

The wealth of Constantinople permanently diverted the warriors of the Fourth Crusade from the Holy Land. The Eastern and Western Churches were temporarily reunited: a Latin patriarch now sat in Constantinople, and a Latin hierarchy presided over a captive Greek Church. Innocent III, who had absolved the crusaders from excommunication after the fall of Zara and had

[3]The Eastern and Western Churches had formally split, amidst mutual recriminations, in 1054 (see p. 229).

excommunicated them anew for attacking Constantinople, readmitted them once again to communion when he realized the "great blessings" that had befallen Christendom by the capture of the schismatic city.

The crusaders, for their part, returned to Europe with immense booty from the Byzantine metropolis: precious gems, money, and gold. The greatest prize of all was the immense store of holy relics that the Westerners liberated from the Byzantine capital and brought home. Bones, heads, and arms of saints, Jesus' crown of thorns, St. Thomas the Apostle's doubting finger, and many similar treasures passed into Western Europe at this time. Perhaps more important, the West was given direct access to the intellectual legacy of Greek and Byzantine civilization. But the old hostility between Greeks and Latins was aggravated by the events of the Fourth Crusade into a virtually insurmountable wall of hatred. On a recent visit to Istanbul (the former Constantinople), I found my local guide still muttering about those accursed crusaders.

Later Crusades

During the thirteenth century, the papacy called for Crusades not only against Muslims in the Holy Land and Spain but also against Albigensian heretics in southern France and even against the Holy Roman emperor. In 1212 a visionary, ill-organized enterprise known as the "Children's Crusade" ended in tragedy. Thousands of boys and girls flocked into the ports of southern Europe, gripped by religious fervor and convinced (wrongly) that the Mediterranean would dry up before them to provide them a miraculous pathway into the Holy Land. Many of them returned home sadder but wiser, and the rest were sold into Muslim slavery.

The next major crusading effort, the Fifth Crusade (1217–1221), was directed not at the Holy Land but at Egypt, the real center of Muslim power in the Near East. The crusaders captured the key Egyptian port of Damietta in 1219 and refused a Muslim offer to trade Jerusalem for it. But dissension tore the crusader ranks, and when they moved against Cairo they were caught between a Muslim army and the flooding Nile. The results were military disaster, the abandonment of Damietta, and another joyless homecoming.

Three additional Crusades of importance were undertaken in the thirteenth century, and together they mark a highly significant shift from papal to royal initiative. The first, led by the brilliant emperor Frederick II, was at once the most fruitful and least violent of the three. Frederick negotiated with the sultan of Egypt rather than fighting him and in 1229 obtained possession of Jerusalem by treaty. The triumph was ephemeral, however, for Jerusalem returned to Muslim hands in 1244. And because of the absence of bloodshed, Frederick II's Crusade was never dignified by being given a number.

The Sixth and Seventh Crusades were led by the saint-king of France, Louis IX. One was undertaken against Egypt in 1248, the other against Tunisia in 1270. Both failed, and the second cost St. Louis his life. Crusades continued to be organized and mounted in subsequent generations, but in 1291 the fall of Acre—the last Christian bridgehead on the Syrian coast—brought an end to the Crusader States in the Holy Land. The reigning pope described this cata-strophe as "a doleful cup of bitterness."

But the Crusades were more than simply a romantic and bloody fiasco. Dur-ing the greater part of the High Middle Ages, Christian lords ruled portions of the Holy Land. Their activities caught the imagination of Europe and held it for two centuries, uniting Western Christendom in a single vast effort. At the same time European merchants established permanent bases in Syria and enormously enlarged their role in international commerce. When the crusaders departed, the merchants remained, continuing their commercial domination of the eastern Mediterranean and, after the capture of Constantinople, the Black Sea as well.

The Crusades gave rise to several religious orders of Christian warriors, bound by monastic rules and dedicated to fighting the Muslims and advancing the crusading cause in every possible way. One such order was the Knights Hos-pitalers, which drew chiefly on the French for its membership. Another was the Knights Templars, an international brotherhood that acquired great wealth through pious gifts and intelligent estate management and gradually became involved in far-flung banking activities. A third order, the Teutonic Knights, was composed chiefly of Germans. In the thirteenth century the Teutonic Knights transferred their activities from the Holy Land to northern Germany, where they devoted themselves to the eastward thrust of German-Christian civilization against the Slavs. Orders of a similar sort arose on other frontiers of Western Christendom. The Knights of Santiago de Compostela, for example, were dedi-cated to fighting the Muslims in Spain and furthering the Christian reconquest of the Iberian Peninsula. These crusading orders, bridging as they did the two great medieval institutions of monasticism and knighthood, represent the ulti-mate synthesis of the military and the Christian life. They were widely admired in their time for "going in war to fight, and returning in peace to rest and pray, so that they behave like knights in battle and like monks in cloister."

THE GERMAN EASTWARD EXPANSION

Eastern Germany was still another area of medieval European expansion. The German eastward drive was not a product of active royal or papal policy but rather a movement led by local nobles, in particular the dukes of Saxony. It was a gradual advance with a great deal of momentum behind it. Over a drawn-out period between about 1125 and 1350, it succeeded in pushing the eastern boundary of German settlement far to the north and east at Slavic expense (see map, p. 205). German military gains were consolidated by the building of innu-merable agrarian villages and by a massive eastward migration of German peasants. Consequently, the new areas were not only conquered; they were in large part Christianized and permanently Germanized.

The Teutonic Knights, who spearheaded the later phases of the German push, penetrated temporarily far northward into Lithuania, Latvia, and Esto-nia, and even made an unsuccessful bid to conquer Russia. During the four-teenth and fifteenth centuries the Teutonic Knights lost some of their conquests, but much of the German expansion proved permanent. The epoch between 1125 and 1350 witnessed the conquest and Germanization of large portions of modern eastern Germany and western Poland.

THE CLOSING OF THE HIGH MEDIEVAL FRONTIERS

In the later thirteenth and early fourteenth centuries European expansion was coming to an end. The internal frontiers of forest and swamp had by then been won. The best farmlands had been reclaimed and resettled, and crowds of Christian peasants no longer flocked into the reconquered districts of Spain and eastern Germany. Europe's frontiers were everywhere hardening, sometimes even receding as in the Holy Land. But by then the high medieval territorial expansion had made its essential contribution to Europe's economic future. The expansion was at once a product of commercial growth and a powerful stimulus to further growth. At a time when European cities were still relatively small, Christian knights won for the Latin West such wealthy metropolises as Palermo, Toledo, Antioch, Cordova, and Constantinople. As a result of their capture, and of the extension of Christian maritime dominion into the eastern Mediterranean and the Black and Baltic seas, money and precious goods flooded back into the towns and river valleys of the European heartland. The Western economy was transformed for all time to come.

CHAPTER 11

New Paths to God: Monks, Friars, and Religious Rebels

THE CHURCH IN THE HIGH MIDDLE AGES

The transformation of values that occurred during the High Middle Ages, resulting in part from economic and demographic expansion, and from the rise of cities, produced fundamental changes in other areas as well. Scholars pioneered across new intellectual horizons; artists and writers added new dimensions to Western culture; administrators pushed forward the art and science of government. And underlying all these changes—which will be explored in the chapters that follow—was a deepening of the religious impulse that expressed itself in many different ways: in the rise of a vigorous papacy dedicated to reform and the creation of a Christian world order (see Chapter 12), in the development of new forms of monasticism, in the rapid expansion of ecclesiastical administration and Church activities, in the intensification of lay piety, and in the growth of heresy.

Medieval religion followed many different paths. It could be devoutly orthodox, it could be anticlerical, and it could be openly heretical. Yet its basic institutional expression was the Catholic Church, and the most obvious characteristic that the vast majority of Western Christians had in common was their Catholicism. Nationalism was just then emerging, and the perspectives and allegiances of most Europeans tended to be at once local and international. In the twelfth and thirteenth centuries the majority of people were still parochial in their outlook. Like children today, they were only vaguely aware of what was going on beyond their immediate surroundings. But alongside their localism was an element of cosmopolitanism—a consciousness of belonging to the international commonwealth of Western Christendom, fragmented politically, but united by a common faith, by the growing power of the papacy, and by a shared enthusiasm toward the Crusades.

The Church in the High Middle Ages was a powerful unifying influence. It had made notable progress since the pre-Carolingian era. A parish system was by now spreading across the European countryside to bring the sacraments and at least some degree of Christian instruction to the peasantry. New bishoprics and archbishoprics were forming, and old ones were becoming steadily more active. The papacy never completely succeeded in breaking the control of kings and secular lords over their local bishops, but by the twelfth century it was coming to exercise a very real authority over European bishops. And the growing efficiency of the papal bureaucracy evoked the envy and imitation of the rising royal governments.

The Sacraments

The buoyancy of high medieval Europe is nowhere more evident than in the accelerating impact of Christian piety on European society. The sacraments of the Church introduced a significant religious dimension into the life of ordinary Europeans: their births were sanctified by the sacrament of *baptism,* in which they were cleansed of the taint of original sin and initiated into the Christian fellowship. At puberty they received the sacrament of *confirmation,* which reaffirmed their membership in the Church and gave them the additional grace to cope with the problems of adulthood. Christian couples were united in the sacrament of *matrimony.* And if a man chose the calling of the Christian ministry, he was spiritually transformed into a priest and "married" to the Church by the sacrament of *holy orders.* As death approached, the sacrament of *extreme unction* prepared the soul for its journey into the next world. And throughout their lives, Christians could receive forgiveness from the damning consequences of mortal sin by repenting their past transgressions and receiving the comforting sacrament of *penance.* Finally they might partake regularly of the central sacrament of the Church—the *Eucharist*—receiving the body of Christ into their own bodies by consuming the Eucharistic bread. Thus, the Church through its seven sacraments brought God's grace to all its members, great and humble, at every critical juncture of their lives. The sacramental system, which assumed final form only in the High Middle Ages, was a source of comfort and reassurance: it made communion with God not merely the elusive goal of a few mystics but the periodic experience of all believers. And, of course, it established the Church as the essential intermediary between God and humanity.

The Evolution of Piety

The ever-increasing scope of the Church, together with the rising self-awareness of the new age, resulted in a deepening of popular piety throughout Western Europe. The High Middle Ages witnessed a shift in religious attitude from the awe and mystery characteristic of earlier Christianity to a new emotionalism and dynamism. This shift is evident in ecclesiastical architecture, as the earthbound Romanesque style gave way during the twelfth century to the tense, upward-reaching Gothic (see pp. 282–289). A parallel change is evident in devotional practice, as the divine Christ sitting in judgment gave way to the tragic figure of the human Christ suffering on the cross for the sins of humanity. And it was in the High Middle Ages that the Virgin Mary came into her own as the compassionate intercessor for hopelessly lost souls. A legend of the age told of the devil complaining to God that the tender-hearted Queen of Heaven was cheating hell of its most promising candidates. Christianity became, as never before, a doctrine of love, hope, and compassion. The God of Justice became the merciful, suffering God of Love.

There was, however, a price to pay for this growing religious sensitivity. As people became increasingly devoted to their Christian faith, they tended to become increasingly intolerant toward those who deviated from its beliefs. Thus, the High Middle Ages witnessed an intensification of hostility toward Jews (as we have seen) and heretics (below), along with a heightening of crusading fervor. The growth of spiritual self-awareness was thus accompanied by the emergence of what one historian has called "a persecuting society," many aspects of which endure to this day.

To say that high medieval Europe was dominated by the Church, although true to a point, is dangerously misleading. The Church was by no means monolithic, nor were its members always obedient to papal commands, or even aware of them. Like all human institutions, the Church functioned imperfectly and often fell short of its ideals. Despite its theoretically centralized command structure (popes to archbishops to bishops to priests), lines of communication had a way of getting clogged. Ecclesiastical courts were deluged with jurisdictional disputes in which abbots sought exemption from the control of bishops, and bishops from archbishops. A bishop who ignored or deliberately "misunderstood" a papal order was difficult to dislodge. And communications could be terribly slow. It might take half a year for an archbishop of Canterbury to journey to Rome, consult with the pope, and return to England.

Furthermore, an immense gulf separated the religious beliefs of popes and theologians from those of common townspeople and peasants. The supernatural ideas of ordinary people in any society, including our own, will include a variety of odd notions (an aunt of mine engages in intense conversations with my grandmother Cora, who has been dead since the late 1930s; a "nonfiction" best-seller insists that the pyramids were built by extraterrestrials). It should come as no surprise that popular attitudes in prescientific societies tend to be at least as implausible. The God of the high medieval theologians was a God of love and reason. But in the popular mind he became a kind of divine magician who could shield his favorites from the hunger, pain, disease, and premature death that afflicted all humanity until quite recent times and afflicts much of humanity still.

To such people, religion offered three desperately needed things: the hope of eternal salvation from a harsh, threatening world; an explanation for human suffering (as a spiritual discipline necessary for paradise); and the promise of a better life here and now. Of course, religion continues to offer these things, but in the Middle Ages, when human need was more intense and more immediate, the popular practice of the Christian religion was quite unlike what it is today. There was a far greater emphasis on acquiring divine favor through mechanical means such as charms, pilgrimages, holy images, and the relics of saints.

The most cherished relics of all were those associated with Christ and the Virgin Mary. Since both were believed to have ascended bodily into heaven, relics of the usual sort were out of reach, but there remained pieces of their clothing, fragments of the True Cross, vials of Christ's blood and the Virgin's milk, Christ's baby teeth, his umbilical cord, and the foreskin removed at his circumcision. Reading Abbey, founded in southern England in the 1120s, had acquired hundreds of relics by the end of the twelfth century, including twenty-nine relics of Christ, six of the Virgin Mary, nineteen of the Old Testament patriarchs and prophets, and fourteen of the apostles. As a result of its avid collecting, Reading became a prosperous pilgrimage center—yet it was merely one of many. Chartres had the Virgin Mary's tunic; Canterbury had the body of St. Thomas Becket; Santiago de Compostela in northwestern Spain had the bones of St. James the Apostle (except for one of his arms, which was at Reading); Paris acquired Christ's crown of thorns after it had been taken from Constantinople following the Fourth Crusade. Indeed, there was scarcely a town or rural district in all Christendom that did not possess some relic or protective image.

Each medieval trade honored its own particular saint. Potters offered special devotions to St. Gore, painters to St. Luke, horse doctors to St. Loy, dentists to St. Apolline. And there was an appropriate saint for almost every known disease. Plague sufferers prayed to St. Roch; St. Romane specialized in mental illnesses, St. Clare in afflictions of the eye, St. Agatha in sore breasts. In southern France a cult developed around a watchdog who was said to have been mistakenly killed by his master while defending his master's infant child; peasants began bringing their sick and deformed children to the grave of the sainted dog in expectation of miraculous healing. The healing powers associated with saints, human or not, satisfied a widespread longing for supernatural protection against dangers and afflictions that seemed beyond human comprehension. The doubts of the theologians were drowned out by the clamor of popular demand.

Such attitudes received encouragement not only from ill-educated parish priests but also from bishops and abbots, who shared the general devotion to relics and who rejoiced in the floods of pilgrims they attracted. The relic cult could be justified up to a point by the Catholic doctrine of the Communion of Saints—the caring fellowship of all Christians, whether in this world or the next. But in its emphasis on the supernatural powers of material objects, popular belief carried a residue from long-ago days of pagan magic.

The high medieval Church suffered not only from popular credulity but from corruption as well. Corrupt churchmen were in evidence throughout the era—a result of the unfortunate necessity of staffing the Church with human beings. Some historians have delighted in cataloging instances of larcenous bishops, gluttonous priests, and licentious nuns. But cases such as these were clearly exceptional. The great shortcoming of the high medieval Church was not gross corruption but rather a creeping complacency that resulted sometimes in a shallow, mechanical attitude toward the Christian religious life and an obsession with ecclesiastical property. The medieval Church had more than its share of saints, but among many of the clergy the profundity of the faith was often lost in the day-to-day affairs of the pastoral office, the management of large estates, disputes over land and privileges, and ecclesiastical status seeking. Anyone familiar with modern politicians and university administrators will appreciate the problem.

Changes in Monastic Life

The drift toward complacency has been a recurring trend in Christian monasticism. Again and again, the idealism of a monastic reform movement was eroded and transformed by time and success until, at length, new reform movements arose in protest against the growing worldliness of old ones. This cycle has been repeated countless times. Indeed, the sixth-century Benedictine movement was itself a protest against the excesses and inadequacies of earlier monasticism. St. Benedict had regarded his new order as a means of withdrawing from the world and devoting full time to communion with God. But despite Benedict's ideal, the order became involved in teaching, evangelism, and ecclesiastical reform, and by the tenth and eleventh centuries the whole Benedictine movement had become immersed in worldly affairs. Benedictine monasteries controlled extensive lands, operated Europe's best schools, supplied contingents of knights to feudal armies, and worked closely with secular princes in affairs of state.

Early in the tenth century the Cluniac movement, which was itself Benedictine in spirit and rule, arose in protest against the worldliness and complacency of contemporary Benedictine monasticism (see pp. 144–145). For more than two centuries thereafter, the congregation of Cluny was a powerful force for Christian reform and social peace, though the monastic devotional life remained uppermost in the minds of Cluniac monks. During the twelfth century, however, Cluniac houses were showing traces of the very complacency against which they had originally rebelled. Prosperous, respected, and secure, Cluny was too content with its majestic abbeys and priories, its elaborate liturgical program, and its bounteous fields to give its wholehearted support to the radical transformation of society for which many Christian reformers were now struggling.

As the twelfth century progressed, the Benedictines saw their educational monopoly gradually eroded by the rising schools and universities of the new towns. These urban schools produced increasing numbers of well-trained scholars who in time rivaled the Benedictines as scribes and advisers to princes. With the steady advance of urbanization, the traditional Benedictine contributions to society were no longer as urgently needed as before.

Still, the Benedictines retained their great landed wealth. The Benedictine monastery was scarcely the sanctuary from worldly concerns that St. Benedict had planned. The larger Benedictine monasteries and nunneries accepted novices only from the aristocracy and required in return a substantial entrance gift from the novice's family, usually a landed estate. Until well into the twelfth century, aristocratic parents had been designating younger offspring for monastic careers at the time of their birth and sending them off to monasteries or nunneries long before adolescence for education and training in the religious life. Thus, future monks and nuns, like future brides and grooms, found their lives shaped by parental decisions based on family strategy. They themselves had little choice in the matter. Some developed into devoted servants of God; others simply went through the motions.

Chronology of High Medieval Monasticism and Heterodoxy

909	Founding of Cluny
1084	Establishment of the Carthusian order
1098	Establishment of Cîteaux
1112–1153	Career of St. Bernard of Clairvaux as a Cistercian
1128	Original Rule of the Knights Templars
c. 1173	Beginning of the Waldensian movement
1208	Innocent III calls the Albigensian Crusade
1210	Innocent III authorizes the Franciscan order
1216	Dominican Rule sanctioned by the papacy
1226	Death of St. Francis

Carthusians and Cistercians

A great many new religious orders emerged during the High Middle Ages. They were founded by ardent reformers and peopled by men and women who had chosen their religious vocations for themselves, as adults. The increasing possibility of career choices resulted, among many, in a heightened sense of self. It was not so much a rise of individualism (in the modern, rather lonely sense) as a new freedom to choose among a number of different kinds of communal life—a discovery of self through community. This opportunity for self-conscious choice was provided by the growing numbers of towns, guilds, newly chartered peasant communes, and, above all, new monastic orders. And the fact that their members had joined out of free choice, and after serious self-examination, gave the new orders a spiritual intensity absent from traditional Benedictine monasticism. Indeed the idea of entering religious life out of free, adult choice was so well attuned to the new thought world of the twelfth century that many of the older Benedictine monasteries, including Cluny itself, ceased to admit child oblates.

Perhaps the most demanding of the new orders, the Carthusians emerged in eastern France in the late eleventh century and spread across Christendom in the twelfth. Isolated from the outside world, the Carthusians lived in small groups, worshiping together in communal chapels, but otherwise living as hermits in individual cells. This austere order has survived to the present day and, unlike most monastic movements, its discipline has seldom waned. Yet even in the spiritually charged atmosphere of the twelfth century it was a small movement, offering a way of life for only a heroically holy minority. Too ascetic for the average Christian, the Carthusian order was much admired but seldom joined.

The greatest monastic force of the twelfth century, the Cistercian order, managed for a time to be both austere and popular. The mother house of the order, Cîteaux, was established by a little group of Benedictine dissenters led by Robert, former abbot of Molême. Robert had first been appointed abbot of St-Michel de Tonnerre, but had become dissatisfied with the luxurious lifestyle of its monks. In about 1075 he led a band of disciples to the wilderness site of Molême, where he founded a new abbey on virgin ground and had his followers build huts of tree limbs. His former abbey of St-Michel de Tonnerre, in keeping with its opulent past, is today a luxury-class hotel with sumptuous bedrooms and a superb Michelin two-star restaurant, one of the best in France. Robert of Molême would have been appalled. But to those with less austere tastes, their coquetiers de homard aux oeufs et caviar are highly recommended.

To Robert, however, even Molême was insufficiently challenging, and in 1098 he led his disciples onward to the wilderness site of Cîteaux. This new abbey became the mother house of what in time became a great Europe-wide congregation of Cistercian houses. The Cistercian order grew slowly at first, then gradually acquired momentum. In 1115 Cîteaux had four daughter houses; by the end of the century it had five hundred.

Cistercian abbeys were stark and undecorated in contrast to the elaborate Cluniac architecture of the time. Cistercian life was stark as well—less severe than that of the Carthusians but far more so than that of the Cluniacs. Like other new orders, the Cistercians admitted no children. The minimum age for entry was fifteen, and new recruits underwent a year-long novitiate (trial period) before taking lifetime vows, so that they would be certain of their religious vocation. The year-long novitiate had been prescribed in the Benedictine Rule but had since been largely ignored.

The Cistercians also admitted peasant lay brothers, known as *conversi,* who worked the Cistercian fields.[1] Some conversi were imported from a distance to till newly cleared lands; others were recruited from the local peasantry who had long been cultivating the fields that the order acquired. The conversi were bound by vows of chastity and obedience but were permitted to follow a less demanding form of the Cistercian spiritual life than the monks. The admission of conversi into the order constituted a compassionate outreach to the illiterate peasantry and, at the same time, a solution to the labor shortage on Cistercian lands.

The Cistercian monks and nuns sought to revive the simple, austere life of the early Benedictines. Their houses were unheated, even in the chill north-European winters; their diet was limited to black bread, water and a few stewed vegetables; they were forbidden to speak except when it was absolutely essential. The numerous Cistercian houses were bound together not by the authority of a central abbot, as at Cluny, but by an annual council of all Cistercian abbots meeting at Cîteaux. Without such centralized control it is unlikely that the individual houses could have clung for long to the strict ascetic ideals on which the order was founded.

The key figure in the twelfth-century Cistercian movement was St. Bernard, an incisive, charismatic leader whom we have already encountered preaching the Second Crusade. Bernard joined the community of Cîteaux in 1112 as a young man; three years later he became the founder and abbot of Clairvaux, one of Cîteaux's earliest daughter houses.

---

[1]Occasionally the Cistercian monks joined the conversi in their labors, but not often.

St. Bernard of Clairvaux was the most admired Christian of his age—a mystic, an eloquent religious orator, an exceptionally gifted and prolific writer, and a crucial figure in the meteoric rise of the Cistercian order. His moral influence was so immense that he became Europe's leading arbiter of political and ecclesiastical disputes. Besides inducing the king of France and the Holy Roman emperor to participate in the Second Crusade, he persuaded Christendom to accept his candidate in the years following a hotly disputed papal election in 1130. On one occasion he even succeeded in reconciling the two great warring families of Germany, the Welfs and Hohenstaufens. He rebuked the pope himself: "Remember, first of all, that the Holy Roman Church, over which you hold sway, is the mother of churches, not their sovereign mistress—that you yourself are not the lord of bishops, but one among them." And he took a firm stand against one of the rising movements of his day: the attempt to reconcile the Catholic faith with human reason, led by the brilliant philosopher Peter Abelard. In the long run Bernard failed to halt the growth of Christian rationalism, but he succeeded in making life miserable for Abelard and in securing the official condemnation of certain of Abelard's teachings (see pp. 304–305).

Above and beyond his obvious talents for diplomacy and persuasion, St. Bernard won the devotion of twelfth-century Europe through his reputation for sanctity. He was widely regarded as a saint in his own lifetime, and stories of his miracles circulated far and wide. Pilgrims flocked to Clairvaux to be healed by his touch. This aspect of Bernard's reputation made his skillful preaching and diplomacy even more effective than it would otherwise have been. For here was a holy man, a miracle worker, who engaged in severe fasts, overworked himself to an extraordinary degree, wore coarse clothing, and devoted himself single-mindedly to the service of God.

When confronting an enemy, Bernard could be absolutely terrifying. On one occasion, for example, he commanded Duke William of Aquitaine to reinstate certain bishops whom the duke had driven from their sees. When, after much persuasion, the duke remained obstinate, St. Bernard celebrated a High Mass for him. Holding the consecrated host in his hands, Bernard advanced from the altar toward the duke and said,

> We have besought you, and you have spurned us. The united multitude of the servants of God, meeting you elsewhere, have entreated you, and you have scorned them. Behold! Here comes to you the Virgin's Son, the Head and Lord of the Church which you persecute! Your Judge is here, at whose name every knee shall bow. . . . Your Judge is here, into whose hands your soul is to pass! Will you spurn him also? Will you scorn him as you have scorned his servants?

The duke threw himself on the ground and submitted to Bernard's demands.

Bernard's career demonstrates the essential paradox of Cistercianism. For although the Cistercians strove to dissociate themselves from the world, Bernard was drawn into the vortex of secular affairs. Indeed, as the twelfth century progressed, the entire Cistercian movement became increasingly involved in the world outside. And like the later Puritans and Quakers, the Cistercians discovered that their twin virtues of austere living and hard work resulted in

an accumulation of wealth and, eventually, a corrosion of their spiritual simplicity. They consolidated their estates and managed them with considerable
skill—introducing improvements in the breeding of horses, cattle, and sheep.
The English Cistercians became the great wool producers of the realm. Altogether the Cistercians exerted a progressive influence on European husbandry
and came to play a prominent role in the agrarian economy. Economic success
brought ever-increasing wealth to the order. Cistercian abbey churches became
more elaborate, and the austerity of Cistercian life was progressively relaxed.
In later years there emerged new offshoots, such as the Trappists, which
returned to the strict observance of the early Cistercians.

Monasticism in the World

The Cistercians had endeavored to withdraw from the world yet became a
powerful force in twelfth-century Europe. At roughly the same time, other
orders were being established with the deliberate aim of participating actively
in society and working toward its regeneration. The Augustinian canons, for
example, submitted to the rigor of a rule, yet carried on normal ecclesiastical
duties in the world, serving in parish churches, hospitals, and cathedrals. The
fusion of monastic discipline and worldly activity culminated in the twelfth-
century crusading orders—the Knights Templars, Knights Hospitalers, Teutonic Knights, and similar groups—whose ideal was a synthesis of the monastic and the military life for the purpose of expanding the political frontiers of
Western Christendom. These and other efforts to direct the spiritual vigor of
monastic life toward the regeneration of Christian society typify the visions
and hopes of the new, emotionally charged piety of twelfth-century Europe.

Heresies and the Inquisition

The surge of popular piety also resulted in a flood of criticism against the
Church itself. It was not that churchmen had grown worse, but rather that the
laity had begun to judge them by more rigorous standards. Popular dissatis-
faction toward the workaday Church spurred the rush toward the austere
twelfth-century monastic orders. Yet the majority of Christians could not
become monks or nuns, and, for them, certain heretical doctrines, old and new,
began to exert a powerful appeal.

The heresies of the High Middle Ages flourished particularly in the rising
towns of southern Europe. The eleventh-century urban revolution had caught
the Church unprepared. The new towns were becoming centers of a burgeoning lay piety, yet the Church, with its roots in the older agrarian order, seemed
unable to minister effectively to the vigorous and widely literate new burgher
class. Too often the urban bishops appeared as political oppressors and enemies
of burghal independence rather than spiritual directors. Too often the Church
failed to understand the town dwellers' problems and aspirations or to antici-
pate their growing suspicion of ecclesiastical wealth and power. Although most
townspeople remained loyal to the Church, a minority, particularly in the

south, turned to new, anticlerical sects. In their denunciation of ecclesiastical wealth, these sects were doing nothing more than St. Bernard and the Cistercians had done. But some of the anticlerical sects crossed the narrow line between orthodox reformism and heresy by preaching without episcopal or papal approval. Far more important, they denied the exclusive right of the priesthood to perform sacraments.

One such sect, the Waldensians, was founded by a merchant of Lyons named Valdez, later known as Peter Waldo. Around 1173, Valdez gave all his possessions to the poor and took up a life of apostolic poverty. He and his followers sought the Church's permission to preach in the towns. The Church refused, after some confusion and delay, because of its uneasiness about the preaching of untrained laypeople who, among the Waldensians, included women as well as men. The Church preferred to leave religious instruction in the hands of ordained males. But Peter Waldo and his followers continued their preaching. This act of defiance, along with their growing doubts about the special spiritual status of the priesthood, earned them the condemnation of the Church.

Similar groups, some orthodox, some heretical, arose in the communes of Lombardy and were known as *Humiliati*. These groups proved troublesome to the local ecclesiastical hierarchies, but generally they escaped downright condemnation, unless they themselves took the step of denying the authority of the Church. Many of them did take that step, however, and by the opening of the thirteenth century, heretical, anticlerical sects were spreading across northern Italy and southern France, and even into Spain and Germany.

The most popular heresy in southern France was associated with a group known as the *Cathari* ("the pure"), or the Albigensians—after the town of Albi where they were particularly strong. The Albigensians represented a fusion of two traditions: (1) the anticlerical protest against ecclesiastical wealth and power and (2) an exotic theology derived originally from Persia. The Albigensians recognized two gods: the god of good who reigned over the universe of the spirit and the god of evil who ruled the world of matter. The Old Testament God, creator of the material universe, was their god of evil; Christ, whom they regarded as a purely spiritual being with a phantom body, was the god of good. The Albigensians believed in reincarnation, and their goal was to break free of the cycle of physical rebirth. Their morality stressed a rigorous rejection of all material things—of physical appetites, wealth, worldly vanities, and sexual intercourse—in the hope of one day escaping from the prison of the body and ascending to the realm of pure spirit. In reality this severe ethic was practiced only by a small elite of spiritual men and women known as *perfecti* ("perfect ones"); the rank and file normally ate well, made love, and participated only vicariously in the rejection of the material world, by criticizing the affluence of the Church. Indeed, their opponents accused them of gross licentiousness. And although such accusations were grotesquely exaggerated, it does seem likely that some Provençal nobles were attracted to the new teaching by the opportunity of appropriating Church lands in good conscience.

As the thirteenth century dawned, the Albigensian heresy was expanding so swiftly that it posed a dangerous threat to the unity of Christendom and the authority of the Church. Orthodox Christians regarded it as a horrible infection spreading through the body of Christendom and threatening it with death. Pope Innocent III, recognizing the gravity of the situation, tried with every means in his power to eradicate the heresy. He pressed for the reform of the southern French clergy by the removal of incompetent and corrupt clerics; he urged the nobility to help suppress the Albigensians (whom he regarded as traitors against God); and he encouraged the revitalization of the faith through orthodox preaching. When none of these measures succeeded, he responded to the murder of a papal legate in southern France in 1208 by summoning a Crusade against the Albigensians, the first crusade ever to be called against European Christians.

The Albigensian Crusade was a savage affair that succeeded only after two decades of bloodshed. The French monarchy intervened in its final stages and brought it to a successful conclusion at last in 1229. Southern France recovered quickly from the ravages of the Crusade, with some help from the kings of France who now extended their authority to the Mediterranean. The power of the Albigensians was crushed, and there remained only the task of mopping up some hard-core survivors and ensuring that the region would thereafter remain staunchly orthodox.

To serve this last end, an institution emerged that exemplifies the medieval Church at its most repressive: the Roman Inquisition. Christian persecution of heretics dates from the fourth century, but it was not until the High Middle Ages that heterodox views presented a serious problem to European society. Traditionally, the task of converting or punishing heretics had been handled by bishops, at the local level. But during the early 1230s, in order to standardize policies and increase efficiency, the papacy established a central tribunal with sweeping powers, staffed by well-educated inquisitors bound by religious vows and responsible to the pope himself. These inquisitors traveled through southern Europe seeking out heretics and judging them. The new inquisitorial procedures that they employed included torture, secret testimony, conviction on the testimony of only two witnesses, the denial of legal council to the accused, and other practices that much exceeded the carefully defined limits of medieval Church law. Many of these procedures, including torture, were drawn from the rules of Roman law. In the context of the thirteenth century they constituted a kind of martial law designed to cope with what was seen as a dire emergency.

The Inquisition aroused strong regional opposition, less on humanitarian grounds than on the grounds that papal officials were usurping the traditional rights of bishops and lay lords. Most inquisitors endeavored to act fairly, and the great majority of persons whom they convicted of heresy were given prison sentences or lesser penances (such as wearing crosses over their clothing) instead of being condemned to death. The Inquisition was the first Western European institution to employ imprisonment on a large scale. And inquisitors often felt frustrated by the difficulty of their task. An inquisitor of the 1230s complained,

Serious problems beset the investigator from every side. On the one hand, his conscience torments him if an individual be punished who has neither confessed nor been proven guilty. On the other, it causes even more anguish to the mind of the inquisitor, familiar through much experience with the falsity, cunning, and malice of such persons, if by their wily astuteness they escape punishment to the detriment of the faith, since they are thereby strengthened, multiplied, and rendered more crafty.

The Roman Inquisition cannot be justified, but like all historical episodes it can be explained. To the medieval Catholic, heresy was a hateful thing, a betrayal of Christ, a source of eternal damnation, a plague spreading its infection to others. The Roman Inquisition would be neither the first nor the last instance of human beings finding themselves unable to respond calmly to attacks on their most cherished beliefs.

DOMINICANS AND FRANCISCANS

The thirteenth-century Church found an answer to the spread of heresy that was more compassionate and effective than the Inquisition. In the opening decades of the century two radically new religious orders emerged—the Dominicans and Franciscans—which devoted themselves to a life of poverty, teaching, and charitable deeds. Rejecting the life of the cloister, they dedicated themselves to religious work in the world, particularly in the towns. Benedictines and Cistercians had traditionally taken vows of personal poverty, but their monasteries could and did acquire great corporate wealth. The Dominicans and Franciscans, on the contrary, were pledged to both personal and corporate poverty. They would accept no lands, whether developed or undeveloped, and they drew their earliest members not from the aristocracy but from middle levels of society. Appropriately, they were known as "mendicants"—"beggars." Through their preaching and works of charity, they drained urban heresy of much of its former allure by demonstrating to townspeople that Christian orthodoxy could be both relevant and compelling.

The Dominicans

St. Dominic (1170–1221), a well-educated Spaniard, spent his early adulthood in Castile serving as an Augustinian canon. While working among the Castilians, Dominic conceived the idea of an order of men trained as theologians and preachers, dedicated to poverty and the simple life and to winning over heretics through argument, oratory, and example. In his mid-thirties he traveled to Rome, met Pope Innocent III, and followed the pope's bidding to preach in southern France against the Albigensians. For the next decade, between 1205 and 1215, he worked among the heretics, leading an austere, humble life. His eloquence and simplicity won him considerable renown, but few converts.

The Dominican order evolved out of a small group of volunteers who joined Dominic in his work among the Albigensians. Gradually Dominic came to see the possibility of a far larger mission: to preach and win converts to the faith throughout the world. In 1215 Dominic's friend, the bishop of Toulouse, gave the group a church and a house in the city, and shortly thereafter the papacy recognized the Dominicans as a separate religious order and approved the Dominican Rule.

The congregation founded by Dominic was to be known as the Order of Friars Preachers. It assumed its permanent shape during the years between its formal establishment in 1216 and Dominic's death in 1221, by which time it had grown to include some five hundred friars and sixty priories organized into eight provinces embracing the whole of Western Europe. The Dominicans stood in the vanguard of thirteenth-century piety. Their order attracted people of imagination and unusual religious dedication who could not be satisfied with the enclosed, tradition-bound life of earlier monasticism but were challenged by the austerity of the Dominican Rule, the disciplined vitality of the order, and the goal of working toward the moral regeneration of society.

The Dominican Rule drew freely from the earlier rule of the Augustinian canons that Dominic had known in his youth, but it added new elements and provided a novel direction for the religious life. The order was to be headed by a minister-general, elected for life, and a legislative body that met annually. It was to include communities of women as well as of men. The friars themselves belonged not to a particular house, but to the order at large. Their place of residence and sphere of activity were determined by the minister-general. Their life included such rigors as midnight services, total abstinence from meat, frequent fasts, and prolonged periods of mandatory silence. And the entire order was strictly bound by the rule of poverty that Dominic had learned from his contemporary, St. Francis. Not only should poverty be the condition of individual Dominicans as it was of individual Benedictines; it was to be the condition of the order itself. The Dominican order was to have no possessions except churches and priories. It was to have no fixed incomes and no manors but was to subsist through charitable gifts.

The order expanded at a phenomenal rate during the course of the thirteenth century. Dominican friars carried their evangelical activities across Europe and beyond, into the Holy Land, central Asia, Tartary, Tibet, and China. Joining the faculties of the rising universities, they became the leading proponents of Aristotelian philosophy and included in their numbers such notable scholars as Albertus Magnus and Thomas Aquinas. Dominic himself had insisted that his followers acquire broad educations before undertaking their mission of preaching and that each Dominican priory maintain a school of theology. Within a few decades after his death his order included some of the foremost intellects of the age.

The Dominicans were, above all, preachers, and their particular mission was to preach among heretics and non-Christians. Their contact with heretics brought them into close involvement with the Inquisition, and they themselves became the leading inquisitors. They took pride in their nickname *Domini canes*— "hounds of God"—which suggested their role as watchdogs of the Catholic faith. To religious rebels, the nickname bore a more ominous connotation.

The order was immensely popular among women as well. In 1207 Dominic founded the first monastery of Dominican nuns for a group of followers that included a number of converted Albigensians, and he subsequently established two more female houses; by the beginning of the fourteenth century the number of Dominican nunneries had soared to over 140. But unlike their male counterparts, Dominican nuns led cloistered lives and were permitted no active ministry. They supported the preaching and teaching mission of the Dominican friars with their prayers, and only in later centuries joined them in teaching and scholarship.

The Dominican order still flourishes. The rule of corporate poverty was softened increasingly; finally, in the fifteenth century, it was dropped altogether in deference to the great truth that scholar-teachers cannot be expected to beg or do odd jobs. But long after their original mendicant ideals were modified, the Dominicans remained committed to their central mission of championing Catholic orthodoxy.

The Franciscans

Dominic's contemporary, St. Francis (c. 1182–1226), is perhaps the most widely admired figure of the Middle Ages. A product of the medieval urban revolution, he was the son of a wealthy cloth merchant of Assisi in central Italy. As a youth he was generous, high-spirited, and popular, and in time he became the leader of a boisterous group of teenagers. As one writer aptly expressed it, he "seems altogether to have been rather a festive figure."

In his early twenties St. Francis underwent a profound religious conversion that occurred in several steps. It began on the occasion of a banquet that he was giving for some of his friends. After the banquet Francis and his companions went into the town with torches, singing in the streets. Francis was crowned with garlands as king of the revelers, but after a time he disappeared and was found in a religious trance. Thereafter, he devoted himself to solitude, prayer, and service to the poor. He went as a pilgrim to Rome, where he is reported to have exchanged clothes with a beggar and spent the day begging with other beggars. Returning to Assisi, he encountered an impoverished leper, and notwithstanding his fear of leprosy, he gave the poor man all the money he was carrying and kissed his hand. Thenceforth he devoted himself to the service of lepers and hospitals.

To the consternation of his bourgeois father, who specialized in fine clothing, Francis now went about Assisi dressed in rags, giving to the poor. His former companions pelted him with mud, and his father, fearing that Francis's almsgiving would consume the family fortune, disinherited him. Francis left home singing a French song and spent the next three years of his life in the environs of Assisi, living in abject poverty. He ministered to lepers and social outcasts and continued to embarrass his family by his unconventional behavior. It was at this time that he began to frequent a crumbling little chapel known as the Portiuncula. One day in 1209, while attending Mass there, he was struck by the words of the Gospel that the priest was reading:

Everywhere on your road preach and say, "The Kingdom of God is at hand." Cure the sick, raise the dead, cleanse the lepers, drive out devils. Freely have you received; freely give. Carry neither gold nor silver nor money in your belts, nor bag, nor two coats, nor sandals, nor staff, for the workman is worthy of his hire.[2]

Francis at once accepted this injunction and immediately thereafter—even though a layman—began to preach to the poor.

St. Francis, Cimabue. This much-restored fresco in the Lower Church of St. Francis of Assisi is the earliest known depiction of St. Francis. It is ascribed to the thirteenth-century Italian painter Cimabue (c. 1240–1302).

[2]Matthew 10:7–10.

Disciples now joined him, and when he had about a dozen followers he is said to have remarked, "Let us go to our Mother, the Holy Roman Church, and tell the pope what the Lord has begun to do through us and carry it out with papal approval." This may seem a naive approach to the masterful, aristocratic Pope Innocent III, yet when Francis came to Rome in 1210, Innocent sanctioned his work. Doubtless the pope saw in the Franciscan mission a potential ortho-dox counterpoise to the Waldensians, Albigensians, and other heretical groups that had been winning masses of converts from the Church by the example of their poverty and simplicity. For here was a man whose loyalty to Catholicism was beyond question and whose own artless simplicity might bring erring souls back into the Church. Already Innocent III had given his blessing to movements similar to that of Francis. An orthodox group of Humiliati had received his sanction in 1201, and in 1208 he permitted a converted Waldensian to found an order known as the "Poor Catholics," which was dedicated to lay preaching. In Francis's movement the pope must have seen still another oppor-tunity to encourage a much-needed wave of reform within the orthodox frame-work. And it may well be that Francis's glowing spirituality appealed to the sanctity of Innocent himself, for the pope, even though a great man of affairs, was deeply pious. However this may be, thirteenth-century Europe deserves some credit for embracing a movement that in many other ages would have been persecuted or ridiculed. Rome crucified Christ; our own society, to its shame, would probably place St. Francis in a mental hospital. But the medieval West took Francis to its heart and made him a saint. In the process, however, the hard edges of Franciscan religious austerity were blunted.

Immediately after the papal interview Francis and his followers returned to the neighborhood of Assisi. They acquired the Portiuncula as their own chapel, and over the years it continued to serve as the headquarters of the Franciscan movement. Around it the friars built huts of branches and twigs. The Portiun-cula was a headquarters but not a home, for the friars were always on the move, wandering in pairs over the country, dressed in peasants' clothing, preaching, serving, and living in conscious imitation of Christ.

During the next decade the order expanded at a spectacular rate. Francis-cans were soon to be found throughout northern Italy; by Francis's death in 1226, Franciscan missions were active in France, Germany, England, Hungary, Spain, Morocco, Turkey, and the Holy Land, and the friars numbered in the thousands. The captivating personality of Francis himself was a crucial factor in his order's popularity, but it also owed much to the fact that its ideals har-monized with the highest religious aspirations of the age. Urban heresy lost some of its allure as the cheerful, devoted Franciscans began to pour into Europe's cities, preaching in the crowded streets and setting a living example of Christian sanctity.

The Franciscan ideal was based above all on the imitation of Christ. Fun-damental to this ideal was the notion of poverty, both individual and corporate. The Franciscans subsisted by working and serving in return for their food and other necessities. Humility also was a part of the ideal; Francis gave his fol-lowers the modest name, "Friars Minor" (little brothers). By their preaching and the unassuming holiness of their lives, they answered an urgent need in the cities where the Church had hitherto responded inadequately to the growing religious hunger of the townspeople. Perhaps most attractive of all was the quality of joyousness, akin to the joyousness that Francis had shown prior to his conversion, but directed now toward spiritual and charitable ends. Contemporaries referred to Francis affectionately as "God's own troubadour."

Pious people of other times have fled the world; the Albigensians renounced it as the epitome of evil. But Francis embraced it joyfully as the handiwork of God. In his "Song of Brother Sun" he expressed poetically his holy commitment to the physical universe:

> Praise be to you, my Lord, for all your creatures,
> Above all Brother Sun
> Who brings us the day, and lends us his light;
> Beautiful is he, radiant with great splendor,
> And speaks to us of you, O most high.
>
> Praise to you, my Lord, for Sister Moon and for the stars;
> In heaven you have set them, clear and precious and fair.
> Praise to you, my Lord, for Brother Wind,
> For air and clouds, for calm and all weather
> By which you support life in all your creatures.
>
> Praise to you, my Lord, for Sister Water
> Which is so helpful and humble, precious and pure.
> Praise to you, my Lord, for Brother Fire,
> By whom you light up the night;
> And fair is he, and joyous, and mighty, and strong.
>
> Praise to you, my Lord, for our sister, Mother Earth,
> Who sustains and directs us,
> And brings forth varied fruits, and plants, and flowers bright.
>
> Praise and bless my Lord, and give him thanks,
> And serve him with great humility.

Early Franciscanism was too good to last. The order was becoming too large to retain its original disorganized simplicity. Francis was no administrator, and well before his death the movement was passing beyond his control. In 1219–1220 he traveled to Egypt in an effort to convert its Muslim inhabitants—a hopeless task, but Francis was never dismayed by the impossible—and while he was away it became apparent that his order required a more coherent organization than he had seen fit to provide it. Many perplexing questions now arose: With thousands of friars invading the begging market, what would become of the common tramp? Would Europe's generosity be overstrained? Above all, how could these crowds of friars be expected to cleave to the ideal without an explicit rule and without Francis's personal presence to inspire and guide them? In short, could the Franciscan ideal be practical on a large scale? For the movement was proliferating at a remarkable rate. Besides the Friars Minor themselves, a second order was established—a female order directed by Francis's friend, St. Clare, and known as the "Poor Clares." And a third group, consisting of part-time Franciscans known as "Tertiaries," dedicated themselves to the Franciscan way while continuing their former careers in the world. The little band of Franciscan brothers had evolved into a holy multitude.

On his return from the Near East, Francis prevailed on a powerful friend, Cardinal Hugolino—later Pope Gregory IX—to become the order's protector. On Hugolino's initiative, a formal rule was drawn up in 1220 that provided a certain degree of administrative structure to the order. A probationary period was established for initiates, who, after completing it, were required to take lifetime vows. And the rule of absolute poverty was softened. In 1223 a shorter, somewhat laxer rule was instituted, and over the years and decades that followed, the movement continued to evolve from the ideal to the practical.

St. Francis himself withdrew more and more from involvement in the order's administration. At the meeting of the general chapter in 1220, he resigned his formal leadership of the movement with the words, "Lord, I give you back this family that you entrusted to me. You know, most sweet Jesus, that I no longer have the power and qualities to continue to take care of it." In 1224 St. Francis underwent a mystical experience atop Mt. Alverno in the Apennines, and legend has it that he received the *stigmata*[3] on that occasion. It is not entirely clear how St. Francis reacted to the evolution of his order, but in his closing years his mysticism deepened, his health declined, and he kept much to himself. At his death in 1226 he was universally mourned, and the order that he had founded remained the most powerful and attractive religious movement of its age.

As Franciscanism became increasingly modified by the demands of practicality, it also became increasingly rent with dissension. Some friars, wishing to bask in Francis's prestige without being burdened with his austere principles, advocated an exceedingly lax interpretation of the Franciscan way. Others insisted on the strict imitation of Francis's life and struggled against its modification. These last, known in later years as "Spiritual Franciscans," sought to preserve the apostolic poverty and artless idealism of Francis himself. By the fourteenth century they had become vigorously antipapal and anticlerical.

The majority of Franciscans, however, were willing to meet reality halfway. Although the order neither acquired nor sought the immense landed wealth of the Benedictines or Cistercians, it soon possessed sufficient means to sustain its members. And although Francis had disparaged formal learning as irrelevant to salvation, Franciscan friars began devoting themselves to scholarship and took their places alongside the Dominicans in the thirteenth- and fourteenth-century universities. Franciscan scholars such as Roger Bacon played a role in the revival of scientific investigation, and the minister-general of the Franciscan order in the later thirteenth century, St. Bonaventure, was one of the most illustrious theologians of the age.

Necessary though they were, these compromises diminished the radical idealism that Francis had instilled in his order. In the progress from huts of twigs to halls of ivy, something precious was left behind. The Franciscans

---

[3]The stigmata, which have been attributed to several saints, consist of wounds or scars, believed to be of supernatural origin, corresponding to those sustained by Christ in his crucifixion.

continued to serve society, but by the end of the thirteenth century they had ceased to inspire it.

CONCLUSION

The pattern of religious reform in the High Middle Ages is one of ebb and flow. A reform movement is launched with high enthusiasm and lofty purpose; it galvanizes society for a time and then succumbs gradually to complacency and gives way to a new and different wave of reform. But with the passing of the High Middle Ages, one can detect a gradual waning of spiritual vigor in orthodox Catholicism. The frontiers were closing as the fourteenth century dawned. Western political power was at an end in Constantinople and the Holy Land, and the Spanish reconquest had stalled. The economic boom was giving way to an epoch of depression, declining population, peasants' rebellions, and debilitating wars. And until the time of the Protestant Reformation, no new religious order was to attain the immense social impact of the thirteenth-century Franciscans and Dominicans. Popular piety remained strong, particularly in northern Europe where succeeding centuries witnessed a surge of mysticism. But in the south a more secular attitude was beginning to emerge. Young men and women no longer flocked into monastic orders; multitudes of soldiers no longer rushed to Crusades; papal excommunications no longer wrought their former terror. The electrifying appeal of a St. Bernard, a St. Dominic, and a St. Francis was a phenomenon peculiar to their age. By the fourteenth century their age was passing.

From Leo IX to Gregory VII

Leo IX labored tirelessly for reform. His vigorous assertion of papal authority aggravated the long and deepening hostility between the Churches of Rome and Constantinople, and in 1054 one of his legates placed a papal bull on the high altar of Hagia Sophia excommunicating the Eastern patriarch and precipitating a split between the Eastern and Western Churches that has never been permanently healed.

More than anything else, Leo struggled to enforce canon law and to purge the Church of simony and clerical marriage. In most of his enterprises he could count on the support of Emperor Henry III, for in these early years Empire and papacy worked hand in glove to raise the moral level of the European Church.

But whatever the success of Leo's reforms, there were those who felt that he was not going far enough. The real evil, in the view of the radical reformers, was lay supremacy over the Church. To them Henry III's domination of papal appointments, however well intentioned, was the supreme example of that evil. A number of ardent reformers were to be found among the cardinals whom Pope Leo appointed and gathered around him. These newcomers, who dominated the reform papacy for the next several decades, came for the most part from monastic backgrounds. Many of them were influenced by the piety surging through the towns of eleventh-century northern Italy and Lorraine, a piety that was stimulating the widespread revival of hermit monasticism.

One such reformer was St. Peter Damiani, a leader of the north-Italian hermit movement before Leo IX brought him to Rome and made him a cardinal. Peter Damiani was a man of many contrasting aspects: a forceful preacher and writer dedicated to the eradication of vices—some of which he described so graphically that a sixteenth-century editor felt constrained to tone down his language. Peter served the reform papacy tirelessly, traveling far and wide to enforce the prohibitions against simony and clerical marriage and to reform the clergy. Yet he drew back from what seemed to him the irresponsible efforts of his more radical associates to challenge and transform the lay-dominated social order.

The leaders of the radical group were Humbert of Silva Candida and Hildebrand. Both were papal officials under Leo IX; both had, like Damiani, left monastic lives to join the Roman curia. Humbert of Silva Candida was a German from Lorraine, probably of aristocratic background, who used his subtle, well-trained intellect to support papal reform in its most radical aspect. He was one of Pope Leo's legates to Constantinople during the dispute with the Eastern Church, where his uncompromising attitudes on papal supremacy clashed with the equally intransigent views of the Eastern patriarch. Indeed, it was Humbert himself who precipitated the schism of 1054 by delivering the papal bull excommunicating the patriarch. A few years later Humbert produced a bitter, closely reasoned attack against the lay-dominated social order in the West, *Three Books against the Simoniacs,* in which he extended the meaning of simony to include not merely the buying or selling of ecclesiastical offices but any instance of lay interference in clerical appointments. In Humbert's view the Church ought to be utterly free of lay control and supreme in European society.

Hildebrand, an Italian monk, lacked Humbert's intellectual depth but had a remarkable ability to draw ideas from the minds of others and formulate them into a clearly articulated program. Intellectually, Hildebrand was a disciple of Humbert, but as a spellbinding leader and mover of events he stood alone. Contemporaries described Hildebrand as a small, ugly, pot-bellied man, but they also recognized that a fire burned inside him—a holy or unholy fire depending on one's point of view. For Hildebrand was the most controversial figure of his age. He was thought to have the power to read minds and may well have believed so himself. Consumed by the ideal of a godly society dominated by the Church and a Church dominated by the papacy, Hildebrand served with prodigious vigor and determination under Pope Leo IX and his successors. At length he became pope himself, taking the name Gregory VII (1073–1085). His pontificate was to be one of the most violent and unforgettable of the Middle Ages.

So long as Henry III lived, radicals such as Humbert of Silva Candida and Hildebrand remained in the background. But in 1056 the emperor died at the age of thirty-nine, leaving behind him a six-year-old heir, Henry IV, and a weak regency government. Henry III's death was a catastrophe for the Empire, but it provided a golden opportunity to the radical reformers, who now took steps to wrest the papacy from imperial control. At the death of Henry III's last papal appointee in 1057, the reform cardinals began electing popes on their own. In 1059, under the influence of Humbert and Hildebrand, they issued a daring declaration of independence known as the "Papal Election Decree," which stated that thenceforth the pope would be chosen by cardinals. The emperor and the Roman laity would merely give formal approval. In the years that followed, this revolutionary proclamation was challenged by both the Empire and the Roman aristocracy, but in the end the reformers won out. The papacy had broken free of lay control; cardinals elected the pope, and the pope appointed the cardinals. The decree of 1059 thus created at the apex of the ecclesiastical hierarchy a reform oligarchy of the most exclusive sort.

The next step in the program of the radical reformers was far more difficult. It involved nothing less than the annihilation of lay control over the Church and the strict subordination of bishops and archbishops to the pope. At a time when the Church possessed perhaps a third of the land in Europe, the full realization of this vision of papal monarchy would cripple secular power, destroy episcopal autonomy, and revolutionize the European political order. Yet only by its realization, so the radical reformers believed, could a justly ordered Christian commonwealth be achieved.

One of the first arenas of conflict was the city of Milan, with its proud archbishopric renowned since St. Ambrose's time. Milan was in the grip of the new commercial revival and, like many other Lombard towns of the eleventh century, seething with activity. The Lombard bishops, who usually cooperated with the Holy Roman Empire and had the support of landholding nobles, opposed reform. But now, throughout Lombardy and especially in Milan, their

Chapter 12   Worlds in Collision: Papacy and Empire

rule was being challenged by the growing class of merchants and artisans, backed by journeymen and peasants. In Milan and elsewhere, these dissidents were referred to by their enemies as *patarenes* ("rag-pickers"). Hostile to the traditional ruling group and fired by the new piety, the patarenes made common cause with the reform papacy against their bishops. The reformers in Rome had no sympathy for the archbishop of Milan who was, in effect, an imperial agent and who, by condoning simony and marriage among his clergy, symbolized the traditional Church at its worst.

In 1059 Cardinal Peter Damiani journeyed to Milan to enforce reform. Backed by the patarenes and the authority of Rome, he humbled the archbishop and the higher clergy, forced them to confess their sins publicly, and made them promise to change their ways. Thus, the Milanese church, despite its friendship with the Empire and its tradition of independence, was made to submit to the power of the papacy. Over the next fifteen years, the patarenes continued their struggle against the noble-ecclesiastical ruling group, and the city was torn by murder and mob violence. When in 1072 the young emperor Henry IV ordered the consecration of an anti-reformer as archbishop of Milan, the patarenes rioted and the pope excommunicated Henry's counselors, forcing him to back down. The episode typifies the close alliance between radical urban piety and papal reform. Having placed themselves at the forefront of the new piety, the reformers were propelled by the revolutionary social-spiritual movement that was sweeping urban Europe. At odds with much of the traditional ecclesiastical establishment, they were in tune with the most vigorous forces of the age.

Gregory VII and Henry IV

The struggle over lay control of ecclesiastical appointments broke out in earnest in 1075 when Hildebrand, now Pope Gregory VII, issued a proclamation banning lay investiture. Traditionally, a newly chosen bishop or abbot was "invested" into office by receiving from his lay lord a ring and a pastoral staff, symbolic of his marriage to the Church and his duty to be a good shepherd to his Christian flock. Gregory attacked this custom of lay investiture as the crucial symbol of lay authority over churchmen. Its prohibition was a challenge to the established social order and a threat to the authority of every ruler in Christendom—none more than the Holy Roman emperor, whose administration was particularly dependent on the German and Lombard bishops.

By Gregory VII's time, Henry IV had grown up and was showing promise of becoming as strong a ruler as his father. When Gregory VII suspended a group of uncooperative, imperially appointed German bishops, Henry IV responded with a vehement letter of defiance. Backed by his bishops, he asserted his authority as a divinely appointed sovereign to lead the German Church without papal interference and challenged Gregory's very right to the papal throne. The letter was insultingly addressed to Gregory under his previous name, "Hildebrand, not pope but false monk." It concluded with the dramatic words, "I, Henry, king by grace of God, with all my bishops, say to you: 'Come down, come down, and be damned throughout the ages.' "

Henry's letter was in effect a defense of the traditional social order of divinely ordained kings, sanctified by the ceremony of holy consecration and anointment that accompanied their coronations, ruling as vicars of God over their lay subjects and their semi-autonomous bishops. Gregory's view of society was vastly different: he denied the sacred qualities of kings and emperors, suggested that most of them were murderous thugs destined for hell, and repudiated their right to question his status or his decrees. Emperors had no power to appoint churchmen, much less depose popes. But the pope, as the ultimate authority in Christendom, had the power to depose not only bishops but kings and emperors as well. Accordingly, Gregory responded to Henry IV's letter with a devastating counterpunch: he excommunicated and deposed Henry IV. It was for the pope to judge whether or not the king was fit to rule, and Gregory had judged.

Radical though it was, the deposition was effective. Under the relatively placid surface of monarchical authority in Germany, aristocratic opposition had long been gathering force. Relatively subdued during the reign of Henry III, local and regional princes asserted themselves during the long regency following his death, and Henry IV, on reaching maturity, had much ground to recover. In 1075 he succeeded in stifling a long, bitter rebellion in Saxony and seemed to be on his way toward reasserting his father's power when the controversy with Rome exploded. Gregory VII's excommunication and deposition—awesome spiritual sanctions to the minds of eleventh-century Christians—unleashed in Germany all the latent hostility that the centralizing policies of the Salian dynasty had evoked. Many Germans, churchmen and aristocrats alike, refused to serve an excommunicated sovereign. The German nobles took the revolutionary step of threatening to elect a new king in Henry's place, thereby challenging the ingrained German tradition of hereditary kingship. The elective principle, which weakened the later medieval and early modern German monarchy, had its real inception at this moment.

Desperate to keep his throne, Henry crossed the Alps into Italy to seek the pope's forgiveness. In January 1077, at the castle of Canossa in northern Italy, the two men met in what was perhaps medieval history's most dramatic encounter—Henry IV, humble and barefoot in the snow, clothed in rough, penitential garments; Gregory VII, torn between his priestly duty to forgive a repentant sinner and his conviction that Henry's change of heart was a mere political subterfuge. Finally Gregory lifted Henry's excommunication and the monarch, swearing to amend his ways, returned to Germany to rebuild his authority.

Throughout the centuries Canossa has symbolized the ultimate royal degradation before the power of the Church. Perhaps it was—but in the immediate political context it was a victory, and a badly needed one, for Henry IV. It did not prevent a group of German nobles from electing a rival king, nor did it restore the powerful centralized monarchy of Henry III, but it did save Henry IV's throne. Restored to communion, he was able to rally support, to check for a time the forces of princely particularism, and to defeat the rival king.

As his power waxed, Henry ignored his promises at Canossa and resumed his struggle against papal reform. Amidst the thunder of armed clashes between the king and a stubborn German opposition, and in the face of renewed papal decrees of deposition and excommunication, Henry IV invaded Italy and led his army toward Rome. Gregory VII responded by calling for help from his Norman ally, Robert Guiscard. This turned out to be a fatal mistake, for although Guiscard's boisterous Normans frightened Henry away, they afterward became involved in a destructive riot against the Roman townspeople, killing many of them and selling others into slavery (see p. 194). The commoners of Rome had always supported Gregory, but now they turned furiously against him and he was obliged, for his own protection, to accompany his Norman "rescuers" when they withdrew to the south. In 1085 Gregory died at Salerno, consumed by bitterness and a conviction of failure. His last words were these: "I have loved justice and hated iniquity; therefore I die in exile."[1]

The Papal Recovery and the Investiture Settlement

Gregory VII failed to transform Europe. "When I look over the lands of the West," he wrote, "I find scarcely any bishops, whether to north or south, who conform to the law." But his vision of papal monarchy long outlived him. The papacy soon fell into the expert hands of Urban II (1088–1099), a former prior of Cluny who had afterward become one of Gregory VII's most faithful and effective cardinals. In calling the First Crusade in 1095, Pope Urban wedded the papal reform movement to the moral fervor of Christian militancy. Ideologically, Urban was a Gregorian, but he was much more practical and diplomatic than his fiery predecessor. He rebuilt the papal administration, which had disintegrated during Gregory's final years, into a smoothly functioning bureaucracy suited to the needs of a centralized papal government in regular communication with the bishops and abbots of Western Christendom. Papal correspondence increased, financial management improved, and the papal tribunal became steadily more active and effective. In the long run, the papal monarchy of the High Middle Ages owed more to its administration than to its excommunications.

Urban II and his successors continued to harass the unlucky Henry IV, stirring up rebellions in Germany and eroding the power of the imperial government. At the emperor's death in 1106, his own son and heir, the future Henry V, was in rebellion against him. Henry V (1106–1125) enjoyed a happier reign than his father's, but only because he forsook his father's struggle to recover the fullness of imperial power as it had existed in the mid-eleventh century. The independence-minded aristocracy consolidated the gains it had made during the preceding era of chaos, and Henry V could do little about it.

Toward the end of his reign, Henry V worked out a compromise settlement with the papacy that brought the investiture contest to an end at last. Already the issue had been resolved in England and France, where the struggle had been considerably less bitter than in Germany. As time progressed both papacy

---

[1]An ironic twist to Psalm 45, verse 7: "You have loved justice and hated iniquity; therefore God, your God, has anointed you with the oil of gladness above all your rivals."

and Empire tended to draw back from the extreme positions they had taken during Gregory VII's pontificate, and in 1122 they reconciled their differences in the Concordat of Worms. Henry V agreed to give up lay investiture, while the pope—a French aristocrat named Calixtus II—conceded to the emperor the important privilege of bestowing on the new prelate the symbols of his territorial and administrative jurisdiction (as distinct from his spiritual authority). Bishops and abbots were thenceforth to be elected according to the principles of canon law, by the monks of a monastery or the canons of a cathedral, but Pope Calixtus conceded that the emperor had the right to be present at such elections and to make the final decision in the event of a dispute. These reservations enabled the emperor to retain a considerable degree of de facto authority over the appointment of important German churchmen. The exercise of royal control over a "canonical election" is illustrated in the later twelfth century by a command of King Henry II of England to the monks at Winchester: "I order you to hold a free election, but nevertheless I forbid you to elect anyone except Richard, my clerk, the archdeacon of Poitiers."

There was no real victor in the investiture controversy. The papacy had won its point—lay investiture was banned—but monarchs still exercised considerable control over their churches. The theory of papal monarchy over a reconstituted Christian society remained unrealized, and the old tradition of peaceful cooperation between kings and prelates was shaken but not destroyed. The papacy, however noble its intentions, had become politicized as never before. And by asserting its authority across Europe, it evoked hostile royalist propaganda and growing opposition.

Still, the papal-imperial balance of power had changed radically since the mid-eleventh century. The papacy was now a major political force in Europe, and the power of the emperor had declined. During the chaotic half-century between the onset of the controversy in 1075 and Henry V's death in 1125, a powerful new aristocracy emerged in Germany. Ambitious landowners rose to great power, built castles, extended their estates, and usurped royal rights. They compelled lesser landholders to become their vassals and, in some instances, forced free peasants to become their serfs. The monarchy was helpless to curb this process of fragmentation.

The investiture controversy resulted in the crippling of imperial authority and episcopal autonomy in northern Italy. The fierce patarene struggle in Milan was repeated throughout Lombardy, and in the anarchy wrought by the papal-imperial conflict, the pro-imperial Lombard bishops lost the wide jurisdictional powers they had formerly exercised over their cities. Lombard burghers, under the banner of papal reform, rebelled against the control of nobles, bishops, and emperor alike, and established quasi-independent city-states. By 1125, Milan and its sister cities were free urban communes, and imperial authority in Lombardy had become nominal.

In Germany and Italy alike, imperial power was receding before the whirlwind of local particularism, fanned by the investiture controversy, the rise of towns, and the soaring popular piety of the age. Well before the Concordat of Worms, the decline of the medieval empire had begun.

Italy in 1303 and took Boniface prisoner at his palace at Anagni with the intention of bringing him to France for trial. Anagni, the antithesis of Canossa, symbolized the humiliation of the medieval papacy. The French plan failed—local townspeople freed Boniface a couple of days later—but the proud old pope died shortly thereafter, outraged and chagrined that armed Frenchmen had dared to lay hands on his sacred person. Contemporaries found it significant that his burial was cut short by a furious electrical storm.

The high tide of papal monarchy now began to recede. In 1305 the cardinals elected the Frenchman Clement V (1305–1314), a native of Gascony, who pursued a policy of cautious accommodation to the French throne. Clement submitted on the question of clerical taxation and publicly burned *Unam Sanctam,* conceding that Philip the Fair, in accusing Pope Boniface, had shown "praiseworthy zeal."

A few years after his election, Clement abandoned faction-ridden Rome for a new papal capital at Avignon on the Rhône river, in present-day southern France, where the papacy remained for several generations. At Avignon the papal administration continued to grow, and papal spiritual prestige continued to dwindle. The town of Avignon belonged to the papacy, not to the French crown, yet France's enemies could never be confident of the Avignon papacy's political impartiality. The French kings were strong, and they were nearby.

It is easy to criticize Boniface VIII's inflexibility or Clement V's eagerness to please, but the waning of papal authority in the later Middle Ages did not result primarily from personal shortcomings. It stemmed from an ever-widening gulf between papal government and the spiritual thirst of ordinary Christians, combined with the hostility to Catholic internationalism on the part of increasingly powerful centralized kingdoms such as England and France. It would be grossly unfair to describe the high medieval papacy as "corrupt." Between 1050 and 1300 men of high purpose sat on the papal throne. Not satisfied merely to chide the society of their day by innocuous moralizing from the sidelines, they plunged into the world and struggled to sanctify it. Tragically, perhaps inevitably, they soiled their hands.

CONCLUSION

The foregoing account of the high medieval papacy has attempted to balance the ideal of ecclesiastical centralization against the untidy local realities of episcopal autonomy, noncompliance with papal commands, and disputes between archbishops, bishops, and abbots. Distances were too great and ecclesiastical egos too tender for the pope to become the great puppeteer of the European Church. And secular rulers were much too strong to permit anything resembling a papal theocracy.

Nevertheless, looking at the Church of high-medieval Western Europe from a global perspective we see a religious institution with a cohesion, independence, and political leverage unmatched in all history. Although popes were never able to dominate kingdoms, at crucial moments they could wrestle with kings on even terms. The papacy was thus able to play a historically unprecedented role in inhibiting the rise of royal absolutism. Unlike the patriarchs of Constantinople, the popes acted independently of imperial control. And they fought tooth and claw to retain their independence against the threat of imperial encirclement—as Frederick II discovered to his sorrow.

Beneath the dust clouds of battles and high politics, the Church sponsored the rise of universities, of schools and hospitals in vast number, of hostels for the poor and refuges for orphans and the physically handicapped. Under papal direction, Church law and doctrine were developed and refined, and theological systems emerged that explored in rational terms the secrets of divine creation. In these and countless other ways the high medieval Church served and shaped the civilization of Western Europe. Notwithstanding historical myths to the contrary, the Church did far more to stimulate European rationalism than to shackle it, to limit autocracy than to encourage it, to affirm human dignity than to diminish it. The impact of medieval Christianity on our modern world is too pervasive and complex to be precisely measured. But it may be more than coincidence that the civilization that has transformed the globe emerged from a society that possessed, in the words of the celebrated historian Sir Richard Southern, "the most elaborate and thoroughly integrated system of religious thought and practice the world has ever known."

CHAPTER 14

Literature, Art, and Thought

OVERVIEW

The revolutionary changes that transformed high medieval Europe's economic, religious, and political institutions were paralleled by deeply significant cultural and intellectual transformations. Europe in the High Middle Ages underwent an artistic and intellectual awakening that affected virtually all forms of expression. Medieval wall paintings, and book illuminations in jewel-like colors, evolved toward realism and elegance. Drama was exemplified in an abundance of highly popular "mystery plays" on religious themes and in the dramatic works of the great twelfth-century polymath, Hildegard of Bingen, which constituted an early form of Christian musical theater. Music itself underwent fundamental advances with the development of the first musical notation and, in twelfth- and thirteenth-century Paris, the earliest complex polyphony (i.e., music with two or more different, interrelated voice lines).

High medieval literature saw the flourishing of warlike *epic* poetry, the rebirth of *lyric* poetry, and the emergence of the *romance*. More sophisticated and sensitive than the epic, the romance was a new literary form that concerned itself with such topics as the courtly deeds of the half-mythical King Arthur and his knights at Camelot, whose stories emerged from the songs and legends of the early medieval Welsh, and the amorous adventures of clandestine lovers: Lancelot and Guinevere, Tristan and Iseult.

Architecture underwent similarly drastic changes as the massive Romanesque style reached its apogee and then evolved into the soaring and delicate Gothic style. With the advent of Gothic architecture in the mid-twelfth century came a new sculptural style in which the characteristic Romanesque qualities of fantasy and distortion gave way to an idealized naturalism unmatched since classical antiquity.

The High Middle Ages witnessed dramatic intellectual developments as well. Schools proliferated in towns and villages all across Western Europe, and the first universities emerged—at Paris, Bologna, Salerno, Oxford, Cambridge, Prague, Montpelier, and elsewhere. Law and medicine became serious intellectual disciplines, the age of European science dawned, and philosopher-theologians such as Thomas Aquinas produced vast, closely reasoned systems of thought that sought to reconcile human reason and the doctrines of the Christian faith.

By the close of the high medieval era, Europe had undergone fundamental changes not only in political, economic, and social organization but in literature, art, and thought as well. The foundations of the Western cultural tradition, scarcely discernible in 1050, were firmly in place by 1300. Limitations of space require that our discussion of high medieval culture and thought be highly selective, providing only a glimpse at the achievements of this deeply creative age.

LITERATURE

The literature of the High Middle Ages was abundant and richly varied. Poets wrote both in the traditional Latin, the universal scholarly language of medieval Europe, and in the vernacular languages of ordinary speech that had long been evolving in the various regions of Christendom. Christian piety found expression in a series of somber and majestic Latin hymns such as *Jerusalem the Golden* from the twelfth century:

> The world is very evil, the times are waxing late.
> Be sober and keep vigil, the judge is at the gate. . . .
> Brief life is here our measure; brief sorrow, short lived care.
> The life that knows no ending, the tearless life, is there.
>
> Jerusalem the golden, with milk and honey blessed,
> Beneath your contemplation sink heart and voice oppressed.
> I know not, O I know not what joys await us there,
> What radiancy of glory, what light beyond compare.

But one also encounters Latin poetry of quite a different sort, composed by young, wandering students and scholars:

> For on this my heart is set, when the hour is nigh me
> Let me in the tavern die, with my ale cup by me,
> While the angels, looking down, joyously sing o'er me. . . .

Another such poem is an elaborate and impudent parody of the Apostles' Creed. A phrase from the Creed, "I believe in the Holy Ghost, the Holy [Catholic] Church . . ." is embroidered as follows:

> *I believe* in wine that's fair to see,
> And in the tavern of my host
> More than *in the Holy Ghost*
> The tavern will my sweetheart be,
> And *the Holy Church* is not for me.

These sentiments do not mark a sweeping trend toward agnosticism but simply reflect the perennial student irreverence toward established institutions.

For all its originality, the Latin poetry of the High Middle Ages was outstripped both in quantity and in variety of expression by vernacular poetry. The drift toward emotionalism, which we have already noted in medieval piety, was closely paralleled by the evolution of vernacular literature from the martial epics of the eleventh century to the sensitive romances of the twelfth and thirteenth.

The Epic

In the eleventh and early twelfth centuries, vernacular epics known as *chansons de geste* ("songs of great deeds") were enormously popular among the northern French aristocracy. Sung aloud by minstrels in the halls of castles, these chansons were rooted in the earlier heroic tradition of the Teutonic north that had produced moody and violent masterpieces such as *Beowulf*. The hero Beowulf is a lonely figure who fights monsters, slays dragons, and pits his strength and courage against a wild, windswept wilderness. The chansons de geste were equally heroic in mood. Like modern epics of outer space, they were packed with action, and their heroes tended to steer clear of sentimental entanglements with women. The battle descriptions, often characterized by gory realism, tell of Christian knights fighting with almost superhuman strength against fantastic odds. The heroes of the chansons are not only proud and loyal to their lords but also capable of experiencing deep emotions—weeping at the deaths of their comrades and appealing to God to receive the souls of the fallen. In short, the chansons de geste mirror the warlike spirit and sense of military brotherhood that characterized the knighthood of eleventh-century Europe.

These qualities find vivid expression in the most famous chanson de geste, the *Song of Roland*, which tells of a bloody battle between a horde of Muslims and the detached rear guard of Charlemagne's army as it was withdrawing from Spain:

> Turpin of Reims, his horse beneath him slain,
> And with four lance wounds he himself in pain,
> Hastens to rise, brave lord, and stand erect.
> He looks on Roland, runs to him, and says
> Only one thing: "I am not beaten yet!
> True man fails not, while life in him is left."
> He draws Almace, his keen-edged steel-bright sword,
> And strikes a thousand strokes amid the press.
>
> Count Roland never loved a recreant,
> Nor a false heart, nor yet a braggart jack,
> Nor knight that was not faithful to his lord.
> He cried to Turpin—churchman militant—
> "Sir, you're on foot, I'm on my horse's back.
> For love of you, here will I make my stand,
> And side by side we'll take both good and bad.
> I'll not leave you for any mortal man. . . ."
>
> Now Roland feels that he is nearing death;
> Out of his ears his brain is running forth.
> So for his peers he prays God call them all,
> And for himself St. Gabriel's aid implores.[1]

Roland and his rear guard are slain to a man, but the Lord Charlemagne returns to avenge them and a furious battle ensues:

---

[1]This and the other translations in this chapter are by C. Warren Hollister.

Both French and Moors are fighting with a will.
How many spears are shattered! lances split!
Whoever saw those shields smashed all to bits,
Heard the bright hauberks grind, the mail rings rip,
Heard the harsh spear upon the helmet ring,
Saw countless knights out of the saddle spilled,
And all the earth with death and deathcries filled,
Would long recall the face of suffering!

The French are victorious. Charlemagne himself defeats the Moorish emir in single combat, and Roland is avenged:

The Muslims fly, God will not have them stay.
All's done, all's won, the French have gained the day.

It should not be supposed that any such battle ever actually occurred. By and large, Charlemagne's Spanish campaign was a fiasco, and it was left to the *Song of Roland* to supply the happy ending (see p. 96).

The Lyric

During the middle and later twelfth century the martial spirit of northern French literature was gradually transformed by the influx of a new, more romantic poetry from southern France. In Provence, Toulouse, and Aquitaine a rich, colorful culture had been developing in the eleventh and twelfth centuries, and out of it came a lyric poetry of remarkable sensitivity and enduring value. The lyric poets of the south were known as "troubadours" (see the box on Bernard of Ventadour on p. 278). Many of them were court minstrels, but some, including Duke William IX of Aquitaine (Eleanor's grandfather), were members of the upper nobility. The wit, delicacy, and romanticism of the troubadour lyrics disclose a more genteel nobility than that of the north—a nobility that preferred songs of love to songs of war. Indeed, some historians have viewed medieval southern France as the source of the romantic-love tradition of Western civilization. It was from there that Europe derived such concepts as the idealization of women, the importance of male gallantry and courtesy, and the impulse to embroider relations between man and woman with emotions of eternal oneness, undying devotion, agony, and ecstasy. One of the favorite themes of the lyric poets was the hopeless love—the unrequited love from afar:

I die of wounds from blissful blows,
And love's cruel stings dry out my flesh,
My health is lost, my vigor goes,
And nothing can my soul refresh.
I never knew so sad a plight,
It should not be, it is not right.

I'll never hold her near to me,
My ardent joy she'll ever spurn,
In her good grace I cannot be,

Nor even hope, but only yearn.
She tells me nothing, false or true,
And neither will she ever do.

The author of these lines, Jaufré Rudel (fl. 1148), unhappily and hopelessly in love, finds consolation in his talents as a poet, of which he has an exceedingly high opinion. The poem concludes on a much more optimistic note:

Make no mistake, my song is fair,
With fitting words and apt design.
My messenger would never dare
To cut it short or change a line.

My song is fair, my song is good,
'Twill bring delight, as well it should.

Many such poems were written in twelfth-century southern France. Their recurring theme is the poet's passionate love for a woman. Occasionally, however, the pattern is reversed, as in this mid-twelfth-century lyric poem by Beatritz, countess of Dia, one of twenty known female troubadours:

I live in grave anxiety
For one fair knight who loved me so.
It would have made him glad to know
I loved him too—but silently.
I was mistaken, now I'm sure,
When I withheld myself from him.
My grief is deep, my days are dim,
And life itself has no allure.

I wish my knight might sleep with me
And hold me naked to his breast,
And on my body take his rest,
And grieve no more, but joyous be.
My love for him surpasses all
The loves that famous lovers knew.
My soul is his, my body, too,
My heart, my life, are at his call.

My most beloved, dearest friend,
When will you fall into my power?
That I might lie with you an hour,
And love you 'till my life should end.
My heart is filled with passion's fire.
My well-loved knight, I grant thee grace
To hold me in my husband's place
And do the things I so desire.

The reversal of roles disclosed in Beatritz of Dia's poem was by no means unusual. Indeed, the idealized qualities of the beloved are often presented with such sexual ambiguity that one cannot tell whether the poet is referring to a man or a woman.

Not every lyric poet took love or life as seriously as Jaufré Rudel or Beatritz of Dia. The following verses by William IX, duke of Aquitaine (1071–1127), parody both the passionate seriousness of the love lyric and the heroic mood of the chanson de geste:

I'll make some verses just for fun,
Not for myself or anyone,
Nor of great deeds that knights have done,
Nor lovers true.
I made them riding in the sun,
My horse helped too.

When I was born I'm not aware;
I'm neither glad nor in despair,
Nor stiff, nor loose, nor do I care,
Nor wonder why.
Since meeting an enchantress fair,
Bewitched am I.

Living for dreaming I mistake,
I must be told when I'm awake.
My mood is sad, my heart may break, such grief I bear!
But never mind, for heaven's sake,
I just don't care.

I'm sick to death, or so I fear;
I cannot see but only hear.
I hope that there's a doctor near, no matter who.
If he can heal me I'll pay dear;
If not, he's through.

My lady fair is far away,
Just who or where I cannot say,
She tells me neither yea nor nay,
Yet I'm not blue,
So long as all those Normans stay
Far from Poitou.

My distant love I so adore,
Though me she has no longing for;
We've never met, and furthermore—to my disgrace—
I've other loves, some three or four, to fill her place.

This verse is done, as you can see,
And by your leave, dispatched 'twill be
To one who'll read it carefully in far Anjou.
Its meaning he'd explain to me if he but knew.

The Romance

Midway through the twelfth century, the southern troubadour tradition began to filter into northern France, England, and Germany. It brought with it a new

Bernard of Ventadour

Bernard of Ventadour (c. 1140–1190) was one of the twelfth century's most celebrated and imitated troubadours. Like other troubadours Bernard was at once a composer and a poet; he created both the music and the lyrics for his songs.

The details of Bernard's life, provided in a biography in the Old Provençal vernacular, may well be embroidered and romanticized, but very little biographical information has survived apart from this one source. It reports that Bernard's mother and father were servants at the castle of the viscount of Ventadour in southern France. At an early age Bernard showed great talent as a poet and musician, and he was singled out by the viscount of Ventadour for training as a troubadour.

The happy days ended abruptly, so the vernacular biography relates, when Bernard's patron, the viscount, found the young boy in bed with the viscountess. Bernard was banished from the castle and was obliged to seek his fortune elsewhere. Undaunted, he presented himself to the greatest artistic patron in Western Europe: Eleanor, duchess of Aquitaine and queen of England.

Queen Eleanor was immediately impressed by Bernard's artistic gifts. He spent a number of years at her court, composing and performing songs for the queen and her entourage. His songs earned him fame and fortune; they were immensely popular in their time and are performed to this day. No fewer than forty-four have survived.

Bernard's songs celebrate the joys and heartaches of romantic love. His basic philosophy, like that of other troubadours of his time, is perfectly epitomized in one of his lyrics:

Singing isn't worth a thing
If the heart sings not the song,

And the heart can never sing
If it brings not love along.

Another of Bernard's songs, "The Lark," available today in several recorded versions, is an evocation of one of the most frequently encountered themes in twelfth-century romantic poetry, the agony of unrequited love:

When I see the lark beat its wings,
Facing the sun's rays,
Forgetting itself, letting itself sing
Of the sweetness that enters its
        heart—
Ah! Such great longing enters me
From the happiness I see,
That only a miracle prevents my heart
From consuming itself with desire.
Alas! I thought I knew so much
        of love,
And I know so little.
For I can't help loving a lady
Whom I cannot attain.
She has all my heart
She has me entirely.
She has left me nothing but desire,
And a foolish heart.

His biographer reported—perhaps indulging in wishful thinking—that Bernard became Eleanor of Aquitaine's lover. Whatever the case, he accompanied the queen and her court on their travels through France, and the evidence suggests that he was in England on at least one occasion.

In later years, Bernard left Queen Eleanor's entourage to join the court of Raymond, count of Toulouse, whose name occurs in several of Bernard's songs. Like other worldly men and women—such as Hugh, earl of Chester, and Bertrada de Montfort—Bernard ended his days in an abbey. He retired to the Cistercian monastery of Dalon in southern France and died there at the age of fifty.

aristocratic ideology of courtly manners, urbane speech, and romantic idealization. These, briefly, were the ideals of what has been called "courtly love." Their impact on the actual behavior of knights was limited, but their effect on the literature of northern Europe was revolutionary. Out of the convergence of vernacular epic and vernacular lyric there emerged a new poetic form known as the "romance."

Like the chanson de geste, the romance was a long narrative; like the southern lyric, it was sentimental and concerned with love. It was commonly based on some theme from the remote past: the Trojan War, Alexander the Great, and above all, King Arthur—the half-legendary sixth-century British king. Arthur was transformed into an idealized twelfth-century monarch surrounded by charming ladies and chivalrous knights. His court at Camelot, as described by the late-twelfth-century French poet, Chrétien de Troyes, was a center of romantic love and refined religious sensibilities where knights worshiped their ladies and went on daring quests in a world of magic and fantasy.

In the chanson de geste the great virtue was loyalty to one's lord; in the romance it was love for one's lady. Several romances portray the old and new values in conflict. An important theme in both the Arthurian romances and the twelfth-century romance of Tristan and Iseult is a love affair between a vassal and his lord's wife. Love and feudal loyalty stand face to face, and love wins out. Tristan loves Iseult, the wife of his lord, King Mark of Cornwall. King Arthur's beloved knight Lancelot loves Arthur's wife, Guinevere. In both stories the lovers are ruined by their love, yet love they must—they have no choice—and although the conduct of Tristan and Lancelot would have been regarded by earlier standards as nothing less than treasonable, both men are presented sympathetically in the romances. Love destroys the lovers in the end, yet their destruction is romantic—even glorious. Tristan and Iseult lie dead together, side by side, and in their very death their love achieves its deepest consummation.

Alongside the theme of love in the romances is the theme of Christian purity and dedication. The rough-hewn knight of old, having been instructed to be courteous and loving, was now instructed to be holy. Lancelot was trapped in the meshes of a lawless love, but his son, Galahad, became the prototype of the Christian knight—worshipful and chaste. And Perceval, another knight of the Arthurian circle, quested not for a lost loved one but for the Holy Grail of the Last Supper.

The romance flourished in twelfth- and thirteenth-century France and among the French-speaking nobility of England. It spread also into Italy and Spain and became a crucial factor in the evolution of vernacular literature in Germany. The German poets, known as "Minnesingers," were influenced by the French lyric and romance but developed these literary forms along highly original lines. The Minnesingers produced their own deeply sensitive and mystical versions of the Arthurian stories that, in their exalted symbolism and deep emotion, rival even the works of Chrétien de Troyes and his French contemporaries.

As the thirteenth century drew toward its close, the romance was becoming conventionalized and drained of inspiration. The love story of Aucassin et Nicolette, which achieved a degree of popularity, was actually a satirical romance in which the hero is much less heroic than heroes usually are, and a battle is depicted in which the opponents cast pieces of cheese at each other. Based on earlier Byzantine material, *Aucassin et Nicolette* makes mortal love take priority over salvation itself. Indeed, Aucassin is scornful of Heaven:

> For into Paradise go only such people as these: There go those aged priests and elderly cripples and maimed ones who day and night stoop before altars and in the crypts beneath the churches; those who go around in worn-out cloaks and shabby old clothing; who are naked and shoeless and full of sores; who are dying of hunger and thirst, of cold and misery. Such folks as these enter Paradise, and I will have nothing to do with them. I will go to hell. For to hell go the fair clerics and comely knights who are killed in tournaments and great wars, and the sturdy archer and the loyal vassal. I will go with them. There also go the fair and courteous ladies who have loving friends, two or three, together with their wedded lords. And there go the gold and silver, the ermine and all rich furs, the harpers and the minstrels, and the happy folk of the world. I will go with these, so long as I have Nicolette, my very sweet friend, at my side.

Another important product of thirteenth-century vernacular literature, the *Romance of the Rose*, was in fact not a romance in the ordinary sense but an allegory of the whole courtly love tradition in which the thoughts and emotions of the lover and his lady are personified in actual characters such as Love, Reason, Jealousy, and Fair-Welcome. Begun by William of Lorris as an idealization of courtly love, the *Romance of the Rose* was completed after William's death by Jean de Meun, a man of limited talent and bourgeois origin. Jean's contribution was long-winded, encyclopedic, and contemptuous of women. The poem as a whole lacks high literary distinction, yet it appealed to contemporaries and enjoyed a great vogue.

Fabliaux and Fables

Neither epic, lyric, nor romance had much appeal below the level of the landed aristocracy. The inhabitants of the rising towns had a vernacular literature all their own. From the bourgeoisie came the high medieval *fabliaux*, short satirical poems filled with vigor and crude humor, which devoted themselves chiefly to ridiculing conventional morality. Priests and monks were portrayed as lechers; merchants' wives, eager for extramarital affairs, were easily and frequently seduced; and clever young men perpetually made fools of sober and stuffy merchants.

Medieval urban culture also produced the fable, or animal story, an allegory in the ancient Greek tradition of *Aesop's Fables*, in which various stock characters in medieval society were presented as animals—thinly disguised. Most of the more popular fables dealt with Renard the Fox and were known collectively as the *Romance of Renard*. These tales constituted a ruthless parody of chivalric ideals in which the clever, unscrupulous Renard persistently outwitted King Lion and his loyal but stupid vassals.

ARCHITECTURE AND SCULPTURE

The Romanesque Style

During the High Middle Ages, stone churches, abbeys, castles, hospitals, and town halls were built in prodigious numbers. More stone was quarried in high medieval France alone than by the pyramid and temple builders across the three-thousand-year history of ancient Egypt. The most celebrated buildings of the High Middle Ages are the great cathedrals and abbeys: Chartres, Mont-St-Michel, Westminster Abbey, Reims, Amiens, Bourges, Notre Dame Paris, and many more. But it is nearly as impressive, driving through the European countryside, to see smaller stone churches of the twelfth and thirteenth centuries still in use in town after town.

Two great architectural styles dominated the age: the Romanesque style flourished in the eleventh century and early twelfth; during the middle decades of the twelfth century it gave way gradually to the Gothic style. From about 1150 to the early 1300s the most famous of the Gothic cathedrals were built. Thereafter the Gothic builders, having exhausted the structural possibilities of their style, turned to decorative elaboration. At its height, Gothic architecture constituted one of humanity's most audacious and successful architectural experiments.

The cathedrals were designed by master architects, some of whose names have come down to us. Cathedral building represented an enormous investment of money and effort: Chartres alone would cost about 120 million dollars to reproduce today. Revenues were raised in a variety of ways—through episcopal taxes and fund drives, through donations by townspeople, guilds, regional lords, and great princes and kings. One of the rose windows of Chartres displays the emblems of two of its benefactors—the Capetian fleur-de-lys of St. Louis, in blue and gold, and the yellow castle on red background identifying the family of his mother, Blanche of Castile. Other Chartres windows depict the symbols of various contributing guilds—tailors, bakers, shoemakers, wheelwrights. Sometimes townspeople and even noble men and women would perform volunteer labor, pulling carts from the stone quarry to the building site, or carrying food and wine to the workers. At other times people objected violently to heavy episcopal taxes, and construction might be long delayed for want of funds. The building of a cathedral could drag on for a century or more, not because of slow work but because of periodic shortages of money necessary to support a construction of such scope. St. Louis' stunning palace church, La Sainte Chapelle, was well financed and completed in half a decade. Conversely, the cathedral of St. John the Divine in New York City, America's largest church, has been under construction for more than 100 years, because of recurring shortages of funds, and is still unfinished.

The evolution of high medieval architecture was shaped by two fundamental trends in medieval civilization. First, the great cathedrals were products of the urban revolution—of rising wealth, civic pride, and intense urban piety. Second, the change from Romanesque to Gothic mirrors the shift in literature,

Romanesque interior: St. Sernin, Toulouse, showing round vaulting and round arcade arches.

Romanesque sculpture: Last Judgment scene from the tympanum over the central portal of St. Foy, Conques. At the upper center is Christ, the judge of all human souls; at bottom left are souls enjoying heaven, and at bottom right are souls being cast through a monster's jaws into hell.

Capital, St. Radegonde, Poitiers. *Adam and Eve.*

piety, and aristocratic lifestyle toward emotional intensity and refinement. Romanesque architecture, though characterized by an exceeding diversity of expression, tended toward the solemnity of earlier Christian piety and the rough-hewn power of the chansons de geste. The Gothic style, on the other hand, is dramatic, upward-reaching, aspiring. It embodies the heightened sensitivity that one finds in the romance.

The development from Romanesque to Gothic can be understood, too, as an evolution in the principles of structural engineering. The key architectural ingredient in the Romanesque churches was the round arch—borrowed from Greco-Roman times—which appears in their portals, their windows, their arcades, and the massive stone vaulting of their roofs. The immense downward and outward thrusts of these heavy stone roofs required massive pillars and thick supporting walls.

The great engineering achievement of Romanesque architects was to replace flat wooden ceilings with stone vaulting, thereby creating buildings less susceptible to fire and more artistically unified. In achieving this goal, the Romanesque builders constructed stone vaults far larger than ever before. The glittering mosaics and wooden roofs that characterized the churches of late Roman, Byzantine, and Carolingian times gave way to the domination of stone as the key material in both Romanesque architecture and Romanesque sculpture. Indeed, the inventive religious sculpture of the age—ornamenting the capitals of Romanesque columns and the semicircular area between the lintel and round arch of the portal (the "tympanum")—was totally architectonic, completely fused into the structure of the church itself.

The Romanesque interior is characterized by heavy masses and relatively small windows. Graceful and richly decorated in southern Europe, the style tends to become increasingly severe as one moves northward. A church in the fully developed Romanesque style conveys a feeling of organic unity and solidity. Its sturdy arches, vaults, and walls, and its somber, shadowy interior give the illusion of mystery and otherworldliness, yet suggest at the same time the steadfast power of the universal Church.

The Gothic Style

During the first half of the twelfth century, new structural elements began to be employed in the building of Romanesque churches: first, ribs of stone that crisscrossed the vaulting; next, pointed arches that permitted greater height in the vaults and arcades. By the middle of the century these novel features—vault rib and pointed arch—were providing the basis for an entirely new style of architecture. They were employed with such effect by Abbot Suger in his new abbey church of St. Denis near Paris around 1140 that St. Denis has been widely regarded as the first true Gothic church.

French Gothic churches of the late twelfth century such as Notre Dame, Paris, disclose the development of vault rib and pointed arch into a powerful, coherent style. During these exciting years, every decade brought new experiments and opened new possibilities in church building; yet Notre Dame, Paris, and the churches of its period and region retain some of the heaviness and solidity of the earlier Romanesque. Not until the 1190s were the full potentialities of Gothic architecture realized. The use of the vault rib and pointed arch, and of a third Gothic structural element—the flying buttress—made it possible to support weights and stresses in a new way. The traditional building, of roof supported by walls, was transformed into a radically new kind of building—a skeleton—in which the stone vault rested not on walls but on slender columns and graceful exterior supports. The walls became mere screens—structurally unnecessary. With the passage of time, they were replaced increasingly by huge windows of stained glass that flooded the church interior with light and color. For concurrent with the Gothic architectural revolution was the development, in twelfth-century Europe, of the new art of stained-glass making. The luminous windows created in the twelfth and thirteenth centuries, with episodes from the Bible and religious legend depicted in shimmering blues and reds, have never been equaled.

The Gothic innovations of vault rib, pointed arch, and flying buttress created the breathtaking illusion of stone vaulting resting on walls of glass. The new churches rose upward in seeming defiance of gravity, losing their earthbound quality and reaching toward the heavens. By about the mid-thirteenth

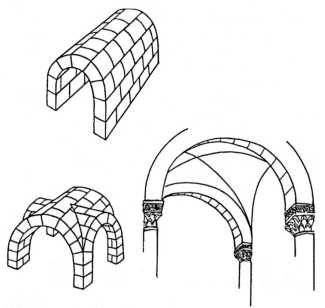

Romanesque barrel and groin vaults.

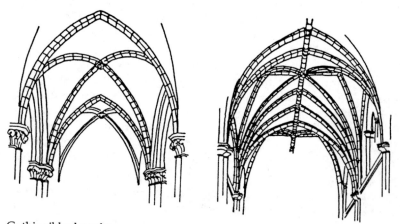

Gothic ribbed vaults.

century all the structural possibilities of the Gothic skeleton design were fully
realized, and in the towns of central and northern France there now rose
churches of delicate, soaring stone with walls of lustrous glass. Never before in
history had windows been so immense or buildings so lofty, and seldom since
has European architecture been at once so daring and so assured.

Gothic sculpture, like Romanesque, was intimately related to architecture,
yet the two styles differed markedly. Romanesque fantasy, exuberance, and distortion gave way to a serene, self-confident naturalism. Human figures were no
longer crowded together on the capitals of pillars; often they stood as statues—

Notre Dame, Paris; nave looking east (showing vault ribs), begun in 1163.

great rows of them—in niches on the cathedral exteriors: saints, prophets, kings, and angels, Christ and the Virgin Mary, depicted as tall, slender figures, calm yet warmly human, often young and sometimes smiling. The greatest Gothic churches of thirteenth-century France—Bourges, Chartres, Amiens, Reims, La Sainte Chapelle—are among the most impressive buildings on earth and are ornamented by some of the greatest works of sculpture ever created. They bring together many separate arts—architecture, sculpture, stained glass, liturgical music—all directed to the single end of providing a majestic background for the central act of Christian worship, the Mass.

High Gothic exterior: Reims Cathedral, showing
the great windows around the rounded east end
and the decorated flying buttresses (thirteenth
century).

High Gothic facade: Amiens
Cathedral, showing the three
west portals decorated with
sculpture (thirteenth century).

High Gothic interior: Beauvais Cathedral,
looking east.

Cathedral Life in the Middle Ages

Stepping inside a medieval cathedral today, one finds an atmosphere of awesome quiet that contrasts sharply with the bustle of the surrounding city. But
in the Middle Ages, cathedrals were centers of urban life rather than refuges
from it. The cathedral bells announced the hours of the business day, called
university students to their studies, and proclaimed great public events—a
victory in battle, the death of a famous person, the birth of a prince or princess.
Townspeople flocked to their cathedral not for the Mass alone, but for marriages, baptisms, funerals, civic and religious festivals, excommunications,
and victory celebrations. Famous traveling preachers addressed huge crowds
from cathedral pulpits and sometimes stirred them into frenzied enthusiasm.
Often a cathedral was the site of a great assembly of nobles and princes or of
a public meeting of the town council. On major feast days—Easter, Christmas,
Pentecost, and others—the cathedral would be ablaze with candles. Colorful
processions would march noisily along its aisles and then out through its portals into the narrow streets of the city.

High Gothic sculpture: Apostle's head from Sens Cathedral, central France (c. 1200).

A cathedral's relics might attract pilgrims from far and wide, many of them crippled or ill, desperate for a miraculous cure. At night, pilgrims might be found sleeping on the cathedral's straw-covered floor in company with local beggars, drunks, and prostitutes. On great feast days, the church would be swarming with pilgrims and local worshippers. Abbot Suger, describing a bois-terous multitude that pressed into his abbey church of St. Denis, complained of "howling men" and of women who screamed "as though they were giving birth." The crowd of visitors, shoving and struggling to see the relics of St. Denis, forced the abbey's monks "to flee through the windows, carrying the precious relics with them."

The Virgin of the Visitation, west facade, Reims Cathedral (c. 1220).

Even larger crowds were drawn to Canterbury Cathedral to visit the wonder-working tomb of St. Thomas Becket. If we could travel backward in time to witness the scene, we would be struck by the sight of the disabled crawling on the floor near the tomb, the ear-shattering cries of the mentally handicapped, the suffocating odor of poverty and disease. We would hear people shouting out their prayers in the half-darkness or see them offering their pennies and homemade candles in desperate appeal for the saint's help. Someone is loudly explaining his miraculous cure to a monk; someone else is vomiting in a corner. Well-dressed nobles are there, too, along with some high

High Gothic sculpture: *Le Beau Dieu*, west portal of Amiens Cathedral (thirteenth century).

officials of the Church; they ignore the crowds of poor and diseased as they await their opportunity to present offerings of silver or gems.

Canterbury Cathedral was a singularly popular pilgrimage center, giving rise to Chaucer's *Canterbury Tales* in the fourteenth century. Few holy relics were as famed for miraculous cures as those of St. Thomas Becket. But all across medieval Europe the cathedrals teemed with women and men from all social levels. One would encounter there the commotion and stench, the hopes and griefs, of a turbulent cross-section of humanity.

THE NEW SCHOOLS

One of the most significant developments in the High Middle Ages was a vast increase in the use of the written word. There was an enormous proliferation of government documents—written commands, property deeds, financial accounts, judicial transcripts—along with records of individual transactions (wills, business records, property transfers) and systematic treatises on philosophy, theology, law, and medicine. Works of literature were committed to writing rather than transmitted by oral tradition. Law came to be based less on local, long-remembered custom, and more on coherent systems of secular and ecclesiastical jurisprudence. This entire process, which has been described as a shift "from memory to written record," resulted in basic changes in attitude and social organization. It encouraged a much more logical and systematic approach to every side of human experience, from the management of a business, farm, or kingdom to philosophical investigation. The ability to reason, read, and compute provided a direct avenue into the governmental institutions of Church and state; it was becoming increasingly evident to young people of ambition that knowledge was power.

Accordingly, schools sprang up everywhere, and skilled teachers found themselves in great demand. The abbot Guibert of Nogent looked back from the early twelfth century to the earlier days of his youth, when "scarcely any teachers could be found in the towns and very few in the cities, and those who by good luck could be found didn't know much: they couldn't be compared with the traveling teachers of these days."

The Rise of Universities

The greatest of the new schools, the universities, were products of the growing cities. The urban revolution brought about the decline of the old monastic schools, which had done so much to preserve and enrich culture over the previous centuries. They were superseded north of the Alps by schools centering on non-monastic churches, often cathedrals, and in Italy by semi-secular municipal schools. Both the cathedral schools and municipal schools had long existed, but only in the eleventh and twelfth centuries did they rise to prominence. Many now became centers of higher learning of a sort that Europe had not known for centuries. Their enrollments increased and their faculties grew until, in the twelfth century, some of them evolved into universities.

In the Middle Ages, "university" was a vague term denoting nothing more than a group of persons associated for any purpose. The word was commonly applied to the merchant and craft guilds of the rising towns. A "guild" or "university" of students and scholars engaged in the pursuit of higher learning was given the more specific name, *studium generale*. When we speak of the medieval university, therefore, we are referring to an institution that would have been called a studium generale at the time. It differed from lesser schools in that students drawn from many lands received instruction from a number of specialized scholars in a variety of disciplines. The studium generale offered a basic

MEDIEVAL UNIVERSITIES

From Greaves, Zaller, Roberts, *Civilization in the West*. Harper Collins, 1992, p. 251.

program of instruction in the traditional "seven liberal arts": astronomy, geometry, arithmetic, music, grammar, rhetoric, and logic; and also instruction in one or more of the "higher" disciplines: law, medicine, and theology (or philosophy). On the successful completion of the liberal arts curriculum, the student could apply for a license to teach but might also wish to continue his studies by specializing in medicine, philosophy, or civil or canon law.

Fundamentally, the medieval university was neither a campus nor a complex of buildings, but a guild—a privileged corporation of teachers, or sometimes of students. With its classes normally held in rented rooms, it was a highly mobile institution, and, on more than one occasion, when a university was dissatisfied with local conditions it won important concessions from the townspeople simply by threatening to move.

In the thirteenth century, universities flourished at Paris, Bologna, Naples, Montpelier, Oxford, Cambridge, and elsewhere. Paris, Oxford, and a number of others were dominated by guilds of instructors in the liberal arts. Bologna, whose pattern was followed by other universities of southern Europe, was governed by a guild of students. The Bologna student guild managed to reduce the exorbitant local prices of food and lodgings by threatening to move collectively to another town and established strict rules of conduct for the instructors. Professors, for example, were placed under the outrageous obligation to begin and end their classes on time and to cover the prescribed curriculum. Since Bologna specialized in legal studies, its pupils were older professional students for the most part—students who had completed their liberal arts curriculum and were determined to secure sufficient training for successful careers in law.

Notwithstanding the enormous differences between medieval and modern university life, the modern university is a direct outgrowth of its high medieval predecessor. We owe to the medieval university such customs as the formal teaching license, the practice—unknown to antiquity—of group instruction, the awarding of academic degrees, the notion of a liberal arts curriculum, and the tradition of honoring commencement day by dressing in priestly garb (caps and gowns).

Student Life at the University of Paris

Let us imagine ourselves at the University of Paris in the days of St. Louis. Here the intellectual environment was alive with philosophical disputes and passionate intellectual rivalries. And besides these battles of words, there were frequent tavern brawls, sometimes exploding into full-scale battles between students and townspeople, or among rival student gangs. New students were hazed unmercifully and imaginatively, while unpopular professors were hissed, shouted down, or, as a last resort, pelted with stones.

Students flocked to the University of Paris from all over Western Christendom. Most of them were about seventeen when they began their studies, and they tended to come from the middle social stratum of town dwellers and lesser landholders. Poor boys occasionally made it, but the sons of the high aristocracy did not pour in until a later era; university educations did not become fashionable in high society until the fourteenth century. And there were no female students at all. (Until fairly recent years women were excluded from most Oxford and Cambridge colleges and denied admission to some of America's foremost private universities, including Harvard and Yale.)

The letters of medieval students to their parents or guardians have a curiously modern ring:

Gratian not only brought together an immense body of canons from a wide variety of sources; he also framed them in a logical, topically organized scheme. Using methods that were just beginning to be employed by scholastic philosophers, he raised questions in logical sequence, quoted the relevant canons, and endeavored to rectify contradictions. The result was an ordered body of general legal principles validated by passages from the Bible, the Fathers, and papal and conciliar decrees. The *Decretum* became the authoritative text in ecclesiastical tribunals and the basis of all future study in canon law.

As time passed, and new decrees were issued, it became necessary to supplement Gratian's *Decretum* by collecting the canons issued after 1140. One such collection was made in 1234 under the direction of the lawyer-pope Gregory IX, another in the pontificate of Boniface VIII, and still others in later generations. Together, the *Decretum* and the supplementary collections were given the title *Corpus Juris Canonici,* and became the ecclesiastical equivalent of Justinian's *Corpus Juris Civilis.* These two great compilations, ecclesiastical and civil, reflect the parallel growth of medieval Europe's two supreme sources of administrative and jurisdictional authority: church and monarchy. They further reflect the high medieval shift toward elaborate intellectual systems, expressed in writing and shaped by rational analysis.

The Background of High Medieval Philosophy

Medieval philosophy, too, is marked by analytical system building. Although every important philosopher in the High Middle Ages was a churchman of one sort or another, ecclesiastical authority did not stifle speculation or limit controversy. Catholic orthodoxy, which would harden noticeably at the time of the sixteenth-century Protestant Reformation, was still relatively flexible in the twelfth and thirteenth centuries, and philosophers were by no means timid apologists for official dogmas. If some of them were impelled to provide the Catholic faith with a logical substructure, others asserted that reason does not lead to the truth of Christian revelation. And among those who sought to harmonize faith and reason there was sharp disagreement as to how it should be done. Their shared faith did not limit their diversity or curb their spirit of intellectual adventure.

The high medieval philosophers drew nourishment from five earlier sources: (1) From the Greeks they inherited the philosophical systems of Plato and Aristotle. At first these two Greek masters were known in the West only through a handful of translations and commentaries dating from late Roman times. By the thirteenth century, however, new and far more complete translations were coming into Christendom from Spain and Sicily, and Aristotelian philosophy became a matter of intense interest and controversy in Europe's universities. (2) From the Islamic world came a flood of Greek scientific and philosophical works that had long before been translated into Arabic and were now retranslated from Arabic into Latin. These works entered Europe accompanied by extensive commentaries and original writings of Arab philosophers and scientists, for the Arabs came to grips with Greek learning long before the West did. Islamic thought made a particularly vital contribution to European science. In philosophy it was enriched by the work of Jewish scholars such as the Spanish philosopher Moses Maimonides (1135–1204), whose *Guide for the Perplexed*—a penetrating reconciliation of Aristotle and Scripture—influenced the work of thirteenth-century Christian philosophers and theologians (see p. 172). (3) The early Church Fathers, particularly Ambrose, Jerome, and Augustine, had been a dominant intellectual force throughout the early Middle Ages and their authority remained strong in the twelfth and thirteenth centuries. St. Augustine retained his singular significance and was, indeed, the chief vessel of Platonic and Neoplatonic thought in the medieval universities. (4) The early medieval scholars themselves contributed significantly to the high medieval intellectual revival. Gregory the Great, Isidore of Seville, Bede, Alcuin, Raban Maur, John the Scot, and Gerbert of Aurillac were all studied in the new universities. The original intellectual contributions of these men were less important, however, than the fact that they and their contemporaries had kept classical learning alive, thus creating the intellectual climate that made possible the reawakening of philosophical speculation in the eleventh century. (5) The high medieval philosophers looked back beyond the scholars of the early Middle Ages, beyond the Fathers of the early Church, to the Hebrew and early Christian religious traditions as recorded in Scripture. Among medieval theologians the Bible, the chief written source of divine revelation, was the fundamental text and the ultimate authority.

Such were the chief elements—Greek, Islamic-Jewish, Patristic, early medieval, and scriptural—that underlay the thought of the scholastic philosophers. Strictly defined, "scholasticism" is simply the philosophical movement associated with the high medieval schools—the cathedral and monastic schools and later the universities. More interestingly, it was a movement concerned above all with exploring the relationship between reason and revelation. All medieval scholastics believed in God; all were committed, to some degree, to the life of reason. Many of them were immensely enthusiastic over the intellectual possibilities inherent in the careful application of Aristotelian logic to basic human and religious problems. Some believed that logic was the master key to a thousand doors and that with sufficient methodological rigor, with sufficient exactness in the use of words, the potentialities of human reason were all but limitless.

The scholastics applied their logical method to a multitude of problems. They were concerned chiefly, however, with matters of basic significance to human existence: the nature of human beings, the purpose of human life, the existence and attributes of God, the fundamentals of human morality, the ethical imperatives of social and political life, the relationship between God and humanity. It would be hard to deny that these are the most profound sorts of questions that one can ask. Many philosophers of our own day are inclined to reject them as unanswerable, but the scholastics, lacking the modern sense of disillusionment, were determined to make the attempt.

The Relationship of Faith and Reason

Among the diverse investigations and conflicting opinions of the medieval philosophers, two central issues deserve particular attention: the degree of inter-relationship between faith and reason and the relative merits of the Platonic-Augustinian and the Aristotelian intellectual traditions. The issue of faith versus reason was perhaps the more far-reaching. Ever since Tertullian in the third century, there had been Christian writers who insisted that God so transcended reason that any attempt to approach him intellectually was useless and, indeed, blasphemous. Tertullian had posed the rhetorical questions:

> What has Athens to do with Jerusalem? What concord is there between the Academy and the Church? . . . Let us have done with all attempts to produce a bastard Christianity of Stoic, Platonic, and dialectic composition. We desire no curious disputation after possessing Christ Jesus, no logical analyses after enjoying the Gospel!

Tertullian had many followers in the Middle Ages. St. Peter Damiani rejected the intellectual road to God in favor of the mystical, insisting that God, whose power is limitless, cannot be bound or even approached by logic. He was followed in this view by such later mystics as St. Hildegard of Bingen (to a degree), St. Bernard of Clairvaux (who denounced his rationalist contemporary Peter Abelard), and St. Francis (who regarded intellectual speculation as irrelevant to salvation). A later spiritual Franciscan, Jacopone da Todi, expressed the position thus:

> Plato and Socrates may often contend,
> And all the breath within their bodies spend,
> Engaged in disputations without end.
> What's that to me?
> For only with a pure and simple mind
> Can one the narrow path to heaven find,
> And greet the King; while lingers far behind,
> Philosophy.

The contrary view was just as old. Third-century theologians such as Clement and Origen in the school of Alexandria had labored to provide Christianity with a sturdy philosophical foundation and did not hesitate to explain the faith by means of Greek—and particularly Platonic—thought. The fourth-century Latin Doctors, Ambrose, Jerome, and Augustine, had wrestled with the problem of whether a Christian might properly use elements from the pagan classical tradition in the service of the faith, and all three ended with affirmative answers. As Augustine expressed it,

> If those who are called philosophers, and especially the Platonists, have said anything that is true and in harmony with our faith, we must not only not shrink from it, but claim it for our own use from those who have unlawful possession of it.

This is the viewpoint that underlies most of high medieval philosophy—that reason has a valuable role to play as a servant of revelation. St. Anselm, following Augustine, declared, "I believe so that I may know." Faith comes first, reason second; faith rules reason, but reason can perform the useful service of illuminating faith. Indeed, faith and reason are separate avenues to a single body of truth. By their very nature they cannot lead to contradictory conclusions, for truth is one. Should their conclusions ever *appear* to disagree, philosophers can be assured that some flaw exists in their logic. Reason cannot err, but our use of it can, and revelation must therefore be the criterion against which reason is measured.

This, in general, became the position of later scholastic philosophers. The intellectual system of St. Thomas Aquinas was built on the conviction that reason and faith were harmonious. Even the arch-rationalist of the twelfth century, Peter Abelard, wrote: "I do not wish to be Aristotle if it must separate me from Christ." Abelard believed that he could at once be a philosopher and a Christian, but his faith took priority.

Among some medieval philosophers the priorities were reversed. Averroës, an astute Aristotelian Muslim of twelfth-century Spain, boldly asserted the superiority of reason over faith. He affirmed the truth of several of Aristotle's conclusions that were directly contrary to Islamic and Christian doctrine: that the world had always existed and was therefore uncreated; that all human actions were determined; that there was no personal salvation but only the return of human raindrops to the divine ocean. In the fourteenth century there emerged a Christian philosophical school known as "Latin Averroism," based in part on the writings of the thirteenth-century Paris theologian, Siger of Brabant. Like Averroës, Siger of Brabant accepted Aristotle's eternally existing world as "logically necessary" yet nevertheless believed firmly in the Christian doctrine of the creation. Expanding on this dilemma, Latin Averroists of the fourteenth century held that reason and revelation produced radically different conclusions. Their position came to be called the doctrine of the "twofold truth."

Platonism-Augustinianism versus Aristotelianism

The conflict between the intellectual systems of Plato-Augustine and Aristotle did not emerge clearly until the thirteenth century when the full body of Aristotle's writings came into the West in Latin translations from Greek and Arabic. Until then, most efforts at applying reason to faith were based on the Platonic tradition transmuted and transmitted by Augustine to medieval Europe. St. Anselm, for example, was a dedicated Augustinian, as were many of his twelfth-century successors. The tradition was carried on in the thirteenth century by the Franciscan St. Bonaventure. Many thoughtful Christians were deeply suspicious of the newly recovered writings of Aristotle. They regarded his work as pagan in viewpoint and dangerous to the faith. Other thirteenth-century philosophers, such as St. Thomas Aquinas, were much too devoted to the goal of reconciling faith and reason to reject the works of a man whom they regarded as antiquity's greatest philosopher. St. Thomas sought to Christianize Aristotle, much as Augustine had Christianized Plato and the Neoplatonists. In the middle decades of the thirteenth century, the Platonic and Aristotelian traditions flourished side by side, and in the works of certain English scientific thinkers of the age they achieved a singularly fruitful synthesis.

The contest between Plato and Aristotle gave rise to a serious philosophical debate over the nature of the Platonic archetypes or, as they were called in the Middle Ages, "universals." Plato had taught that terms such as "dog" or "cat" not only describe particular creatures but also are language-symbols for things that have reality in themselves—that individual cats are imperfect reflections of a model cat, an archetypal or universal cat. Similarly, there are many examples of circles, squares, or triangles. Were we to measure these individual figures with sufficiently refined instruments we would discover that they were imperfect in one respect or another. No circle in this world is absolutely round. No square or triangle has perfectly straight sides. They are merely approximations of a perfect "idea." In "heaven," Plato would say, the perfect triangle exists. It is the source of the concept of triangularity that lurks in our minds and of all the imperfect triangles that we see in the physical world. The heavenly triangle is not only perfect but *real*. The earthly triangles are less real, and less worthy of our attention. Or, to take still another example, we call certain acts "good" because they partake, imperfectly, of a universal good that exists in heaven. In short, these universals—cat, dog, circle, triangle, beauty, goodness, etc.—exist apart from the multitude of individual dogs, cats, circles, triangles, and beautiful and good things in this world. And the person who seeks knowledge ought to meditate on these universals rather than study the world of phenomena in which they are only imperfectly reflected.

St. Augustine accepted Plato's theory of universals but not without amendment. Augustine taught that the archetypes existed in the mind of God instead of in Plato's abstract "heaven." And whereas Plato has ascribed our knowledge of the universals to dim memories from a prenatal existence, Augustine maintained that God puts a knowledge of universals directly into our minds by a process of "divine illumination." Plato and Augustine agreed, however, that the universal existed apart from the particular and, indeed, was *more real* than the particular. In the High Middle Ages, those who followed the Platonic-Augustinian approach to universals were known as "Realists": they believed that universals were real.

The Aristotelian tradition brought with it another viewpoint on universals: they existed, to be sure, but only in the particular. Only by studying particular things in the world of phenomena could one gain a knowledge of universals. The human mind drew its knowledge of the universal from its observation of the particular by a process of abstraction. The universals were real, but in a sense less real—or less independently real—than Plato and Augustine believed. Accordingly, philosophers who inclined toward the Aristotelian position have been called "Moderate Realists."

As early as the eleventh century the philosopher Roscellinus rejected both these views, declaring that universals were not real at all. "Dog," "cat," and "triangle" are mere words—names that we have concocted for bunches of individual things that we have lumped into arbitrary categories. These categories, or universals, have no objective existence whatever. Reality is not to be found in them, but rather in the multiplicity and variety of individual objects that we can see, touch, and smell in the world around us. Those who followed Roscellinus in this view were known as "Nominalists": for them, the universals had no reality apart from their *nomina*—"names." Nominalism remained in the intellectual background during the twelfth and thirteenth centuries but was revived in the fourteenth. Many churchmen regarded it as a dangerous doctrine, since its emphasis on the particular over the universal seemed to suggest that the Church was not, as Catholics believed, a single universal body but rather a vast accumulation of individual Christians.

PHILOSOPHERS AND MYSTICS

St. Anselm

The Scholastic philosophers first made their appearance in the later eleventh century as an aspect of Europe's intellectual reawakening. The first major figure was St. Anselm (c. 1033–1109), the Italian philosopher who became abbot of Bec and later, as archbishop of Canterbury, brought the investiture controversy into England (see pp. 251–252).

As an Augustinian, Anselm took the realist position on the problem of universals. It was from Augustine, too, that he derived his attitude on the relationship of faith and reason. He taught that faith must precede reason but that reason could serve to illuminate faith. His conviction that reason and faith were compatible made him a singularly important pioneer in the development of high medieval rationalism. He worked out several proofs of God, based on abstract reasoning rather than observation. And in his important theological treatise, *Cur Deus Homo (Why God Became Man)*, he subjected the doctrines of the incarnation and atonement to rigorous logical analysis.

Anselm's emphasis on reason, employed within the framework of a firm Christian conviction, set the stage for the significant philosophical developments of the following generations. With Anselm, who was possessed of one of the most penetrating intellects in human history, Western Christendom regained at last the intellectual level of the fourth-century Latin Doctors.

Abelard

The twelfth-century philosophers were intoxicated by the seemingly limitless possibilities of reason and logic. The most audacious of them all was Peter Abelard (1079–1142), whose dazzling career ended ingloriously.

Abelard is perhaps best known for his love affair with his young student Heloise. Although this was possibly the most celebrated romance of the Middle Ages, the fact that Abelard was twenty years older than Heloise, and was her teacher, suggests a situation that could well be described today as sexual harassment. The two lovers did eventually marry, but Heloise's uncle remained so angry that he arranged to have Abelard castrated by hired thugs. The lovers separated permanently, both taking monastic vows, and in later years Abelard wrote regretfully of the affair in his autobiographical *History of My Calamities*. There followed a touching correspondence in which Heloise, now an abbess, confessed her enduring love—"I am tortured by passion and the fires of memory." In reply Abelard offered her spiritual consolation but, of necessity, nothing more.

Abelard was the supreme logician of the twelfth century. Writing several decades before the great influx of Aristotelian thought in Latin translation, he anticipated Aristotle's position on the question of universals by advocating a theory similar to Aristotle's moderate realism. Universals, Abelard believed, have no separate existence; our knowledge of them is derived from particular things by a process of abstraction. In a famous work entitled *Sic et Non (Yes and No)*, Abelard collected opinions from the Bible, the Latin Fathers, the councils of the Church, and the decrees of the papacy on a great variety of theological issues, demonstrating that these authorities disagreed on such issues as whether it is ever permissible to lie, whether anything happens by chance, and whether sin is or is not pleasing to God. Others before him had collected authoritative opinions on theological and legal issues, but never so systematically. Abelard, in his *Sic et Non*, employed a method of inquiry that was developed and perfected by canon lawyers and philosophers over the next several generations. We have already seen how the canonist Gratian, in his *Decretum*, used the device of lining up conflicting authorities and reconciling them. Similarly, Abelard's successors in theology sought to reconcile contradictions and arrive at conclusions. But Abelard himself had left the issues unresolved, arguing that students should reason them out for themselves. Abelard was a devoted Christian, if something of an intellectual show-off, but many regarded him as a budding skeptic. Thus he left himself open to attacks by St. Bernard, who was hostile to the Christian rationalist movement and called Abelard's theology (not very cleverly) a "foolology." The brilliant teacher was driven from one place to another until at length his opinions were condemned by an ecclesiastical council in 1141. Retiring to Cluny, he died there in 1142. The abbot of Cluny wrote Heloise a touching letter praising Abelard's late-blooming humility and assuring her that they would be reunited on the day of the Lord's coming.

Twelfth-century rationalism was far more than a solo performance, and the attacks on Abelard failed to halt its growth. His student Peter Lombard (c. 1100–1160) produced an important theological text, the *Book of Sentences*, which set off conflicting opinions on the pattern of the *Sic et Non*, but which, like Gratian's *Decretum*, took the further step of reconciling the contradictory authorities. Lombard's *Books of Sentences* remained for centuries a fundamental text in schools of theology.

Hildegard of Bingen: Rationalism, Art, and Mystical Union

A contemporary of Peter Lombard's, the German nun Hildegard of Bingen (1098–1179), was both a rationalist and a mystic. Indeed, had she not been a woman her many talents would have earned her, more than anyone else in her century, the title of "Renaissance Man" (see p. 272). She was a great composer, whose religious opera, the *Ordo Virtutum*, left songwriters such as King Richard the Lion-Hearted and Emperor Henry VI far back in the dust. The *Ordo Virtutum* is often performed to this day and is available on compact disc (and highly recommended!). Hildegard of Bingen was also a scholar of medical science (see p. 297), a prophet, and a political scientist whose advice was sought out by the major leaders of church and state in her time.

Mysticism had always been an element in Christian devotional life. During the twelfth century and especially in the thirteenth, the most celebrated mystical visionaries were women. As the authority of the clergy increased with the development of canon law and the growth of the Church bureaucracy, religious women—who were denied the priestly commission to preach and consecrate the Eucharist—found an alternative and more immediate source of divine authorization in their mystical union with Christ. Hildegard of Bingen, for example, was consulted by theologians on thorny points of doctrine and by popes and emperors on questions of high politics. Her divine revelations had impressed St. Bernard of Clairvaux so deeply that he addressed her as a "prophetess of God." A century later, at the thirteenth-century abbey of Helfta in Saxony, Gertrude of Helfta (d. 1301/2) and several other nuns of her community had visions of a Christ who was at once regal and lovingly approachable; their writings express what has aptly been called "a poised, self-confident, lyrical female mysticism."

The nuns of Helfta may themselves have been influenced by the mystical writings of pious laywomen known as "Beguines," whose loosely organized groups grew to considerable numbers during the thirteenth and early fourteenth centuries in the towns of Germany and the Netherlands. The Beguines adopted the idea of loving service to others in imitation of Christ—a kind of evangelism inspired by St. Francis that was denied to the strictly cloistered female Franciscans, the Poor Clares (see p. 222). Living by no papally sanctioned religious rule and taking no lifetime vows, the Beguines were alternately praised and condemned by ecclesiastical authorities, but they continued to flourish into the late Middle Ages, representing a kind of mystical lay piety that grew increasingly significant.

The goal of imitating Christ gave rise in many thirteenth-century Beguine communities to powerful mystical experiences, expressed in vernacular prose and poetry of great immediacy and intensity. The Beguine Mechthild of Magdeburg (d. c. 1282), whose *Flowing Light of Divinity* is a vivid and deeply personal description of her experiences of divine union, ended her days as a nun of Helfta and was probably a source of inspiration for the outpouring of mystical writings there.

Like other pioneers, Grosseteste followed many false paths. He was better at formulating a scientific methodology than in applying it to specific problems, and his explanations of such phenomena as heat, light, color, comets, and rainbows were rejected in later centuries. But the experimental method that he formulated was to become in time a powerful intellectual tool. The problem of the rainbow, for example, was largely solved by the fourteenth-century scientist Theodoric of Freiburg, who employed a refined version of Grosseteste's experimental methodology. The great triumphs of European science lay far in the future, but with the work of Robert Grosseteste the basic instrument had been forged.

Grosseteste's work was carried further by his disciple, the Oxford Franciscan Roger Bacon (c. 1214–1294). The author of a fascinating body of scientific sense and nonsense, Roger Bacon dabbled in the mysteries of alchemy, and his curiosity carried him along strange roads. He was critical of the deductive logic and metaphysical speculations that so fascinated his scholastic contemporaries: "Reasoning," he wrote, "does not illuminate these matters; experiments are required, conducted on a large scale, performed with instruments and by various necessary means."

At his best, Roger Bacon was almost prophetic:

Experimental science controls the conclusions of all other sciences. It reveals truths which reasoning from general principles would never have discovered. Finally, it starts us on the way to marvelous inventions which will change the face of the world.

CONCLUSION

Underlying the achievements of the high medieval logicians, scientists, and system builders was a basic change in attitude toward the world. The best minds of the twelfth and thirteenth centuries were coming to view God's created universe as a natural order, functioning according to consistent, divinely constituted laws and therefore open to rational inspection. Abelard was an early exponent of this new naturalism, but it is also to be found in the writings of many others. The collapse of the central tower of Winchester Cathedral in 1107 was attributed by some to the fact that the blaspheming King William II lay entombed beneath it, but the historian William of Malmesbury had his doubts: "The structure might have fallen because of faulty construction, even if the king had never been buried there." Similarly, a passage from the thirteenth-century *Romance of the Rose* ridicules the notion that storm damage is the work of demons,

With their hooks and cables, or their teeth and nails;
Such an explanation isn't worth
Two turnips; those accepting it are wrong.
For nothing but the tempest and the wind
Are needed to explain the havoc wrought.
These are the things that cause the injury.

God as Architect, demonstrating the viewpoint that
the creation of the universe was a rational process
based on principles of mathematics and geometry.
[Joan Evans, ed., *The Flowering of the Middle Ages,*
p. 83.]

In the view of the scholastics, a rational, loving God had created a world
that was both intelligible and good. The goodness of nature found its most
eloquent expression in St. Francis's "Song of Brother Sun"; it also inspired the
idealized naturalism of the Gothic sculptors, the poems of Dante in praise of
Beatrice, and the philosophy of Thomas Aquinas.

Many people would long continue to regard the world as threatening and
unpredictable, governed by supernatural forces and possessed by the devil.
Such was the traditional view, and some might agree with it even today. But
during the cultural awakening of the High Middle Ages it was diminishing. A
poet of the thirteenth century celebrated both the beauty of nature and the high
medieval awakening in his ovation to springtime:

> The earth's ablaze again with lustrous flowers.
> The fields are green again, the shadows deep.
> Woods are in leaf again, and all the world
> Is filled with joy again; this long-dead land
> Now flames with life again: the passions surge,
> Love is reborn, and beauty wakes from sleep.

The Popes of the Middle Ages*

Sylvester I, 314–335
Mark, 336
Julius I, 337–352
Liberius, 352–366
(Felix II, 355–365)
Damasus I, 366–384
Siricius, 384–399
Anastasius I, 399–401
Innocent I, 401–417
Zosimus, 417–418
Boniface I, 418–422
Celestine I, 422–432
Sixtus III, 432–440
Leo I, the Great, 440–461
Hilary, 461–468
Simplicius, 468–483
Felix III, 483–492
Gelasius I, 492–496
Anastasius II, 496–498
Symmachus, 498–514
Hormisdas, 514–523
John I, 523–526
Felix IV, 526–530
Boniface II, 530–532
John II, 533–535
Agapitus I, 535–536
Silverius, 536–537
Vigilius, 537–555
Pelagius I, 555–561
John III, 561–574
Benedict I, 575–579
Pelagius II, 579–590
Gregory I, 590–604
Sabinianus, 604–606

Boniface III, 607
Boniface IV, 608–615
Deusdedit, 615–618
Boniface V, 619–625
Honorius I, 625–638
Severinus, 640
John IV, 640–642
Theodore I, 642–649
Martin I, 649–655
Eugenius I, 654–657
Vitalian, 657–672
Adeodatus II, 672–676
Donus, 676–678
Agatho, 678–681
Leo II, 682–683
Benedict II, 684–685
John V, 685–686
Conon, 686–687
Sergius I, 687–701
John VI, 701–705
John VII, 705–707
Sisinnius, 708
Constantine, 708–715
Gregory II, 715–731
Gregory III, 731–741
Zacharias, 741–752
Stephen II, 752–757
Paul I, 757–767
Stephen III, 768–772
Hadrian I, 772–795
Leo III, 795–816
Stephen IV, 816–817
Paschal I, 817–824
Eugenius II, 824–827

*Antipopes are in parentheses.

Valentine, 827
Gregory IV, 827–844
Sergius II, 844–847
Leo IV, 847–855
Benedict III, 855–858
Nicholas I, 858–867
Hadrian II, 867–872
John VIII, 872–882
Marinus I, 882–884
Hadrian III, 884–885
Stephen V, 885–891
Formosus, 891–896
Boniface VI, 896
Stephen VI, 896–897
Romanus, 897
Theodore II, 897
John IX, 898–900
Benedict IV, 900–903
Leo V, 903
(Christopher, 903–904)
Sergius III, 904–911
Anastasius III, 911–913
Lando, 913–914
John X, 914–928
Leo VI, 928
Stephen VII, 928–931
John XI, 931–935
Leo VII, 936–939
Stephen VIII, 939–942
Marinus II, 942–946
Agapitus II, 946–955
John XII, 955–964
Leo VIII, 963–965
Benedict V, 964–966
John XIII, 965–972
Benedict VI, 973–974
(Boniface VII, 974 and 984–985)
Benedict VII, 974–983
John XIV, 983–984
John XV, 985–996
Gregory V, 996–999
(John XVI, 997–998)
Sylvester II, 999–1003
John XVII, 1003
John XVIII, 1004–1009
Sergius IV, 1009–1012
Benedict VIII, 1012–1024
John XIX, 1024–1032
Benedict IX, 1032–1048
Sylvester III, 1045

Gregory VI, 1045–1046
Clement II, 1046–1047
Damasus II, 1048
Leo IX, 1049–1054
Victor II, 1055–1057
Stephen IX, 1057–1058
(Benedict X, 1058–1059)
Nicholas II, 1059–1061
Alexander II, 1061–1073
Gregory VII, 1073–1085
(Clement III, 1080 and 1084–1100)
Victor III, 1086–1087
Urban II, 1088–1099
Paschal II, 1099–1118
(Theodoric, 1100)
(Albert, 1102)
(Sylvester IV, 1105–1111)
Gelasius II, 1118–1119
(Gregory VIII, 1118–1121)
Calixtus II, 1119–1124
Honorius II, 1124–1130
Innocent II, 1130–1143
(Anacletus II, 1130–1138)
Celestine II, 1143–1144
Lucius II, 1144–1145
Eugenius III, 1145–1153
Anastasius IV, 1153–1154
Hadrian IV, 1154–1159
Alexander III, 1159–1181
(Victor IV, 1159–1164)
(Paschal III, 1164–1168)
(Calixtus III, 1168–1178)
(Innocent III, 1179–1180)
Lucius III, 1181–1185
Urban III, 1185–1187
Gregory VIII, 1187
Clement III, 1187–1191
Celestine III, 1191–1198
Innocent III, 1198–1216
Honorius III, 1216–1227
Gregory IX, 1227–1241
Celestine IV, 1241
Innocent IV, 1243–1254
Alexander IV, 1254–1261
Urban IV, 1261–1264
Clement IV, 1265–1268
Gregory X, 1271–1276
Innocent V, 1276
Hadrian V, 1276
John XXI, 1276–1277

Appendix 1   The Popes of the Middle Ages

Nicholas III, 1277–1280
Martin IV, 1281–1285
Honorius IV, 1285–1287
Nicholas IV, 1288–1292
Celestine V, 1294
Boniface VIII, 1294–1303
Benedict XI, 1303–1304
Clement V, 1305–1314
John XXII, 1316–1334
Benedict XII, 1334–1342
Clement VI, 1342–1352
Innocent VI, 1352–1362
Urban V, 1362–1370
Gregory XI, 1370–1378
Urban VI, 1378–1389†
Clement VII, 1378–1394*
Boniface IX, 1389–1404*

Benedict XIII, 1394–1423†
Innocent VII, 1404–1406*
Gregory XII, 1406–1415*
(Alexander V, 1409–1410)
(John XXIII, 1410–1415)
Martin V, 1417–1431
(Clement VIII, 1423–1429)
(Benedict XIV, 1425–1430?)
Eugenius IV, 1431–1447
(Felix V, 1439–1449)
Nicholas V, 1447–1455
Calixtus III, 1455–1458
Pius II, 1458–1464
Paul II, 1464–1471
Sixtus IV, 1471–1484
Innocent VIII, 1484–1492
Alexander VI, 1492–1503

*Popes at Rome.
†Popes at Avignon.